Essay Index

GREAT ENGLISHMEN OF THE SIXTEENTH CENTURY

Sir Philip Sidney.

From the miniature by Isaac Oliver,
in the Royal Library at Windsor Castle.

GREAT ENGLISHMEN

OF THE

SIXTEENTH CENTURY

BY

SIDNEY LEE

Essay Index

KENNIKAT PRESS
Port Washington, N. Y./London

GREAT ENGLISHMEN OF THE SIXTEENTH CENTURY

First published in 1904
Reissued in 1972 by Kennikat Press
Library of Congress Catalog Card No: 77-159708
ISBN 0-8046-1655-8

Manufactured by Taylor Publishing Company   Dallas, Texas

ESSAY AND GENERAL LITERATURE INDEX REPRINT SERIES

PREFACE

THE contents of this volume are based on a series of eight lectures which I delivered, by invitation of the Trustee, at the Lowell Institute, Boston, in the spring of last year. I paid a first visit to America for the purpose of fulfilling that engagement. My reception was in all ways of the pleasantest, and I feel especially grateful to my Boston audience for the considerate attention which they extended to me.

In preparing the lectures for the press I have adhered to the main lines which I followed in their delivery. But I have judged it necessary to make sweeping alterations in form and detail. I have introduced much information which was scarcely fitted for oral treatment. I have endeavoured to present more coherently and more exhaustively the leading achievements of the Renaissance in England than was possible in the time at the disposal of a lecturer. I have tried, however, to keep in view the requirements of those to whom the lectures were originally addressed. Though I have embodied in my revision the fruits of some original research, I have not overloaded my pages with recondite references. My chief aim has been to interest the cultivated reader of general intelligence rather than the expert.

The opening lecture of my course at Boston surveyed

in general terms the uses to the public (alike in England and America) of the *Dictionary of National Biography*. Of that lecture I have only printed a small section in this volume. I have substituted for it, by way of introduction, a sketch of the intellectual spirit which was peculiar to the sixteenth century. This preparatory essay, which is practically new, gives, I trust, increased unity to the general handling of my theme.

The six men of whom I treat are all obviously, in their several ways, representative of the highest culture of sixteenth-century England. But they by no means exhaust the subject. Many other great Englishmen of the sixteenth century—statesmen like Wolsey and Burghley, theologians like Colet and Hooker, dramatists like Marlowe and Ben Jonson, men of science like William Gilbert, the electrician, and Napier of Merchiston, the inventor of logarithms—deserve association with them in any complete survey of sixteenth-century culture. In choosing five of the six names, I was moved by the fact that I had already studied, with some minuteness, their careers and work in my capacity of contributor to the *Dictionary of National Biography*. I wrote there the lives of Sir Thomas More, Sir Philip Sidney and Shakespeare, and I collaborated with others in the biographies of Sir Walter Ralegh and Edmund Spenser. I have not written at any length on Bacon before; but it is obvious that not the briefest list of great Englishmen of the sixteenth century would be worthy of attention were he excluded from it. I hope that, by presenting Bacon in juxtaposition with Shakespeare, I may do something to dispel the hallucination which would confuse the achievements of the one with those of the other.

Any who desire to undertake further study of the men who form my present subject may possibly derive some guidance from the bibliographies prefixed to each chapter. There I mention the chief editions of the literary works which I describe and criticise, and give references to biographies of value. For full bibliographies and exhaustive summaries of the biographical facts, the reader will do well to consult, in each case, the article in the *Dictionary of National Biography*. My present scheme only enables me to offer my readers such information as illustrates leading characteristics. I seek to trace the course of a great intellectual movement rather than attempt detailed biographies of those who are identified with its progress.

In the hope of increasing the usefulness of the volume I have supplied a somewhat full preliminary analysis of its contents, as well as a chronological table of leading events in European culture from the introduction of printing into England in 1477 to Bacon's death in 1626. I have also added an index. In preparing these sections of the book, I have been largely indebted to the services of Mr. W. B. Owen, B.A., late scholar of St. Catherine's College, Cambridge. I have at the same time to thank my friend Mr. Thomas Seccombe for reading the final proofs.

October 1, 1904.

CONTENTS

III

SIR PHILIP SIDNEY

IV

SIR WALTER RALEGH

V

EDMUND SPENSER

VI

FRANCIS BACON

VII

SHAKESPEARE'S CAREER

CONTENTS

VIII

FOREIGN INFLUENCES ON SHAKESPEARE

LIST OF ILLUSTRATIONS

CHRONOLOGICAL TABLE

OF LEADING EVENTS IN THE HISTORY OF ENGLISH AND EUROPEAN CULTURE FROM THE INTRODUCTION OF PRINTING INTO ENGLAND TO THE DEATH OF FRANCIS BACON

1477. Caxton sets up a printing-press at Westminster.
Birth of Titian.
1478. Birth of Sir Thomas More.
1480. Birth of Bandello, the Italian novelist.
1483. Birth of Raphael.
Birth of Luther.
Birth of Rabelais.
1484. Birth of Julius Cæsar Scaliger.
1485. Death of Richard III.
Accession of Henry VII.
1486. Birth of Andrea del Sarto.
1491. Copernicus studies optics, and mathematics at Cracow.
1492. Columbus's first voyage to West Indies.
1493. Columbus' second voyage to West Indies.
1494. Death of Politian.
1497. John Cabot sights Cape Breton and Nova Scotia.
Vasco da Gama rounds the Cape of Good Hope.
Birth of Holbein.
1498. Columbus discovers South America.
Erasmus first visits England.
Death of Savonarola.
1499. Cabot follows North American coast from 60° to 30° N. lat.
Leonardo da Vinci's 'Last Supper.'

1499. Birth of Charles V.
1502. Columbus sails in the Gulf of Mexico.
1504. More enters Parliament.
More's first marriage.
Leonardo da Vinci paints 'Mona Lisa.'
Sanazzaro's *Arcadia*.
1506. Death of Columbus.
1508. Michael Angelo decorates the roof of the Sistine Chapel.
1509. Death of Henry VII.
Accession of Henry VIII.
Erasmus's *Encomium Moriæ* published.
Raphael decorates the Vatican.
Birth of Calvin.
1510. More Under-Sheriff of London.
Ariosto's *Orlando Furioso*.
Titian paints 'Sacred and profane Love.'
Death of Botticelli.
1511. More's second marriage.
1512. Death of Amerigo Vespucci.
1513. Leo X. Pope.
Wolsey chief minister in England.
Machiavelli's *Prince* composed.
1515. More sent as envoy to Flanders.
Raphael's 'Sistine Madonna.'
1516. Erasmus issues revised Greek text of New Testament.

1516. More's *Utopia*.
1517. Erasmus finally leaves England.
    Luther nails his challenge to the Pope on Wittenberg Church door.
1518. Birth of Tintoretto.
1519. Death of Leonardo da Vinci.
    Charles v. elected emperor.
1520. Death of Raphael.
    Luther burns papal bull condemning him.
1521. More knighted.
    Luther translates Scriptures into German.
    Death of Leo x.
1522. Luther attacks Henry viii.
1523. Lord Berners's translation of Froissart's *Chronicles* (1st vol.) published.
    More Speaker of the House of Commons.
    Titian's 'Bacchus and Ariadne.'
1524. Birth of Ronsard.
1525. Tyndale translates the New Testament into English.
    Lord Berners's translation of Froissart's *Chronicles* (2nd vol.) published.
    More Chancellor of the Duchy of Lancaster.
1526. Sebastian Cabot visits La Plata in behalf of Charles v. of Spain.
1527. Holbein visits England.
    Death of Machiavelli (*æt.* 58).
1528. Birth of Albert Dürer.
    Birth of Paul Veronese.
1529. More succeeds Wolsey as Lord Chancellor.
1530. Copernicus (*De Revolutionibus*) completes description of solar system.
    The Augsburg Confession embodies Luther's final principles.
1532. More resigns office of Lord Chancellor.
    Machiavelli's *Prince* published.
    Rabelais' *Pantagruel* and *Gargantua*.
    Birth of Jean Antoine de Baif.

1533. Separation of English Church from Rome.
    Divorce of Queen Catherine.
    Death of Ariosto.
    Birth of Montaigne.
1534. Henry viii. made supreme Head of the Church of England.
    The Nun of Kent denounces Henry viii.
    More sent to the Tower.
1535. Execution of More.
    Coverdale's translation of the Bible (first complete Bible printed in English).
1536. English Bible issued by Rogers.
    Dissolution of lesser monasteries.
    Pope Paul iii. issues bull of deposition against Henry viii.
    Death of Erasmus.
    Calvin's *Christianæ Religionis Institutio* published.
1539. Suppression of greater abbeys in England.
1540. Order of Jesuits instituted.
1542. Montemayor's *Diana*.
    Inquisition established in Rome.
1543. Death of Copernicus.
    Death of Holbein.
1544. Birth of Tasso.
1546. Michael Angelo designs the dome of St. Peter's, Rome.
    Death of Luther.
    Birth of Tycho Brahe.
    Birth of Philippe Desportes.
1547. Death of Henry viii.
    Accession of Edward vi.
    Birth of Cervantes.
1549. English Book of Common Prayer issued.
    Ronsard's first poem published.
    Du Bellay's *Defense et illustration de la langue Française*.
1550. Monument to Chaucer erected in Westminster Abbey.
    Inauguration of the French Pléiade.
1551. English translation of More's *Utopia*.
1552. English Prayer Book revised by Cranmer.

1552. Birth of Edmund Spenser.
Birth of Sir Walter Ralegh.
1553. Death of Edward vi.
Coronation of Lady Jane Grey.
Accession of Mary, who restores
the Catholic religion.
Death of Rabelais.
1554. Birth of Sir Philip Sidney.
Bandello's *Novelle* published.
1555. Persecution of Protestants in
England.
1556. Death of Cranmer.
Death of Ignatius Loyola, founder
of the Jesuits.
1558. England loses Calais.
Death of Queen Mary.
Accession of Queen Elizabeth, who
restores Protestantism in England.
Death of Julius Cæsar Scaliger.
1560. The Geneva (Breeches) Bible.
First collective edition of the
works of Ronsard.
Death of Du Bellay.
Death of Bandello, the Italian
novelist.
1561. Birth of Francis Bacon.
Scaliger's *Poetics* published.
1562. Tasso's epic *Rinaldo* written.
1563. The Thirty-nine Articles imposed
on the English Clergy.
1564. Birth of Shakespeare.
Birth of Marlowe.
Death of Michael Angelo.
Death of Calvin.
Birth of Galileo.
1565. Cinthio's *Hecatommithi* published.
1568. The 'Bishops' Bible' published.
1571. Bull of deposition issued by Pope
Pius v. against Queen Elizabeth.
Birth of Kepler.
1572. The St. Bartholomew Massacre in
Paris.
1573. Sidney in Germany and Italy.
1574. Death of Cinthio, the Italian
novelist.
1576. First public theatre opened in
London.
Death of Titian.

1576. Festivities at Kenilworth in honour
of Queen Elizabeth.
Spenser becomes M.A.
1577. Sidney on diplomatic mission in
Germany.
Birth of Rubens.
1578. Sidney visits William of Orange
at Antwerp.
1579. Gosson's *School of Abuse.*
North's English translation of
Plutarch's *Lives.*
Spenser's *Shepheards Calender*
published.
Sidney and Spenser become members of the 'Areopagus.'
Birth of John Fletcher.
1580. Lyly's *Euphues* published.
Spenser settles in Ireland in
Government service.
Sir F. Drake returns to England
after his circumnavigation.
Kepler and Tycho Brahe's Astro-
nomical Tables published.
Montaigne's *Essais* (i. ii.) pub-
lished.
1581. Sidney's *Arcadia* finished, his
Sonnets and *Apologie for Poetrie*
begun.
Tasso's *Gerusalemme Liberata*
published, and *Aminta* written.
1582. Shakespeare marries Anne Hatha-
way.
Bible translated by English Cath-
olics at Rheims.
1583. Bruno visits England.
Sidney knighted: becomes Joint-
Master of Ordnance and marries
Frances Walsingham.
Sir Humphrey Gilbert voyages to
Newfoundland.
Grant to Sidney of land in
America.
Galileo discovers the principle of
the pendulum.
1584. Bacon enters Parliament.
Ralegh's colonisation of Virginia
begins.
Birth of Francis Beaumont.
1585. Death of Ronsard (27th December).

1585. Guarini's *Pastor Fido* acted.
Cervantes' first work, *Galatea*, published.

1586. Shakespeare leaves Stratford-on-Avon for London.
Hooker's *Ecclesiastical Polity* begun.
Bacon becomes a member of Gray's Inn.
English army supports Protestants of Low Countries.
Sidney Governor of Flushing.
Tobacco and potatoes introduced into England.

1587. Marlowe's *Tamburlaine* produced.
Marlowe, Lodge, Greene, and Peele begin writing for English stage.
Execution of Mary Queen of Scots.

1588. Defeat of Spanish Armada.
Death of Paul Veronese.
Montaigne's *Essais* (iii.) published.

1589. Bacon's *Advertisement touching Controversies of the Church.*
Drake plunders Corunna.
Lope de Vega commences his great series of dramas.
Death of Jean Antoine de Baif.

1590. Sidney's *Arcadia* published.
Spenser revisits London, and publishes his *Faerie Queene* (i.-iii.).
Death of Walsingham.

1591. Bacon enters service of the Earl of Essex.
Spenser receives a pension from the Queen.
Sidney's *Astrophel and Stella.*
Spenser's *Daphnaida* and *Complaints.*
Shakespeare's *Love's Labour's Lost* written.

1592. Shakespeare remodels *Henry VI.*
Death of Montaigne.
Galileo supports Copernican theory in lectures at Padua.

1593. Death of Marlowe.
Shakespeare's *Venus and Adonis* published.

1594. Shakespeare's *Lucrece* published.
Shakespeare acts at Court.

1594. Spenser marries Elizabeth Boyle.
Death of Tintoretto.

1595. Ralegh sails to Guiana.
Sidney's *Apologie for Poetrie* published.
Spenser's *Colin Clout, Amoretti,* and *Epithalamion* published.
Death of Tasso.

1596. Death of Sir Francis Drake.
Ralegh's *Discovery of Guiana* written (published, 1606).
Spenser's *View of the State of Ireland* completed, *Faerie Queene* (iv.-vi.) and *Prothalamion* published.

1597. First edition of Bacon's *Essays.*
Shakespeare writes 1 *Henry IV.,* and purchases New Place, Stratford-on-Avon.

1598. Globe Theatre built.
Death of Lord Burghley.
Spenser Sheriff of Cork.
Sidney's *Arcadia* edited in folio.
Jonson's *Every Man in His Humour* acted.

1599. Death of Spenser and burial in Westminster Abbey.
Expedition of Earl of Essex in Ireland.

1600. William Gilbert's *De Magnete* published.
Death of Hooker.
Birth of Calderon.
Fairfax's translation of Tasso's *Jerusalem Delivered* published.
Giordano Bruno burned at Rome.
Earl of Essex's rebellion and execution.

1601. Death of Tycho Brahe; he is succeeded by Kepler as astronomer to the Emperor Rudolph II.

1602. *Hamlet* produced.

1603. Death of Queen Elizabeth.
Accession of James I.
Florio's translation of Montaigne published.

1603. Ralegh condemned for alleged treason and imprisoned in the Tower of London.

1604. *Hamlet* published in quarto.

England makes peace with Spain.

Kepler's *Optics* published.

1605. Bacon's *Advancement of Learning* published.

Bacon marries Alice Barnham.

Cervantes' *Don Quixote*, Part i., published.

Death of Desportes.

1607. Bacon Solicitor-General.

1608. *King Lear* published in quarto.

Birth of Milton.

1609. Spenser's *Works* published in folio.

Shakespeare's *Sonnets*, *Troilus and Cressida*, and *Pericles* published in quarto.

Kepler publishes first and second laws of astronomical calculation.

Galileo discovers the satellites of Jupiter.

1611. Shakespeare's *Tempest* probably written; after which the dramatist retires to Stratford.

Authorised Version of Bible issued.

1612. Second edition of Bacon's *Essays*.

Death of Robert Cecil, Earl of Salisbury.

1613. Bacon Attorney-General.

Death of Guarini.

1614. Ralegh's *History of the World* published.

1615. Cervantes' *Don Quixote*, Part ii., published.

1616. Bacon privy-councillor.

Death of Shakespeare.

Death of Francis Beaumont.

Death of Cervantes.

1617. Bacon Lord Keeper.

Expedition of Ralegh to the Orinoco.

Galileo submits to the ecclesiastical authorities.

1619. Bacon Lord Chancellor, and raised to peerage as Lord Verulam.

Ralegh's execution.

1619. Harvey reveals his discovery of the Circulation of the Blood.

Kepler publishes third law in his *Harmonia Mundi*.

1620. Landing of Pilgrim Fathers in New England.

Bacon's *Novum Organum* published.

1621. Bacon made Viscount St. Alban; charged with corruption, convicted, and degraded.

1622. Bacon's *Henry VII.* published.

Othello published in quarto.

1623. Shakespeare's First Folio published.

Bacon's *De Augmentis* published.

1624. Bacon writes *New Atlantis*.

1625. Third and final edition of Bacon's *Essays*.

Death of James i.

Death of John Fletcher.

1626. Death of Bacon (April 9).

GREAT ENGLISHMEN OF THE SIXTEENTH CENTURY

I

THE SPIRIT OF THE SIXTEENTH CENTURY

> 'What a piece of work is man! How noble in reason!
> how infinite in faculty! in form, in moving how express
> and admirable! in action how like an angel! in apprehen-
> sion how like a god! the beauty of the world! the paragon
> of animals!'
>
> SHAKESPEARE, *Hamlet*, II. ii. 323-8.

> 'Nam ipsa scientia potestas est.'
>
> BACON, *Meditationes Sacrae.*

[BIBLIOGRAPHY.—The subject of the European Renaissance may
be studied at length in Burckhardt's *Civilisation of the Period of
the Renaissance in Italy* (English ed. 1890); in J. A. Symonds's
Renaissance in Italy (7 vols. ed. 1898); and in the *Cambridge
Modern History*, vol. i., 1902. Important phases of the movement are well illustrated in Walter Pater's collection of Essays
called *The Renaissance* (1877).]

I

In the *Dictionary of National Biography* will be found the
lives of more than two thousand Englishmen and Englishwomen who flourished in England in the sixteenth National
century. It is the first century in our history Biography
and
which offers the national biographer subjects sixteenth-
century
reaching in number to four figures. The English- England.
men who attained, according to the national biographer's
estimate, the level of distinction entitling them to biographic commemoration were in the sixteenth century

thrice as numerous as those who reached that level in the fourteenth or fifteenth century.

The number of distinguished men which a country produces depends to some extent, but to some extent only, on Causes of its population. England of the sixteenth century distinctive was more populous than England of the four-achieve-ment. teenth or fifteenth, but the increase of population is not as three to one, which is the rate of increase in the volume of distinctive achievement. Probably the four millions of the fifteenth century became five millions in the sixteenth, a rate of increase of twenty-five per cent., an infinitesimal rate of increase when it is compared with the gigantic increase of three hundred per cent., which characterises the volume of distinctive achievement. One must, therefore, look outside statistics of population for the true cause of the fact that for every man who gained any sort of distinction in fifteenth century England, three men gained any sort of distinction in the sixteenth century. It is not to the numbers of the people that we need direct our attention; it is to their spirit, to the working of their minds, to their outlook on life, to their opportunities of uncommon experience that we must turn for a solution of our problem.

Englishmen of the sixteenth century breathed a new atmosphere intellectually and spiritually. They came under The Re- a new stimulus, compounded of many elements, naissance. each of them new and inspiring. To that stimulus must be attributed the sudden upward growth of distinctive achievement among them, the increase of the opportunities of famous exploits, and the consequent preservation from oblivion of more names of Englishmen than in any century before. The stimulus under which Englishmen came in the sixteenth century may be summed up in the familiar word

Renaissance. The main factor of the European Renaissance, of the New Birth of intellect, was a passion for extending the limits of human knowledge, and for employing man's capabilities to new and better advantage than of old. New curiosity was generated in regard to the dimensions of the material world. There was a boundless enthusiasm for the newly discovered art and literature of ancient Greece. Men were fired by a new resolve to make the best and not the worst of life upon earth. They were ambitious to cultivate as the highest good the idea of beauty.

All the nations of Western Europe came under the sway of the mighty movement of the Renaissance, and although national idiosyncrasies moulded and coloured its development in each country, there was every- *Unity of the movement.* where close resemblance in the general effect. The intellectual restlessness and recklessness of sixteenth-century England, with its literary productivity and yearning for novelty and adventure, differed little in broad outline, however much it differed in detail, from the intellectual life of sixteenth-century France, Italy, Spain, or even Germany. It was the universal spirit of the Renaissance, and no purely national impulse, which produced in sixteenth-century England that extended series of varied exploits on the part of Englishmen and Englishwomen, the like of which had not been known before in the history of our race. That series of exploits may be said to begin with the wonderful enlightenment of Sir Thomas More's *Utopia,* and to culminate in the achievements of Bacon and Shakespeare; sharply divided as was the form of Shakespeare's work from that of Bacon's, each was in spirit the complement of the other.

Bacon ranks in eminence only second to Shakespeare among the English sons of the Renaissance, and his Latin

apophthegm, 'nam ipsa scientia potestas est'—'for knowledge is power'—might be described as the watchword

'Know-
ledge is
power.'

of the intellectual history of England, as of
all Western Europe, in the sixteenth century.
The true sons of the Renaissance imagined that
unrestricted study of the operations of nature, life, and
thought could place at their command all the forces which
moved the world.   The Renaissance student's faith was
that of Marlowe's *Faustus :*

> 'Oh, what a world of profit and delight,
> Of power, of honour, and omnipotence,
> Is promised to the studious artisan !
> All things that move between the quiet poles
> Shall be at my command ; emperors and kings
> Are but obeyed in their several provinces ;
> But his dominion that exceeds in this,
> Stretcheth as far as doth the mind of man.'[1]

Knowledge was the ever present quest.   Study yielded
'godlike recompense,' which was worthy of any exertion.
Men drank deep of the fountains of knowledge and were
still insatiate.   Extravagant conceptions were bred of the
capabilities of man's intellect which made it easy of belief
that omniscience was ultimately attainable.

II

Here and there a painful scholar of the Renaissance was
content to seek knowledge in one direction only ; such an

Width of
outlook.

one cheerfully forwent the joys of life in the
hope of mastering in all minuteness a single
branch of learning, or of science.   But the meticulous scholar
was not typical of the epoch.   The children of the Renaissance scorned narrowness of outlook.   They thirsted for

[1] Marlowe, *Faustus*, Sc. i. 54 *sq*.

universal knowledge; they pursued with equal eagerness practice and theory. Natural science was not divorced from literature. The study of mathematics was a fit pursuit for the artist. The greatest painter of the age, Leonardo da Vinci, was also poet, mathematician, engineer, expert indeed in all branches of physical science. The poet and the scholar were ambitious to engage in affairs of the world—in war or politics. It was no part of a man, however richly endowed by genius, to avoid the active business of life. Dialecticians of the time credited all goals of human endeavour with inherent unity. They repeatedly argued, for example, that skill with the pen was the proper complement of skill with the sword. Poetry, according to Sir Philip Sidney, an admirable representative of Renaissance aspirations, was the rightful 'companion of camps,' and no soldier could safely neglect the military teachings of Homer. Avowed specialism was foreign to the large temper of the times. Versatility of interest and experience was the accepted token of human excellence.

There are obvious disadvantages in excessive distribution of mental energy. The products of diversified endeavour are commonly formless, void, and evanescent. But the era of the Renaissance had such abundant stores of intellectual energy that, in spite of all that was dissipated in the vain quest of omniscience, there remained enough to vitalise particular provinces of endeavour with enduring and splendid effect. The men of the Renaissance had reserves of strength which enabled them to master more or less specialised fields of work, even while they winged vague and discursive flights through the whole intellectual expanse. Leonardo da Vinci was an excellent mathematician and poet, but despite his excellence in these directions, his supreme power was concentrated on

Checks on distribution of mental energy.

painting. Prodigal as seemed the expenditure of intellectual
effort, there was a practical economy in its application. In
the result its ripest fruit was stimulating and lasting, more
stimulating and lasting than any which came of the more
rigid specialism of later epochs.

More and Ralegh, Sidney and Spenser, Bacon and Shakespeare, all pertinently illustrate the versatility of the age,
Versatility of great English-men of the epoch. the bold digressiveness of its intellectual and
imaginative endeavour. To varying extents
omniscience was the foible of all and carried with
it the inevitable penalties. Each set foot in more
numerous and varied tracts of knowledge than any one man
could thoroughly explore. They treated of many subjects,
of the real significance of which they obtained only the
faintest and haziest glimpse. The breadth of their intellectual
ambitions at times impoverished their achievement. The
splendid gifts of Sidney and Ralegh were indeed largely
wasted in too wide and multifarious a range of work. They
did a strange variety of things to admiration, but failed to do
the one thing of isolated pre-eminence which might have
rewarded efficient concentration of effort. Shakespeare's
intellectual capacity seems as catholic in range as Leonardo
da Vinci's, and laws that apply to other men hardly apply
to him ; but there were tracts of knowledge, outside even
Shakespeare's province, on which he trespassed unwisely.
His handling of themes of law, geography, and scholarship,
proves that in his case, as in that of smaller men, there
were limits of knowledge beyond which it was perilous
for him to stray. With greater insolence Bacon wrote of
astronomy without putting himself to the trouble of appre-
hending the solar system of Copernicus, and misinterpreted
other branches of science from lack of special knowledge.
But in the case of Bacon and Shakespeare, such errors are

spots on the sun. As interpreter in drama of human nature Shakespeare has no rival; nor indeed among prophets of science has any other shown Bacon's magnanimity or eloquence. Although nature had amply endowed them with the era's universality of intellectual interests, she had also given them the power of demonstrating the full force of their rare genius in a particular field of effort. It was there that each reached the highest pinnacle of glory.

III

In a sense the sixteenth century was an age of transition, of transition from the ancient to the modern world, from the age of darkness and superstition to the age of light and scientific knowledge. A mass of newly discovered knowledge lay at its disposal, but so large a mass that succeeding centuries had to be enlisted in the service of digesting it and co-ordinating it. When the sixteenth century opened, the aspects of human life had recently undergone revolution. The old established theories of man and the world had been refuted, and much time was required for the evolution of new theories that should be workable, and fill the vacant places. The new problems were surveyed with eager interest and curiosity, but were left to the future for complete solution. The scientific spirit, which is the life of the modern world, was conceived in the sixteenth century; it came to birth later.

The transitional aspect of the century.

The causes of the intellectual awakening which distinguished sixteenth-century Europe lie on the surface. Its primary mainsprings are twofold. On the one hand a distant past had been suddenly unveiled, and there had come to light an ancient literature and an ancient philosophy which proved the human intellect

Primary causes of the awakening.

to possess capacities hitherto unimagined. On the other hand, the dark curtains which had hitherto restricted man's view of the physical world to a small corner of it were torn asunder, and the strange fact was revealed that that which had hitherto been regarded by men as the whole sphere of physical life and nature was in reality a mere fragment of a mighty universe of which there had been no previous conception.

Of the two revelations—that of man's true intellectual capacity and that of the true extent of his physical environment—the intellectual revelation came first. The physical revelation followed at no long interval. It was an accidental conjuncture of events. But each powerfully reacted on the other, and increased its fertility of effect.

The priority of the intellectual revelation.

It was the discovery anew by Western Europe of classical Greek literature and philosophy which was the spring of the intellectual revelation of the Renaissance. That discovery was begun in the fourteenth century, when Greek subjects of the falling Byzantine empire brought across the Adriatic manuscript memorials of Greek intellectual culture. But it was not till the final overthrow of the Byzantine empire by the Turks that all that survived of the literary art of Athens was driven westward in a flood, and the whole range of Greek enlightenment—the highest enlightenment that had yet dawned in the human mind—lay at the disposal of Western Europe. It was then there came for the first time into the modern world the feeling for form, the frank delight in life and the senses, the unrestricted employment of the reason, with every other enlightened aspiration that was enshrined in Attic literature and philosophy. Under the growing Greek influence, all shapes of literature and specu-

The discovery of Greek literature and philosophy.

lation, of poetry and philosophy, sprang into new life in Italy during the fourteenth and fifteenth centuries. In the sixteenth century the torch was handed on by Italy to Spain, France, Germany, and England. In each of those countries the light developed in accord with the national idiosyncrasy, but in none of them did it wholly lose the Italian hue, which it acquired at its first coming into Western Europe. It was mainly through Florence that the newly released stream of Hellenism flowed northwards.

The Italian influence.

From another quarter than the East came, a little later, the physical revelation which helped no less to mould the spirit of the era. Until the extreme end of the fifteenth century, man knew nothing of the true shape or extent of the planet on which his life was cast. Fantastic theories of cosmography had been evolved, to which no genuine test had been applied. It was only in the year 1492 that Western Europe first learned its real place on the world's surface. The maritime explorations which distinguished the decade 1490-1500 unveiled new expanses of land and sea which reduced to insignificance the fragments of earth and heaven with which men had hitherto been familiar.

The physical revelation.

To the west was brought to light for the first time a continent larger than the whole area of terrestrial matter of which there was previous knowledge. To the south a Portuguese mariner discovered that Africa, which was hitherto deemed to be merely a narrow strip of earth forming the southern boundary wall of the world, was a gigantic peninsula thrice the size of Europe, which stretched far into a southern ocean, into the same ocean which washed the shores of India.

Maritime exploration.

Such discoveries were far more than contributions to the

science of geography. They were levers to lift the spirit

The dis-
covery of
the solar
system.

of man into unlooked-for altitudes. They gave new conceptions not of earth alone, but of heaven. The skies were surveyed from points of view which had never yet been approached. A trustworthy study of the sun and stars became possible, and in the early years of the sixteenth century, a scientific investigator deduced from the rich array of new knowledge the startling truth that the earth, hitherto believed to be the centre of the universe, was only one—and that not the largest—of numerous planetary bodies rotating about the sun. If Columbus and Vasco da Gama, the discoverers of new lands and seas, deserve homage for having first revealed the true dimensions of the earth, to Copernicus is due the supreme honour of having taught the inhabitants of the earth to know their just place in the economy of the limitless firmament, over which they had hitherto fancied that they ruled. Whatever final purpose sun, planets and stars served, it was no longer possible to regard them as mere ministers of light and heat to men on earth.

So stupendous was the expansion of the field of man's thought, which was generated by the efforts of Columbus

The expan-
sion of
thought.

and Copernicus, that only gradually was its full significance apprehended. All branches of human endeavour and human speculation were ultimately remodelled in the light of the new physical revelation. The change was in the sixteenth century only beginning. But new ideals at once came to birth, and new applications of human energy suggested themselves in every direction.

Dreamers believed that a new universe had been born, and that they were destined to begin a new manner of human life, which should be freed from the defects of the old. The intellectual revelation of a new culture power-

fully reinforced the physical revelation of new heavenly
and earthly bodies. Assured hopes of human perfectibility
permeated human thought. The unveiling of the measure-
less expanse of physical nature made of man, physically
considered, a pigmy, but the spirited enterprises whereby
the new knowledge was gained combined with the revelation of the intellectual achievements of the past to generate
the new faith that there lurked in man's mind a power
which would ultimately yield him mastery of all the hidden
forces of animate and inanimate nature.

IV

The mechanical invention of the printing press almost
synchronised with the twofold revelation of new realms of
thought and nature. The ingenious device came   The inven-
slowly to perfection, but as soon as it was   tion of
perfected, its employment spread with amazing   printing.
rapidity under stress of the prevailing stir of discovery. The
printing press greatly contributed to the dissemination of
the ideas, which the movement of the Renaissance bred.
Without the printing-press the spread of the movement
would have been slower and its character would have been
less homogeneous. The books embodying the new spirit
would not have multiplied so quickly nor travelled so far.
The printing-press distributed the fruit of the new spirit
over the whole area of the civilised world.

In every sphere of human aspiration through Western
Europe the spirit of the Renaissance made its presence felt.
New ideas invaded the whole field of human effort   The Re-
in a tumbling crowd, but many traditions of the   naissance
ancient régime, which the invasion threatened to   and the
                                                    Church of
displace, stubbornly held their ground. Some   Rome.
veteran principles opposed the newcomers' progress and

checked the growth of the New Birth of mind. The old Papal Church of Rome at the outset absorbed some of its teaching. The Roman Church did not officially discourage Greek learning and it encouraged exploration. There were humanists among the Popes of the fifteenth and sixteenth centuries. But the new spirit, in the fulness of time, demanded concessions of the Church which struck at the root of her being. The Church peremptorily refused to remodel her beliefs on the liberal lines that the new spirit laid down. Ultimately she declared open war on the enlightened thought of the Renaissance. Some essayed the subtle task of paying simultaneous allegiance to the two opposing forces. Erasmus's unique fertility of mental resource enabled him to come near success in the exploit. But most found the attempt beyond their strength, and, like Sir Thomas More, the greatest of those who tried to reconcile the irreconcilable, sacrificed genius and life in the hopeless cause.

The Papacy had more to fear from the passion for inquiry and criticism which the Renaissance evoked than from the positive ideals and principles which it generated. The great Protestant schism is sometimes represented, without much regard for historic truth, as a calculated return to the primitive ideals of a distant past, as a deliberate revival of a divinely inspired system of religion which had suffered eclipse. Its origin is more complex. It was mainly the outcome of a compromise with the critical temper, which the intellectual and physical revelations of the Renaissance imposed on men's mind. Protestantism, in the garb in which it won its main triumph, was the contribution of Germany to the spiritual regeneration of the sixteenth century, and a Teutonic cloudiness of sentiment overhung its foundations. Protestantism ignored large tracts of the new teaching and a mass of the new ideas which the Italian Renaissance brought to birth and cherished. But

*The com-
promise of
Protes-
tantism.*

Protestants were eager to mould their belief in some limited agreement with the dictates of reason.   They acknowledged, within bounds, the Renaissance faith in the power and right of the human intellect to grapple with the mysteries of nature.   The dogmas and ceremonies of the old system which signally flouted reason were denounced and rejected. A narrow interpretation of the Renaissance theory of human perfectibility coloured new speculations as to the efficacy of divine grace.   But Protestantism declined to take reason as its sole guide or object of worship.   Protestantism was the fruit of a compromise between the old conception of faith and the new conception of reason.   The compromise was widely welcomed by a mass of inquirers who, though moved by the spirit of the age, were swayed in larger degree by religious emotion, and cherished unshakable confidence in the bases of Christianity.   But the Protestant endeavour to accommodate old and new ideas was not acceptable in all quarters.   A bold minority in Italy, France and England, either tacitly or openly, spurned a compromise which was out of harmony with the genuine temper of the era.   While Roman Catholicism fortified its citadels anew, and Protestantism advanced against them in battle array in growing strength, the free thought and agnosticism, which the unalloyed spirit of the Renaissance generated, gained year by year fresh accession of force in every country of Western Europe.

On secular literature the religious reformation, working within its normal limits, produced a far-reaching effect. The qualified desire for increase of knowledge, Literary which characterised the new religious creeds, influence of the widely extended the first-hand study of the Holy Bible. Scriptures, which enshrined the title-deeds of Christianity. Translations of the Bible into living tongues were encouraged by all Protestant reformers, and thereby Hebraic sublimity and intensity gained admission to much Renaissance literature.   It was owing to such turn of events that there met, notably in the great literature of sixteenth-century England, the solemnity of Hebraism, with the Hellenist love of beauty and form.

v

The incessant clash of ideas—the ferment of men's thought—strangely affected the moral character of many

The ethical paradox of the era. leaders of the Renaissance in England no less than in Europe.   Life was lived at too high a pressure to maintain outward show of unity of purpose.   A moral chaos often reigned in man's being and vice was entangled inextricably with virtue.

Probably in no age did the elemental forces of good and evil fight with greater energy than in the sixteenth century

The alliance of good and evil. for the dominion of man's soul.   Or rather, never did the two forces make closer compact with each other whereby they might maintain a joint occu-pation of the human heart.   Men who were capable of the noblest acts of heroism were also capable of the most con-temptible acts of treachery.   An active sense of loyalty to a throne seemed no bar to secret conspiracy against a sovereign's life.   When Shakespeare described in his sonnets the two spirits—'the better angel' and 'the worser spirit,' both of whom claimed his allegiance—he repeated a conceit which is universal in the poetry of the Renaissance, and repre-sents with singular accuracy the ethical temper of the age.

Among the six men whose life and work are portrayed in

The major paradox of More, Bacon, and Ralegh. this volume, three—More, Bacon, and Ralegh —forcibly illustrate the mutually inconsistent characteristics with which the spirit of the Re-naissance often endowed one and the same man. More, who proved himself in the *Utopia* an enlightened champion of the freedom of the intellect, and of religious

toleration, laid down his life as a martyr to superstition and
to the principle of authority (in its least rational form) in
matters of religion.   Ralegh, who preached in his *History of
the World* and in philosophic tracts a most elevated altruism
and philosophy of life, neglected the first principles of
honesty in a passionate greed of gold.   Bacon, who rightly
believed himself to be an inspired prophet of science, and
a clear-eyed champion of the noblest progress in human
thought, stooped to every petty trick in order to make
money and a worldly reputation.

Happily the careers of the three remaining subjects—
Sidney, Spenser, and Shakespeare—are paradoxical in a minor
degree.   But the paradox which is inherent in the   The minor
spirit of the time cast its glamour to some extent   paradox of
Sidney,
even over them.   The poets Sidney and Spenser,   Spenser,
and Shake-
who preached with every appearance of conviction   speare.
the fine doctrine that the poets' crown is alone worthy the
poets' winning, strained their nerves until they broke in
death, in pursuit of such will-o'-the-wisps as political or
military fame.   Shakespeare, with narrow personal experiences of life, and with worldly ambitions of commonplace
calibre, mastered the whole scale of human aspiration and
announced his message in language which no other mortal
has yet approached in insight or harmony.   Shakespeare's
career stands apart from that of his fellows and defies
methods of analysis which are applicable to theirs.   But he,
no less than they, was steeped in the spirit of the Renaissance.   In him that spirit reached its apotheosis.   With it,
however, there mingled in his nature a mysteriously potent
element, which belonged in like measure to none other.
The magic of genius has worked miracles in individual
minds in many epochs, but it never worked greater miracle
than when it fused itself in Shakespeare's being with the
ripe temper of Renaissance culture.

II

SIR THOMAS MORE

Thomae Mori ingenio quid unquam finxit natura vel mollius, vel dulcius, vel felicius?'—[Than the temper of Thomas More did nature ever frame aught gentler, sweeter, or happier?]

Erasmi Epistolae, Tom. III., No. xiv.

[BIBLIOGRAPHY.—The foundation for all lives of Sir Thomas More is the charming personal memoir by his son-in-law, William Roper, which was first printed at Paris in 1626, and after passing through numerous editions was recently re-issued in the 'King's Classics.' Cresacre More, Sir Thomas' great-grandson, a pious Catholic layman, published a fuller biography about 1631 ; this was reissued for the last time in 1828. The Letters of Erasmus, *Erasmi Epistolae*, Leyden 1706, which J. A. Froude has charmingly summarised, shed invaluable light on More's character. Mr. Frederic Seebohm's *Oxford Reformers* (Colet, Erasmus and More) vividly describes More in relation to the religious revolution of his day. The latest complete biography, by the Rev. W. H. Hutton, B.D., appeared in 1895. The classical English translation of More's *Utopia*, which was first published in 1551, has lately been re-edited by Mr. Churton Collins for the Oxford University Press. More's English works have not been reprinted since they were first collected in 1557. The completest collection of his Latin works was issued in Germany in 1689.]

I

SIR THOMAS MORE was a Londoner. He was born in the heart of the capital, in Milk Street, Cheapside, not far from Bread Street, where Milton was born more than a century later. The year of More's birth carries us back to 1478, to the end of the Middle Ages, to the year when the Renaissance was looming on England's intellectual horizon, but was as yet shedding a vague and

More's birth, 7th Feb. 1478.

SIR THOMAS MORE
AT THE AGE OF 49.

From the portrait by Holbein in the possession of Edwa·d Huth, Esq.

flickering light. The centre of European culture was in
distant Florence, and England's interests at home were still
mainly absorbed by civil strife. Though by 1478 the acutest
phases of that warfare were passed, it was not effectually
stemmed till Henry VII. triumphed at Bosworth Field and
More was seven years old. Much else was to change before
opportunity for great achievement should be offered More
in his maturity.

It was in association with men and movements for the
most part slightly younger than himself that More first
figured on life's stage. He set forth on life in the vanguard
of the advancing army of contemporary progress, but destiny
decreed that death should find him at the head of the
opposing forces of reaction.

Of the leading actors in the drama in which More was to
play his great part, two were at the time of his birth unborn,
and two were in infancy. Luther, the practical
leader of the religious revolution by which More's
career was moulded, did not come into the world
until More was five; nor until he was thirteen was there born
Henry VIII., the monarch to whom he owed his martyrdom.
To only two of the men with whom he conspicuously worked
was he junior. Erasmus, one of the chief emanci-
pators of the reason, from whom More derived
abundant inspiration, was his senior by eleven
years; Wolsey, the political priest, who was to give England
ascendency in Europe and to offer More the salient opportunities of his career, was seven years his senior.

Senior of Luther and Henry VIII.

The junior of Erasmus and Wolsey.

One spacious avenue to intellectual progress was indeed
in readiness for More and his friends from the
outset. One commanding invention, which exerted unbounded influence—the introduction into
England by Caxton of the newly invented art of printing—

The invention of printing.

was almost coincident with More's birth. A year earlier
Caxton had set up a printing-office in Westminster, and produced for the first time an English printed book there.
That event had far-reaching consequences on the England
of More's childhood. The invention of printing was to the
sixteenth century what the invention of steam locomotion
was to the nineteenth.

The birth in England of the first of the two great influences which chiefly stimulated men's intellectual development, during More's adolescence, was almost simultaneous
with the introduction of printing. Greek learning and
literature were first taught in the country at Oxford in the
seventh decade of the fifteenth century. It was not till the
last decade of that century that European explorers set foot
in the New World of America, and, by compelling men to
reconsider their notion of the universe and pre-existing
theories of the planet to which they were born, completed
the inauguration of the new era of which More was the
earliest English hero.

II

More's family belonged to the professional classes, whose
welfare depends for the most part on no extraneous
More's advantages of inherited rank or wealth, but
father. on personal ability and application. His father
was a barrister who afterwards became a judge. Of humble
origin, he acquired a modest fortune. His temperament
was singularly modest and gentle, but he was blessed with
a quiet sense of humour which was one of his son's most
notable inheritances. The father had a wide experience of
matrimony, having been thrice married, and he is credited
with the ungallant remark that a man taking a wife is like
one putting his hand into a bag of snakes with one eel

among them; he may light on the eel, but it is a hundred
chances to one that he shall be stung by a snake.

Of the great English public schools only two—Winchester
and Eton—were in existence when More was a boy, and
they had not yet acquired a national repute. At school
Up to the age of thirteen More attended a small in London.
day school—the best of its kind in London. It was St.
Anthony's school in Threadneedle Street, and was attached
to St. Anthony's Hospital, a religious and charitable foundation for the residence of twelve poor men. Latin was the
sole means and topic of instruction.

Cardinal Morton, the Archbishop of Canterbury, was wont
to admit to his household boys of good family, to wait on
him, and to receive instruction from his chap- In the
lains. More's father knew the Archbishop and service of
the Arch-
requested him to take young Thomas More into bishop.
his service. The boy's wit and towardness delighted the
Archbishop. 'At Christmastide he would sometimes suddenly
step in among the players and masquers who made merri-
ment for the Archbishop, and, never studying for the
matter, would extemporise a part of his own presently
among them, which made the lookers-on more sport than
all the players besides.' The Archbishop, impressed by the
lad's alertness of intellect, 'would often say of him to the
nobles that divers times dined with him "This child here
writing at the table, whoever shall live to see it, will prove
a marvellous man." '

The Archbishop arranged with More's father to send him
to the University of Oxford, and, when little more than fourteen, he entered Canterbury Hall, a collegiate
At Oxford.
establishment which was afterwards absorbed in
Cardinal Wolsey's noble foundation of Christ Church.

More's allowance while an Oxford student was small.

Without money to bestow on amusements, he spent his time in study to the best advantage. At Oxford More came under the two main influences that dominated his life.

Oxford has often been called by advanced spirits in England the asylum of lost causes, but those who call her so have studied her history superficially. Oxford is commonly as ready to offer a home to new intellectual movements as faithfully to harbour old causes. Oxford has a singular faculty of cultivating the old and the new side by side with a parallel enthusiasm. The University, when More knew it, was proving its capacity in both the old and the new directions. It was giving the first public welcome in England to the new learning, to the revival of classical, and notably of Greek, study. It was helping to introduce the modern English world to Attic literature, the most artistically restrained, the most brilliantly perspicuous body of literature that has yet been contrived by the human spirit. Greek had been lately taught there for the first time by an Italian visitor, while several Oxford students had just returned from Italy burdened with the results of the new study. More came under the travelled scholars' sway, and his agile mind was filled with zeal to assimilate the stimulating fruits of pagan intellect. He read Greek and Latin authors with avidity, and essayed original compositions in their tongues. His scholarship was never very exact, but the instinct of genius revealed to him almost at a glance the secrets of the classical words. His Latin verse was exceptionally facile and harmonious. French came to him with little trouble, and, in emulation of the frequenters of the Athenian Academy, he sought recreation in music, playing with skill on the viol and the flute.

His conservative father, who knew no Greek, was alarmed by his son's enthusiasm for learning, which did not come

The influence of Oxford.

within his own cognisance.   He feared its influence on
the boy's religious orthodoxy, and deemed it safer to
transfer him to the study of law.   Recalling A student
him from Oxford, he sent him to an Inn of of law.
Court in London before he was twenty, to pursue his own
legal profession.   More, with characteristic complacency,
adapted himself to his new environment.   Within a year
or two he proved himself an expert and a learned
lawyer.

But his father had misunderstood Oxford, and had misunderstood his son.   At the same time as the youth imbibed at Oxford a passion for the new learning, Spiritual
he had also imbibed a passion there for the old question-
religion.   Oxford, with its past traditions of un- ings.
swerving fidelity to the Catholic Church, had made More a
religious enthusiast at the same time as her recent access of
intellectual enlightenment had made him a zealous humanist.
While he was a law student in London, the two influences
fought for supremacy in his mind.   He extended his knowledge of Greek, making the acquaintance of other Oxford
students with like interests to his own.   Colet, Linacre,
Grocyn, and Lily, all of whom had drunk deep of the new
culture of the Renaissance, became his closest associates.   He
engaged with them in friendly rivalry in rendering epigrams
from the Greek anthology into Latin, and he read for himself
the works of the great Florentine humanist and mystical
philosopher, Pico della Mirandola, who had absorbed the
idealistic teachings of Plato.   But spiritual questionings at
the same time disturbed him.   Every day he devoted many
hours to spiritual exercises.   He fasted, he prayed, he kept
vigils, he denied himself sleep, he wore a shirt of hair next
his skin, he practised all manner of austerities.   He gave
lectures on St. Augustine's Christian ideal of a 'City of God'

in a London city church ; he began to think that the priest-
hood was his vocation.

But before he was twenty-five he had arrived at a
different conclusion. He resolved to remain at the bar and
in secular life ; he thought he had discovered a *via media*
whereby he could maintain allegiance to his two-fold faith
in Catholicism and in humanism. The breadth of his intellect permitted him the double enthusiasm, although the
liability of conflict between the two was always great. While
moderating his asceticism, he continued scrupulously regular
in all the religious observances expected of a pious Catholic.
But he pursued at the same time his study of Lucian and
the Greek anthology, of Pico della Mirandola and the
philosophic humanists of modern Italy. He made, to his
own satisfaction, a working reconciliation between the old
religion and the new learning, and imagined that he could
devote his life to the furtherance of both causes at once.
There was in the resolve a fatal miscalculation of the force
of his religious convictions. There was inconsistency in the
endeavour to serve two masters. But miscalculation and
inconsistency were the moving causes of the vicissitudes of
Thomas More's career.

III

Probably the main cause of More's resolve to adhere to
the paths of humanism, when his religious fervour inclined
him to abandon them, was his introduction to
the great scholar of the European Renaissance,
Erasmus, who came on a first visit to England
about the year that More reached his majority. Erasmus,
a Dutchman about eleven years More's senior, became a
first-rate Greek scholar when a student at Paris, and gained
a thorough mastery of all classical learning and literature.

The influ-
ence of
Erasmus.

Taking priest's orders he was soon a learned student of divinity, and an enlightened teacher alike of profane and sacred letters. His native temperament preserved him from any tincture of pedantry, and implanted in him a perennially vivid interest in every aspect of human endeavour and experience. Above all things he was a penetrating critic—a critic of life as well as of literature, and he was able to express his critical views with an airiness, a charm, a playfulness of style, which secured for his conclusions a far wider acceptance than was possible to a more formal, more serious, and more crabbed presentation. He was an adept in the use of banter and satire, when exposing the abuses and absurdities whether of religious or secular society of his time. But he met with the usual fate of independent and level-headed critics to whom all extremes are obnoxious, and whose temperament forbids them to identify themselves with any distinctly organised party or faction. In the religious conflicts of the hour Erasmus stood aloof from Protestant revolutionaries like Luther, and from orthodox champions at the Paris Sorbonne of the ancient faith of papal Rome. In the struggle over the progress of humanistic learning, he treated with equal disdain those who set their faces against the study of pagan writers, and those who argued that the human intellect should be exclusively nurtured on servile imitation of classical style. As a consequence Erasmus was denounced by all parties, but he was unmoved by clamour, and remained faithful to his idiosyncrasy to the last. In the era of the Renaissance he did as much as any man to free humanity from the bonds of superstition, and to enable it to give free play to its reasoning faculties.

Erasmus spent much time in England while More's life

was at its prime, and the two men became the closest of

Erasmus's
friendship
for More.

friends. Erasmus at once acknowledged More's fascination. 'My affection for the man is so great,' he wrote, in the early days of their acquaintance, 'that if he bade me dance a hornpipe, I should do at once what he bid me.' Until death separated them, their love for one another knew no change. Erasmus's enlightened influence and critical frankness offered the stimulus that More's genius needed to sustain his faith in humanism at the moment that it was threatened by his religious zeal.

Neither More's spiritual nor his intellectual interests detached him from practical affairs. His progress at the

At the Bar
and in
Parliament.

bar was rapid, and after the customary manner of English barristers, he sought to improve his worldly position by going into politics and obtaining a seat in Parliament. He was a bold and independent speaker, and quickly made his mark by denouncing King Henry vii.'s heavy taxation of the people. A ready ear was given to his argument by fellow members of the House of Commons, and they negatived, at his suggestion, one of the many royal appeals for money. The King angrily expressed astonishment that a beardless boy should disappoint his purpose, and he invented a cause of quarrel with More's father by way of revenge.

IV

Meanwhile More married. As a wooer he seems to have been more philosophic than ardent. He made the acquain-

Marriage.

tance of an Essex gentleman named Colte, who had three daughters, and the second daughter, whom he deemed 'the fairest and best favoured,' moved affection in More. But the young philosopher curbed his passion; he 'considered that it would be both great grief and some shame also to the eldest to see her younger sister preferred before her in marriage.' Accordingly 'of a certain pity' he 'framed his fancy towards' the eldest daughter, Jane. He married her in 1505. The union, if the fruit of compassion, was most satisfactory in result. His wife was very young, and quite uneducated, but More was able, according to his friend Erasmus, to shape her character after his own pattern. Teaching her books and music, he made her a true companion. Acquiring a house in the best part of the City of London, in Bucklersbury, More delighted in his new domestic life. He reckoned 'the enjoyment of his family a necessary part of the business of the man who does not wish to be a stranger in his own house,' and such leisure as his professional work allowed him was happily divided between the superintendence of his household and literary study. Unluckily his wife died six years after marriage. She left him with a family of four children. More lost no time in supplying her place. His second wife was a widow, who, he would often His second wife. say with a laugh, was neither beautiful nor well educated. She lacked one desirable faculty in a wife, the ability to appreciate her husband's jests. But she had the virtues of a good housewife, and ministered to More's creature comforts. He ruled her, according to his friend Erasmus, with caresses and with jokes the point of which she missed. Thus he kept her sharp tongue under better control than sternness and assertion of authority could achieve. With characteristic sense of humour, More made her learn harp, cithern, guitar and (it is said) flute, and practise in his presence every day.

More, after his second marriage, removed from the bust-

ling centre of London to what was then the peaceful river-
side hamlet of Chelsea.   There he lived in simple
patriarchal fashion, surrounded by his children.
Ostentation was abhorrent to him, but he quietly gratified his
love for art and literature by collecting pictures and books.

Settlement at Chelsea.

More prospered in his profession.   The small legal post of
Under-Sheriff, which he obtained from the Corporation of
London, brought him into relations with the merchants, who admired his quickness of wit.   The
Government was contemplating a new commercial
treaty with Flanders, and required the assistance of a representative of London's commercial interest with a view to
improving business relations with the Flemings.   More was
recommended for the post by a city magnate to Henry VIII.'s
great Minister, Cardinal Wolsey, and he received the appointment.   Thus, not long after he had fallen under the
sway of the greatest intellectual leader of the day, Erasmus,
did he first come under the notice of the great political
chieftain.

Under-Sheriff of London.

v

But for the present Wolsey and More worked out their
destinies apart.   The duties of the new office required More
to leave England.   For the first time in his life he
was brought face to face with Continental culture.
He chiefly spent his time in the cities of Bruges,
Brussels and Antwerp, all of which were northern strong-
holds of the art and literature of the Italian Renaissance.
More's interests were widened and stimulated by the enlightened society into which he was thrown.   But he had
his private difficulties.   His salary was small for a man with
a growing family, and he humorously expressed regret at

First visit to the Continent.

the inconsiderateness of his wife and children in failing to
fast from food in his absence.

But, however ill More was remunerated at the moment,
this first visit to the Continent invigorated, if it did not
create, a new ideal of life, and impelled him to
offer his fellow-men a new counsel of perfection,
which, although it had little bearing on the practical course of his own affairs, powerfully affected his reputation with posterity. At Antwerp More met a thoroughly
congenial companion, the great scholar of France and friend
of Erasmus, Peter Giles or Egidius. Versatility of interest
was a mark of Renaissance scholarship. With Giles, More
discussed not merely literary topics but also the contemporary politics and the social conditions of England and the
Continent. In the course of the debates the notion of
sketching an imaginary commonwealth, which should be
freed from the defects of existing society, entered More's
brain.

*Social re-
creation at
Antwerp.*

VI

From Antwerp More brought back the first draft of his
Utopia. That draft ultimately formed the second book of
the completed treatise. But the first and shorter
book which he penned after his return home
merely served the purpose of a literary preface
to the full and detailed exposition of the political and social
ideals which his foreign tour had conjured up in his active
mind.

*First draft
of the
Utopia.*

Increasing practice at the Bar, and the duties of his
judicial office in the City, delayed the completion of the
Utopia, which was not published till the end of 1516, a year
after More's return.

The *Utopia* of Sir Thomas More is the main monument

of his genius. It is as admirable in literary form as it is

original in thought. It displays a mind revelling

Detach-
ment of the in the power of detachment from the sentiment
Utopia.

and the prejudices which prevailed in his personal
environment. To a large extent this power of detachment
was bred of his study of Greek literature. Plato, the great
philosopher of Athens, had sketched in detail an imaginary
republic which was governed solely by regard for the moral
and material welfare of the citizens. To Plato's republic is
traceable More's central position. Equality in all things is
the one and only way to ensure the well-being of a community. All men should enjoy equal possessions and equal
opportunities. On that revolutionary text, which defied the
established bases of contemporary society, More preached
a new and unconventional discourse which ranks with the
supreme manifestations of intellectual fertility.

VII

The prefatory book of the *Utopia* is a vivid piece of fiction
which Defoe could not have excelled. More relates how he

The First accidentally came upon his scholarly friend Peter
Book. Giles in the streets of Antwerp, in conversation
with an old sailor named Raphael Hythlodaye. The sailor
had lately returned from a voyage to the New World
under the command of Amerigo Vespucci, America's epony-
mous hero. Raphael had been impressed by the beneficent
forms of government which prevailed in the New World.
He had also visited England, and had noted social evils there
which called for speedy redress. The degradation of the
masses was sapping the strength of the country. Capital
punishment was the invariable penalty for robbery, and it
was difficult to supply sufficient gibbets whereon to hang

the offenders. The prevalence of crime Raphael assigned to want of employment among the poor, to the idleness and the luxury of the well-to-do, to the recklessness with which the rulers engaged in war, and to the readiness with which merchants were converting arable land into pasture ; villages were laid waste and the opportunity of labour was greatly diminished, in order to fill the coffers of capitalists. Discharged soldiers, troops of dismissed retainers from the households of the nobility and gentry, who, after a life of idleness, were thrown on their own resources, ploughmen and peasants, whose services were no longer required by the sheep-farmers, perilously swelled the ranks of the unemployed and made thieving the only means of livelihood for thousands of the population. A more even distribution of wealth was necessary to the country's salvation. To this end were necessary the enjoyment of the blessings of peace, restrictions on the cupidity of the capitalist, improved education of the humbler classes, and the encouragement of new industries. Crime could be restrained by merciful laws more effectually than by merciless statutes.

This fearless and spirited exposure of the demoralisation of English society, which is set in the mouth of the sailor from the world beyond the Atlantic, potently illustrates the stimulus to thought in the social and political sphere which sprang from the recent maritime discoveries. The abuses which time had fostered in the Old World could alone be dispersed by acceptance of the unsophisticated principles of the New World. The sailor's auditors eagerly recognise the worth of his suggestions, and the sailor promises to report to them the political and social institutions which are in vogue in the land of perfection across the seas. He had lived in such a country. He had made his way to the island of Utopia when, on

The ideal of the New World.

his last voyage, he had been left behind by his comrades at his own wish on the South American coast near Cape Frio, off Brazil.

The second book of More's *Utopia* describes the ideal commonwealth of this imaginary island of No-where (Οὐ τόπος), and in it culminate the hopes and aspirations of all Renaissance students of current politics and society. The constitution of the country is an elective monarchy, but the prince can be

deposed if he falls under suspicion of seeking to

The Second Book of the Utopia. enslave the people. War is regarded as inglorious, and no leagues or treaties with foreign powers are permitted. The internal economy is of an exceptionally enlightened kind. The sanitary arrangements in towns are the best imaginable. The streets are broad and well watered. Every house has a garden. Slaughter-houses are placed outside the wall. Hospitals are organised on scientific principles. The isolation of persons suffering from contagious diseases is imperative.

The mind is as wisely cared for as the body. All children whether girls or boys are thoroughly and wisely educated.

Care of the mind. They are apt to learn, and find much attraction in Greek authors, even in Lucian's merry conceits and jests. At the same time labour is an universal condition of life. Every man has to work at a craft, as well as to devote some time each day to husbandry, but no human being is permitted to become a mere beast of burden. The hours of manual labour are strictly limited to six a day. A large portion of the people's leisure is assigned to intellectual pursuits, to studies which liberalise the mind. Offenders against law and order are condemned to bondage. But redemption was assured bondmen when they gave satisfactory promise of mending their ways, and of making fit use of liberty.

Contempt for silver and gold and precious stones is especially characteristic of the Utopians. Diamonds and pearls are treated as children's playthings. Crim- inals are chained with golden fetters by way of indicating the disrepute attaching to the metal. Ambassadors arriving in Utopia from other countries with golden chains about their necks, and wearing robes ornamented with pearls, are mistaken by the Utopians for degraded bondmen, who among the Utopians are wont to cherish in adult years a childish love for toys.

Contempt for the precious metals.

To find happiness in virtuous and reasonable pleasure is the final aim of the Utopian scheme of life. The Utopians declare that 'the felicity of man' consists in pleasure. But 'they think not,' More adds, 'felicity to consist in all pleasure but only in that pleasure that is good and honest.' They define virtue to be 'life ordered according to nature, and that we be hereunto ordained even of God. And that he doth follow the course of nature, who in desiring and refusing things is ruled by reason.' The watchword of Utopia declares reason and reason alone to be the safe guide of life. Even in the religious sphere principles of reason's fashioning are carried to logical conclusions without hesitation or condition.

Utopian philosophy.

The official religion of More's imaginary world is pure Pantheism. But differences on religious questions are permitted. The essence of the Utopian faith is 'that there is a certain godly power unknown, far above the capacity and reach of man's wit, dispersed throughout all the world, not in bigness, but in virtue and power. Him they call Father of all. To Him alone they attribute the beginnings, the increasings, the proceedings, the changes, and the ends of all things. Neither give they any divine honours to any other than Him.' The state

Utopian religion.

organises public worship of an elementary Pantheistic pattern. It only concerns itself with first principles about which differences of opinion are barely conceivable. In other regards differences of view are encouraged.

Nowhere indeed has the great doctrine of religious toleration been expounded with greater force or fulness than in the *Utopia*. The bases of morality are duly safeguarded, but otherwise every man in Utopia is permitted to cherish without hindrance the religious belief that is adapted to his idiosyncrasy. Reason, the sole test of beneficent rule, justifies no other provision.

VIII

More wrote his romance of *Utopia* in Latin, and addressed it to the educated classes of Europe. It was published at *Utopia published on the Continent.* the end of 1516, at Louvain, a prominent centre of academic learning. A new edition came four months later from a famous press of Paris, and then within a year the scholar printer, Froben of Basle, produced a luxurious reissue under the auspices of Erasmus and with illustrations by Erasmus's friend and chief exponent of Renaissance art in Germany, Hans Holbein. The brightest influences of the new culture pronounced fervent benedictions on the printed book, and the epithets which the publishers bestowed on its title-page, 'aureus,' 'salutaris,' 'festivus'—golden, healthful, joyous—were well adapted to a manifesto from every sentence of which radiated the light and hope of social progress.

None who read the *Utopia* can deny that its author drank deep of the finest spirit of his age. None can question that he foresaw the main lines along which the political and social ideals of the Renaissance were to develop

in the future.   There is hardly a scheme of social or
political reform that has been enunciated in later epochs
of which there is no definite adumbration in More's pages.
But he who passes hastily from the speculations of More's
Utopia to the record of More's subsequent life and writings
will experience a strange shock.   Nowhere else is he likely
to be faced by so sharp a contrast between precept and
practice, between enlightened and vivifying theory in the
study and adherence in the work-a-day world to the unin-
telligent routine of bigotry and obscurantism.   By the
precept and theory of his *Utopia,* More cherished and added
power to the new light.   By his practical conduct in life
he sought to extinguish the illuminating forces to which his
writing offered fuel.

The facts of the situation are not open to question.   More
was long associated in the government of his country on
principles which in the *Utopia* he condemned.   Contrast
He acquiesced in a system of rule which rested   between
                                                  Utopian
on inequalities of rank and wealth, and made   precepts
no endeavour to diminish poverty.   In the sphere   and More's
                                                     personal
of religion More's personal conduct most con-   practice.
spicuously conflicted with the aspirations of his Utopians.
So far from regarding Pantheism, or any shape of un-
dogmatic religion, as beneficial, he lost no opportunity of
denouncing it as sinful; he regarded the toleration in practical life of differences on religious questions as sacrilegious.
He actively illustrated more than once his faith in physical
coercion or punishment as a means of bringing men to a
sense of the only religion which seemed to him to be true.
Into his idealistic romance he had introduced a saving clause
to the effect that he was not at one with his Utopians at all
points.   He gave no indication that by the conduct of his
personal life he ranked himself with their strenuous foes.

The discrepancy is not satisfactorily accounted for by the theory that his political or religious views suffered change after the *Utopia* was written. No man adhered more rigidly through life to the religious tenets that he had adopted in youth. From youth to age his dominant hope was to fit himself for the rewards in a future life of honest championship of the Catholic Christian faith. No man was more consistently conservative in his attitude to questions of current politics. He believed in the despotic principle of government and the inevitableness of class distinctions. But the breadth of his intellectual temper admitted him also to regions of speculation which were beyond the range of any established religious or political doctrines. He was capable of a detachment of mind which blinded him to the inconsistencies of his double part. The student of More's biography cannot set the *Utopia* in its proper place among More's achievements unless he treat it as proof of his mental sensitiveness to the finest issues of the era, as evidence of his gift of literary imagination, as an impressively fine play of fancy, which was woven by the writer far away from his own work-a-day world in a realm which was not bounded by facts or practical affairs, as they were known to him. Whatever the effects of More's imaginings on readers, whatever their practical bearing in others' minds on actual conditions of social life, the *Utopia* was for its creator merely a vision, which melted into thin air in his brain as he stood face to face with the realities of life. When the dream ended, the brilliant pageant faded from his consciousness and left not a wrack behind.

The Utopia a dream of fancy.

IX

Very soon after the *Utopia* was written, More descended swiftly from speculative heights. His attention was absorbed by the religious revolution that was arising in Germany. He heard with alarm and incredulity of the attempt of Luther, the monk of Wittenberg, to reform the Church by dissociating it from Rome. Like his friend Erasmus, More was well alive to the defects in the administration of the Catholic Church. The ignorance of many priests, their lack of spiritual fervour, their worldly ambition, their misapprehension of the significance of ceremonies, their soulless teaching of divine things, all at times roused his resentment, and he hoped for improvement. But in the constitution of the great Roman hierarchy, under the sway of St. Peter's vicegerent, the Pope, he had unswerving faith. It never occurred to him to question the belief in the Pope. Against any encroachment on the Pope's authority every fibre of his mind and body was prepared to resist to the last. From first to last he exhausted the language of invective in denouncing the self-styled reformers of religion. The enlightened principles of reason and tolerance which he had illustrated with unmatchable point and vivacity in the *Utopia* were ignored, were buried. As soon as the papal claim to supremacy in matters of religion was disputed, every pretension of the papacy seemed to take, in More's mind, the character of an indisputable law of nature. To challenge it was to sin against the light. No glimmer of justice nor of virtue could his vision discover in those who took another view.

Meanwhile More was steadily building up a material fortune and practical repute. His success as a diplomatist at Antwerp reinforced his reputation as a lawyer in London. He showed gifts of oratory which especially gratified the public ear. The King's great minister, Wolsey, anxious to absorb talent which the public recognised, deemed it politic to offer him further public employment.　Unexpected favour was shown him.　His ability and reputation led to his appointment to a prominent Court office, a Mastership of Requests, or Examiner of Petitions that were presented to the King on his progresses through the country.　The duties required More to spend much time at Court, and he was thus brought suddenly and unexpectedly into relation with the greatest person in the State—with the King.

According to Erasmus, More was 'dragged' into the circle of the Court.　'" Dragged " is the only word,' wrote

His atti-
tude to
politics.
his friend, 'for no one ever struggled harder to gain admission there than More struggled to escape.'　Secular politics always seemed to More a puny business.　He always held a modest view of his own capacities, and despite his literary professions in the *Utopia*, he never entertained the notion that from the heights of even supreme office could a statesman serve his country to much purpose.　By lineage he was closely connected with the people.　No ties of kinship bound him to a privileged nobility.　He instinctively cherished a limited measure of popular sympathy.　He desired all classes of society to enjoy to full extent such welfare as was inherent in the established order of things.　Above all, he was by tempera-ment a conservative.　He had little faith in the efficacy of new legislation to ameliorate social or political conditions. He had no belief in heroic or revolutionary statesmanship. At most the politician could prevent increase of evil.　He could not appreciably enlarge the volume of the nation's virtue or prosperity.　To other activities than those of states-men, to religious and spiritual energy and endeavour, More alone looked in the work-a-day world for the salvation of man and society.　' It is not possible,' he wrote complacently, ' for all things to be well unless all men are good ; which I

think will not be yet these many years.' Study of precedents, experience, reliance on those religious principles which had hitherto enjoyed the undivided allegiance of his countrymen, these things alone gave promise of healthful conduct of the world's affairs. It was neither a fruitful nor a logical creed, when applied to politics, but it was one to which More, despite the professions of his imaginary spokesman in his great romance, clung throughout his political career with unrelaxing tenacity.

The established principles of absolute monarchy More accepted intuitively. He respected the authority of the King with a whole heart. Henry VIII.'s private character illustrated the inconsistency of conduct which prevailed among the children of the Renaissance. *His loyalty.* He could be ' wise, amaz'd, temperate and furious, loyal and neutral in a moment.' But there was much in Henry VIII.'s personality to confirm More's instinctive reverence for the head of the State. The King was well educated, and encouraged pursuit of the New Learning. If he had disappointed the hopes of those, who, at his succession, prophesied that his reign would inaugurate peace and goodwill at home and among the nations, he was reckoned to have at heart, provided his autocratic pretensions went unquestioned, the welfare of his people. His geniality attracted all comers, and diverted condemnation of his sensuality and tyranny. For the main dogmas and ceremonial observances of the Church of his fathers he professed reverent loyalty. The King bade More, at the outset of his Court career, look first unto God, and after God unto the King. Such conventional counsel was in complete accord with More's working views of life.

More's personal fascination at once put him on intimate terms with his sovereign. His witty conversation, his wide knowledge, delighted Henry, who treated his new counsellor with much familiarity, often summoning him to his private The King's favour. room to talk of science or divinity, or inviting him to supper with the King and Queen in order to enjoy his merry talk. At times Henry would go to More's own house and walk about the garden at Chelsea with him. But More did not exaggerate the significance of these attentions. He had no blind faith in the security of royal favour. Whatever his respect for the kingly office, he formed no exaggerated estimate of the magnanimity of its holder. ' If my head should win him a castle in France,' More once remarked to his son-in-law, ' it should not fail to go.'

x

More's ascent of the steps of the official ladder was very rapid. He was knighted in the spring of 1521, and each of Rapid preferment. the ten years that followed saw some advance of dignity. From every direction came opportunities of preferment. The King manifested the continuance of his confidence by making him sub-Treasurer of the Household. To Cardinal Wolsey's influence he owed one session's experience of the Speakership of the House of Commons. He was employed on many more diplomatic missions abroad, and in 1525 became chancellor of the duchy of Lancaster.

The smiles of fortune engendered no pride in More. The Cardinal expressed surprise that he did not press his advan- More's humility. tage with greater energy or seek larger pecuniary rewards for his service. Independence was of greater value to him than wealth or titles, and he made the Cardinal often realise that he was a fearless if witty critic whom no bribe could convert into a tool.

Had Wolsey foreseen events, he might have had good ground for fearing More's advancement. Wolsey suddenly

forfeited the royal favour and was deprived of his high office
of Lord Chancellor in the autumn of 1529.   Six days later
—on 25th October—greatly to More's surprise,   *More made*
the King invited him to fill the vacant place.   *Lord*
The Lord Chancellor is the head of the legal   *Chancellor*
profession in England—the chief judge, the adviser   *25th Oct.*
1529.
of the King in all legal business, who is popularly called
keeper of the King's conscience.   More's appointment
was an exceptional proceeding from every point of view.
Lord Chancellors, though their business was with law, had
of late invariably been dignitaries of the Church, who in
the Middle Ages were the chief lawyers.   Doubtless the
King's motive in promoting to so high an office a man of
comparatively humble rank was in order to wield greater
influence over the Chancellor, and to free himself of the
bonds that had been forged for him by Wolsey, whose
powerful individuality and resolute ambition seems to find
among modern statesmen the closest reflection in Prince
Bismarck.

More's father, Sir John More, was still judge when he first
occupied the woolsack, and Sir John remained on the bench
till his death a year later.   Sir Thomas's affection
for his father was deep and lasting, and during   *More and*
the first year of his Chancellorship, while he and   *his father*
as judges.
his father were both judges at the same time, it was the
Chancellor's daily practice to visit his father in the lower
court in order to ask a blessing as he passed down Westminster Hall on the way to his superior court of Chancery.
With like humility More bore himself to all on reaching
the goal of a lawyer's mundane ambition.   Nor did his
dignities repress his mirthful geniality in intercourse either
with equals or inferiors.

The King had need of subservient instruments in his great

offices of State.　He was contemplating a great revolution in
his own life and in the life of the nation.　He had
determined to divorce his wife, Queen Catherine,
and to marry another, Anne Boleyn.　The purpose
was not easy of fulfilment.　The threatened Queen had
champions at home and abroad, with whom conflict was perilous.　Charles v., the Emperor of the Holy Roman Empire,
Henry's most persistent rival in his efforts to dominate
Europe, was his wife's nephew.　Divorce was a weapon that
could only be wielded by the Pope, and it was known that
the Pontiff was not inclined to forward Henry's wish.　It
was this intricate coil of circumstance which encumbered
More's great elevation.　The clouds deepened in the years
that followed, and ultimately cast the shadow of tragedy
over the tenor of More's life.

*The King
and the
Reforma-
tion.*

XI

Soon after More became Chancellor, the King lightly consulted him on the projected divorce.　More frankly declared
himself opposed to the King's design.　Henry for
the time was complacent, and told his new Chancellor he was free to hold his own opinion.　But
the King recognised the existence of no obstacle,
however formidable it might prove, to the fulfilment of his
will.　No authority, not even that of the Pope, was powerful
enough to deflect his settled purpose.　To him the
conclusion was inevitable that if the Pope would
not go with him on an errand to which he was
committed, he must go without the Pope.　An upheaval of
the ecclesiastical and political constitution of the State which
should put heavy strain on the conscience of a large section
of his people was a price that Henry was prepared to pay
with equanimity for the accomplishment of his desires.　The

*More's
view of
the King's
projected
divorce.*

*The King's
supreme
power.*

sanction of the papacy was to be abrogated in his dominions, if it failed to accommodate itself to the royal resolve.

Apart from his obstinate faith in his own personal power, the King knew that he possessed in the sympathy which the Lutheran movement in Germany bred among a small class of his subjects a powerful lever which might easily be worked to bring about England's separation from Rome. *The growth of Protestantism.* Hitherto he had done what he could to discourage the spread of the Lutheran movement at home, and the mass of the people had proved loyal to the papacy. But controversy respecting the precise grounds of the Pope's claim in England to the supreme authority in matters of religion had already sown seeds of alienation between England and Rome; were those seeds fostered by royal influence, there would be placed in the royal hand a formidable weapon of offence. The cry of national independence always quickened the people's spirit, and it could readily be made the watchword of opposition to the papal pretensions. The King's position as champion of his people against foreign domination was difficult of assault.

The constitution of the country was, too, easily adaptable to Henry's purposes. Parliament, which as yet knew little of its strength, was usually eager to give effect to a popular King's wishes. His wishes were indeed hardly distinguishable from commands. *Hopelessness of resistance.* As soon as the King's mind was made up, it was easy for him to secure parliamentary enactments which should disestablish the papacy in England and abolish its sovereignty. At a word from the King Parliament could be reckoned on to remove all the obstacles that papal obduracy put in the way of the legal accomplishment of his plan of divorce. Officers of State, and indeed the people at large, might disapprove of such parliamentary action, but they could only stand aside or acquiesce. The King, whose liking for More was not easily dispelled, applied no compulsion to him either to accept his master's policy or to declare his convictions. He was at liberty, he was told, to stand aside.

Neutrality for More on matters touching his innermost beliefs was out of the question. For him to remain in office when the Government was irretrievably committed to heresy was to belie his conscience. To condemn himself to silence in any relation of life was contrary to his nature. Tacitly to accept the revolution in religion, which was henceforth to identify England with Protestantism, was in his eyes a breach of the laws of morality. As soon, therefore, as Parliament was invited to set aside papal power in England, More retired from his high office. He had held the Chancellorship, when he resigned it in the spring of 1532, for two and a half years. In spite of all his early hopes and ambitions, it was with a profound sense of relief that he brought his official career to an end.

More's conscientious scruples.

His resignation of the Woolsack.

Loyalty to the King was still a cherished doctrine of More's practical philosophy, even when loyalty was avowedly in conflict with his principles. The inconsistent attitude of mind was unchangeable till death. To preserve his sense of loyalty from decay now required of him, he perceived, a serious effort. The proper course, to his mind, was to abstain henceforth from affairs of State, and to keep his mind fixed exclusively on spiritual matters. Pitfalls encircled him, but he was sanguine enough to believe that, despite all that had happened in the past or might happen in the future, he might as a private citizen reconcile his duty to his God with his duty to his King.

His spiritual ambition.

To Erasmus he wrote on the day of his resignation.

'That which I have from a child unto this day continually wished, that being freed from the troublesome businesses of public affairs I might live somewhile only to God and myself, I have now by the especial grace of Almighty God, and the favour of my most indulgent prince obtained.' He told his friend that he was sick at heart, and that his physical strength was failing. Apprehension of the trend of public affairs shook his nerve, but there was no infirmity in his convictions.

XII

The abandonment of his career meant for More a serious reduction of income, and entailed upon him the need of living with great simplicity. He adapted his household expenses to his diminished revenues with alacrity, but showed the utmost consideration for all retainers whom he was compelled to dismiss.[1] He called all his children together and reminded them that he had mounted to the highest degree from the lowest, and that he had known all manner of fare from the scantiest to the most abundant—the fare of a poor Oxford student, of a poor law student, of a junior barrister, and finally of a great officer of state. He hardly knew how far his resources would go; he would not at the outset adopt the lowest scale of living with which youthful experience had familiarised him; he would make trial of the fare to which his earnings as barrister had accustomed him; but he warned his hearers that, if his revenues proved insufficient to maintain that level of expenditure

More's impaired resources.

---

[1] When dismissing the gentleman and yeomen of his household, he endeavoured to find situations for them with bishops and noblemen. He seems to have presented his barge to his successor in the Chancellorship, Sir Thomas Audley, with the request that the new chancellor would retain in his service the eight bargemen who had served his predecessor.

after a year's experiment, he should promptly descend in the scale, with risk of a further descent, should prudence require it. He jested over the necessity which he suffered of selling his plate; he cheerfully declared that a hundred pounds a year was adequate for any reasonable man's requirements.

More's chief interests were for the time absorbed in the erection of a tomb for himself in Chelsea Church. For the monument he prepared a long epitaph, in which he announced the fulfilment of his early resolves to devote his last years to preparation for the life to come.

The Chelsea tomb.

From the worldly points of view—public or private—More's premature withdrawal from the office of Lord Chancellor was regrettable. The chief duty of a Lord Chancellor is to act as a judge in equity, to dispense justice in the loftiest and widest sense. For the performance of such a function More had first-rate capacity, and the wisdom of his judgments rendered his tenure of the Chancellorship memorable in the annals of English law. He worked with exceptional rapidity, and, as long as he held office, freed the processes of law from their traditional imputation of tardiness. On one occasion he cleared off the business of his court before ten o'clock in the morning. A popular rhyme long ran to the effect:—

His work as Chancellor.

> 'When More some time had Chancellor been
>   No more suits did remain,
> The like will never more be seen
>   Till More be there again.'

We are told that 'The poorest suitor obtained ready access to him and speedy trial, while the richest offered presents in vain, and the claims of kindred found no favour.' More's son-in-law and biographer wrote 'That he would for no respect digress from justice well appeared by a plain example of his son-in-law Mr. Giles Heron. For when the son having a matter before his father-in-law in the Chancery, presuming too much of his father-in-law's favour, would by him in no wise be persuaded to agree to any indifferent order, then made the Chancellor in conclusion a flat decree against his son-in-law.'

More took the widest views of his duty, and ignored all restrictive formalities. It was not only in his court that he was prepared to dispense justice to the people whom he served. 'This Lord Chancellor,' wrote His accessibility his son-and-law, 'used commonly every afternoon as judge. to sit in his open hall, to the intent, if any person had any suit unto him, they might the more boldly come to his presence, and there open complaints before him. His manner was also to read every bill or cause of action himself, ere he would award any subpœna, which bearing matter sufficient worthy a subpœna, would he set his hand unto, or else cancel it.' Constantly did he point out to his colleagues that equitable considerations ought to qualify the rigour of the law.

But high as was More's standard of conduct on the judicial bench, he did not escape censure. In the stirring contro versy, to one side of which he was deeply committed, every manner of calumnious suspicion Censure of his judicial was generated. There were vague charges conduct. brought against him of taking bribes. But these hardly admit of examination. More serious were the persistent reports that he had used his judicial power in order to torture physically those who held religious opinions differing from his own. There seems little question that at times he endeavoured to repress the spread of what he regarded as heresy or irreligion by cruel punishment of offenders.

But the evidence against him comes from opponents who were resolved to put the worst construction on all he did. His alleged acts of tyranny have been misrepresented. He had an old-fashioned belief in the value of corporal punishment. A boy in his service who talked lightly of sacred things to a fellow-servant was whipped by his orders. A madman who brawled in churches was sentenced by him to be beaten. He honestly thought that in certain circumstances physical torture and even burning at the stake was likely to extirpate heretical doctrine. The fervour of his religious faith inclined him to identify with crime obstinate defiance of the ancient dogmas. His native geniality was not proof against the consuming fire of his religious zeal. But the ultimate humaneness of his nature was not subdued to what it worked in.

XIII

In his retirement, More studied the writings of the Protestant controversialists, and sought to meet their arguments in a long series of tracts in which he expressed himself with heat and vehemence. He abandoned the Latin language, in which he had penned his great romance of *Utopia*, and wrote in English in order to gain the ear of a wider public.

More engages in theological controversy.

The chief object of his denunciation was the Protestant translator of the Bible into English, and the foremost of the early champions of the English Reformation, William Tyndale. In the opposite camp Tyndale faced, with a resolution equal to More's, poverty, danger and death in the service of what he held to be divine truth. Already in the height of his prosperity had More opened fire on Tyndale ; as early as 1529, the year of his

The attack on Tyndale.

accession to the Chancellorship, he had passionately defended the cause of Rome against the 'pestilent sect of Luther and Tyndale.' Before More's withdrawal from public life, Tyndale replied with much cogency and satiric bitterness, although he wrongly suspected More of having sold his pen to his royal employer. More, by his retirement from public life, effectively confuted such suspicion. When in his time of leisure he renewed the attack on the foe, he gave him no quarter. Tyndale's writings were declared to be a 'very treasury and well-spring of wickedness.' The reformer and friends were of all 'heretics that ever sprang in Christ's church the very worst and the most beastly.' More did not object to translations of the Bible into English, provided they were faithful renderings. But Tyndale's version of the New Testament had (he argued) altered 'matters of great weight,' and was only worthy of the fire. Erasmus wisely thought his friend would have been more prudent in leaving theology to the clergy. It was under stress of an irresistible impulse which reason could not moderate that More fanned with his pen the theological strife.

More's time was fully occupied in his library and chapel, and he sought no recreation abroad. He studiously avoided the Court, where the predominance of the King's new wife, Anne Boleyn, intensified his misgivings of the course of public affairs. But he was discreetly silent when friends invited his opinion on political topics. His mind, however, was always alert, and his rebellious instincts were not always under control. In spite of himself he was drawn from his retreat into the outer circle of the political whirlpool, and was soon engulfed beyond chance of deliverance.

More seeks to ignore political affairs.

In 1533, England was distracted by a curious imposture.

A young woman, Elizabeth Barton, who became known as the Holy Maid of Kent, was believed to be possessed of the gift of prophecy. She prophesied that the King had ruined his soul and would come to a speedy end for having divorced Queen Catherine. She was under the influence of priests, who were resentful at the recent turn of affairs, and were sincerely moved by the unjust fate that the divorced Queen Catherine had suffered. The girl's priestly abettors insisted that she was divinely inspired, and information of her sayings was forwarded to More. He showed interest in her revelations, and did not at the outset reject the possibility that they were the outcome of divine inspiration. He visited her when she was staying with the monks of the Charterhouse at Sion House, London. He talked with her, and was impressed by her spiritual fervour, but he was prudent in the counsel that he offered her. He advised her to devote herself to pious exercises, and not to meddle with political themes. He committed himself to little in his interview with her. It was, however, perilous to come into close quarters with her at all. The nation was greatly roused by her utterances, which were fully reported and circulated by her priestly friends. The new Protestant Minister of the King, Cromwell, deemed it needful to take legal proceedings against her and her allies. She and the priests were arrested. By way of defence they asserted that More, the late Lord Chancellor, was one of the Holy Maid's disciples.

More and the Maid of Kent.

The Minister, Cromwell, sent to More for an explanation; More repeated what he knew of the woman, and Cromwell treated his relations with her as innocent. More soon learned the dishonest tricks by which the Maid of Kent's influence had been spread by the priests, and he at once admitted that he had been the victim

Cromwell invites explanations.

of a foolish imposture. But at the trial of the Holy Maid of Kent, proofs were adduced of the reverence in which More's views were held by disaffected Catholics. The King's suspicions were aroused. He dreaded More's influence, and, in defiance of his personal feeling for him, could not bring himself to neglect the opportunity of checking his credit which the proceedings against the Holy Maid seemed to offer.

More was charged with conniving at treason through his intercourse with the Holy Maid. Summoned before a Committee of the Privy Council, he was asked an irrelevant question which was embarrassing. It had no concern with the charges of treason brought against him, yet it went to the root of the situation. Had he declined to acknowledge the wisdom and necessity of the King's abjuration of the Pope's authority in England? More quietly replied that he wished to do everything that was acceptable to the King; he had explained his views freely to him, and he knew not that he had incurred the royal displeasure. There the matter was for the moment suffered to rest. But very ominous looked the future. The charge of treason was not pressed further. Its punishment might have been death; it would certainly have been fine and imprisonment. For the time More was safe. The warning, however, was unmistakable. More's eyes were opened to the peril which menaced him. His friend the Duke of Norfolk reminded him that the anger of a King means death. More received the remark with equanimity. 'Is that all, my Lord?' he answered, 'then, in good faith, between your Grace and me is but this, that I shall die to-day, and you to-morrow.'

The threat of prosecution.

More conscious of his danger.

XIV

Rulers in those days believed that coercion gave ultimate security to uniformity of opinion.　Henry was not willing to tolerate dissent from his policy, though he bore More no ill-will.　On his own terms the King was always ready to welcome his ex-Chancellor's return to the royal camp, but he felt embarrassment, which was easily convertible into resentment, at More's remaining in permanence outside.　Having now divorced Queen Catherine, and married Queen Anne, Henry had caused a bill to be passed through Parliament vesting the succession to the Crown in Anne's children, and imposing as a test of loyalty an oath on all Englishmen, by which they undertook to be faithful subjects of the issue of the new Queen.

The triumph of Anne Boleyn.

Commissioners were nominated to administer this oath, and they interpreted their duties liberally.　They added to it words by which the oath-taker abjured any foreign potentate, *i.e.* the Pope.　More was summoned before the new Commissioners, at whose head stood Cromwell the Minister, and the Archbishop of Canterbury, Cranmer.　After hearing Mass, and taking the Holy Communion, he presented himself to the Archbishop and his fellow Commissioners at the Archbishop's Palace of Lambeth.　The ex-Chancellor was requested to subscribe to the new oath in its extended form.　The demand roused his spirit; he was in no temper to sacrifice his principles.　He declared himself ready to take the oath of fidelity to the Queen's children, but he declined to go further. He was bidden take an oath that impugned the Pope's authority.　He refused peremptorily.　He was told that he was setting up his private judgment against the nation's wisdom as expressed in Parliament.　More replied that the

The oath abjuring the Pope.

council of the realm was setting itself against the general council of Christendom. The Commissioners were uncertain what step to take next. They ordered More for the present into the custody of one of themselves, the Abbot of Westminster Abbey. The Archbishop was inclined to a compromise. What harm would come of permitting More to take the oath with the reservations which he had claimed? The King was consulted; he also expressed doubt as to the fit course to pursue. The new Queen, Anne Boleyn, had, however, made up her mind that More was a dangerous enemy. At her instance the King and his Minister declared that no exception could be made in favour of More. By their order he was committed to the Tower of London as a traitor, and there he remained a prisoner until his death, some fifteen months later. An old friend, John Fisher, Bishop of Rochester, had of late gone through the same experience as More, and he was already in the Tower to welcome the arrival of his companion in the faith.

More's detention.

Lawyers generally doubted whether the oath of fidelity to the new Queen's issue, as defined in the Act of Parliament, included any repudiation of the Pope; and Parliament was invited to solve this doubt by passing a resolution stating that the double-barrelled oath, as it had been administered to More and Fisher, was the very oath intended by the Act of Succession. More's position was thereby rendered most critical. There was no longer any doubt that he was putting himself in opposition to the law of the land. Legal definition was given to his offence. A bill of indictment was drawn against him; it declared him to be a sower of sedition, and guilty of ingratitude to his royal benefactor.

The oath of the Act of Succession.

Adversity as it deepened had no terrors for More. His passage from palace to prison did not disturb his equanimity.

He had already written in verse of the vicissitudes of fortune. He had represented the scornful goddess as More's distributing among men 'brittle gifts,' bestowing resignation. them only to amuse herself by suddenly plucking them away—

> 'This is her sport, thus proveth she her might ;
> Great boast she mak'th if one be by her power
> Wealthy and wretched both within an hour.
>
> Wherefore if thou in surety lust to stand,
> Take poverty's part and let proud fortune go,
> Receive nothing that cometh from her hand.
> Love manner and virtue ; they be only tho,
> Which double Fortune may not take thee fro' :
> Then may'st thou boldly defy her turning chance,
> She can thee neither hinder nor advance.'

There was no affectation in the lines. More wrote from his heart. It was with a smile on his lips that he returned Fortune's ugliest scowl.

XV

. In the Tower More's gaolers treated him with kindness. His health was bad, but his spirits were untamable, and In the when his friends and his wife and children visited Tower. him in his cell his gaiety proved infectious. In the first days of his imprisonment he wrote many letters, punctually performed his religious duties, and penned religious tracts. There was no hope of his giving way. His wife urged him to yield his scruples, ask pardon of the King, and gain his freedom. He replied that prison was as near Heaven as his own house, and he had no intention of quitting his cell. His children petitioned the King for pardon on the ground of his ill-health and their poverty, and they re-asserted that his offence was not of malice or obstinacy, but of such a long-continued and deep-rooted

scruple as passeth his power to avoid and put away. His
relatives were forced to submit to painful indignities. They
had to pay for his board and lodging, and their resources
were small. More's wife sold her clothes in order to pay
the prison fees.

Henry, under the new Queen's influence, was now at
length incensed against More. The likelihood of his mercy
was small. Parliament was entirely under his The King
sway. In the late autumn of 1534 yet a new Act and the
was passed to complete the separation of England of the
from Rome. There was conferred on the King the Church.
title of Supreme Head of the Church in place of the Pope,
and that title, very slightly modified, all Henry viii.'s successors have borne. The new Act made it high treason
maliciously to deny any of the royal titles. Next spring
Minister Cromwell went to the Tower and asked More his
opinion of this new statute ; was it in his view lawful or no ?
More sought refuge in the declaration that he was a faithful
subject of the King. He declined further answer. Similar
scenes passed in the months that followed. But More was
warned that the King would compel a precise answer.

More's fellow-prisoner Fisher was subjected to like trials,
and they compared their experiences in correspondence with
each other. More also wrote in terms of pathetic His corre-
affection to his favourite daughter, Margaret Roper, spondence.
and described the recent discussions in his cell. He received replies. In the result his correspondence was declared
to constitute a new offence ; it amounted to conspiracy.
The prisoner was unmoved by the baseless insinuation. His
treatment became more rigorous. Deprived of writing
materials and books, he could only write to his wife,
daughter, or friends on scraps of paper with pieces of coal.

More cheerfully abandoned hope of freedom. He caused

the shutters of the cell to be closed, and spent his time in
contemplation in the dark.   His end was, indeed,
near.   Death had been made the penalty for
those who refused to accept the King's supremacy.   On the
25th June 1535, Fisher suffered for his refusal on the
scaffold.   On the 1st July 1535, More was brought to Westminster Hall to stand his trial for having infringed the
Act of Supremacy, disobedience to which was now high
treason.   The Crown relied on his answer to his examiners
in the prison, and on his correspondence with Fisher.   He
was ill in health, and was allowed to sit.   He denied the
truth of most of the evidence.   He had not advised his
friend Fisher to disobey the new Act ; he had not described
that new Act as a two-edged sword, approval of which ruined
the soul, while disapproval of it ruined the body.   The
outcome was not in doubt.   A verdict of guilty was returned,
and More, the faithful son of the old Church and the disciple
of the new culture, was sentenced to be hanged at Tyburn.
As he left the Court he remarked that no temporal lord
could lawfully be head of the Church ; that he had studied
the history of the papacy, and was convinced that it was
based on Divine authority.

His trial.

With calm and unruffled temper, More faced the end.   As
he re-entered the Tower he met his favourite daughter who
asked his blessing.   The touching episode is thus
narrated by William Roper, husband of More's
eldest daughter, who wrote the earliest biography
of More :—' When Sir Thomas More came from Westminster to the Tower-Ward again, his daughter, my wife,
desirous to see her father, whom she thought she should
never see in this world after, and alsoe to have his final blessing, gave attendance about the Tower wharf where she knew
he should pass before he could enter into the Tower.   There

*The fare-
well to his
daughter.*

tarrying his comming, as soon as she saw him, after his blessing upon her knees reverentlie received, she hasting towards
him, without consideracion or care of her selfe, pressing in
amongst the midst of the throng and company of the guard,
that with halberds and bills went round about him, hastily
ran to him, and there openly in sight of them embraced him
and took him about the neck and kissed him. Who well
liking her most natural and dear daughterly affecion towards
him gave her his fatherly blessing and many godly words of
comfort besides. From whom after she was departed, she
was not satisfied with the former sight of him, and like one
that had forgotten herself being all ravished with the entire
love of her father, having respect neither to herself nor to
the press of the people and multitude that were there about
him, suddenly turned back again, ran to him as before, took
him about the neck and divers times kissed him lovingly, and
at last with a full and heavy heart was fain to depart from
him : the beholding whereof was to many that were present
so lamentable that it made them for very sorrow therof to
weep and mourn.'

XVI

The King commuted the sentence of hanging to that of
beheading, a favour which More grimly expressed the hope
that his friends might be spared the need of More's
asking. Early on the morning of the 6th July execution.
he was carried from the Tower to Tower Hill for execution. His composure knew no diminution. 'I pray thee,
see me safely up,' he said to the officer who led him from the
Tower, up the steps of the frail scaffold, 'as for my coming
down, I can shift for myself.' He encouraged the headsman
to do his duty fearlessly : 'Pluck up thy spirits, man ; be not
afraid to do thine office ; my neck is very short.' He

seemed to speak in jest as he moved his beard from the
block, with the remark that it had never committed treason.
Then with the calmness of one who was rid of every care he
told the bystanders that he died in and for the faith of the
Catholic Church, and prayed God to send the King good
counsel.

His body was buried in the Tower of London. The tomb
that he had erected at Chelsea never held his remains. His

Preservation of his head by Margaret Roper.

head was placed, according to the barbarous
custom of that day, on a pole on London Bridge,
but his favourite daughter, Margaret Roper,
privately purchased it a month later, and preserved it in spices till her death, nine years afterwards.
Tennyson commemorated her devotion in his great poem
' A Dream of Fair Women,' where he describes her as the
woman who clasped in her last trance of death her murdered
father's head.

> ' Morn broaden'd on the borders of the dark
>   Ere I saw her, who clasp'd in her last trance
> Her murdered father's head.'

The head is said to have long belonged to her descendants,
and to have been finally placed in the vault belonging to her
husband's family in a church at Canterbury.

More's piteous fate startled the world. His meekness at
the end, the dignified office which he once enjoyed, the fine
temper of his intellect, his domestic virtues seemed to plead
like angels trumpet-tongued against the deep damnation of
his taking off. To onlookers it appeared as if virtue and
wisdom in a champion of orthodoxy had whetted the fury of
a schismatic tyrant. To the principle and sentiment of the
Catholic peoples a desperate challenge had been offered.
' The horrid deed was blown in every eye, and tears

drowned the wind' of every country of Western Europe.
Catholics in Europe freely threatened the King (Henry VIII.)
with reprisals. The Emperor, Charles V., declared he would
have rather lost his best city than such a coun- The recep-
sellor. The Pope prepared a bull and interdict tion abroad
of deposition which was designed to cut King his death.
Henry off from the body of Christ, to empower his subjects to expel him from the throne and to cast his soul in
death into hell for ever. English ambassadors abroad were
instructed, without much effect, to explain that More had
suffered justly the penalty of the law, and that the legal
procedure had been perfectly regular. In all countries
poets likened him to the greatest heroes of antiquity, to
Socrates, Seneca, Aristides and Cato. Few questioned the
declaration of his friends that angels had carried his soul
into everlasting glory, where an imperishable crown of
martyrdom adorned his brow.

XVII

More's devotion to principle, his religious fervour, his
invincible courage, are his most obvious personal characteristics, but with them were combined a series of More's
qualities which are rarely to be met with in the character.
martyrs of religion. There was no gloom in his sunny nature.
He was a wit, a wag, delighting in amusing repartee, and
seeking to engage men in all walks of life in cheery talk.
It was complained of him that he hardly ever opened his
mouth except to make a joke, and his jests on the scaffold
were held by many contemporary critics to be idle im-
pertinences. Yet his mode of life could stand His mode
the severest tests; he lived with great simplicity, of life.
drinking little wine, avoiding expensive food, and dressing

carelessly. He hated luxury or any sort of ostentation in his home life. At Chelsea he lived in patriarchal fashion, with his children and their husbands or wives and his grandchildren about him. He rarely missed attendance at the Chelsea Parish Church, and would often sing in the choir, wearing a surplice. He encouraged all his household to study and read, and to practise liberal arts. He was fond of animals, even foxes, weasels, and monkeys. He was a charming host to congenial friends, though he disliked games of chance, and eschewed dice or cards.

At the same time More never ceased to prove himself a child of the Renaissance. All forms of Art strongly appealed to him. He liked collecting curious furniture and plate. 'His house,' wrote Erasmus, 'is a magazine of curiosities, which he rejoices in showing.' He delighted in music, and persuaded his uncultivated wife to learn the flute and other instruments with him. Of painting he was an expert critic. The great German artist, Holbein, was his intimate friend, and, often staying with him at Chelsea, acknowledged More's hospitality by painting portraits of him and his family.

His love of art.

As a writer, More's fame mainly depended on his political romance of *Utopia*, which was penned in finished Latin. His Latin style, both in prose and verse, is of rare lucidity, and entitles him to a foremost place among English contributors to the Latin literature of the Renaissance. His *Utopia* is an admirable specimen of fluent and harmonious Latin prose. With the popular English translation of his romance, which was first published sixteen years after his death, he had no concern. Much English verse as well as much Latin verse came from More's active pen. Critics have usually ignored or scorned his English poetry. Its theme is mainly the fickleness of

His Latin writing.

His English poetry.

fortune and the voracity of time. But freshness and sincerity characterise his treatment of these well-worn topics, and, though the rhythm is often harsh, and the modern reader may be repelled by archaic vocabulary and constructions, More at times achieves metrical effects which *His English* adumbrate the art of Edmund Spenser. Of *prose.* English prose More made abundant use in treating both secular and religious themes. There is doubt as to his responsibility for the 'History of Richard III.,' which ordinarily figures among his English prose writings. Archbishop Morton has been credited, on grounds that merit *History of* attention, with the main responsibility for its com- *Richard III.* position. It is an admirable example of Tudor prose, clear and simple, free from pedantry and singularly modern in construction. Similar characteristics are only a little less conspicuous in More's authentic biography of Pico, *Pico's Life.* the Italian humanist, who, like More himself, yielded to theology abilities that were better adapted to win renown in the pursuit of profane literature.

It is, however, by the voluminous polemical tracts and devotional treatises of his closing career that More's English prose must be finally judged. In controversy *Contro-* More wrote with a rapidity and fluency which put *versial* dignity out of the question. Very often the tone *theology.* is too spasmodic and interjectional to give his work genuine literary value. In the heat of passion he sinks to scurrility which admits of no literary form. But it is only episodically that his anger gets the better of his literary temper. His native humour was never long repressible, and some homely anecdote or proverbial jest usually rushed into his mind to stem the furious torrents of his abuse. When the gust of his anger passed, he said what he meant with the simple directness that comes of conviction, unconstrained by fear.

Vigour and freedom are thus the main characteristics of his controversial English prose.

There is smaller trace of individual style in his books of religious exhortation and devotion, but their pious placidity does not exclude bursts both of eloquence and of anecdotal reminiscence which prove his wealth of literary energy and of humoursome originality. To one virtue as a writer in English he can make no claim : pointed brevity was out of his range. In Latin he could achieve epigrams, but all his English works in prose are of massive dimensions, and untamable volubility.

His devotional treatises.

For two centuries after his death More was regarded by Catholic Europe as the chief glory of English literature. In the seventeenth century the Latin countries deemed Shakespeare and Bacon his inferiors. It was his Latin writing that was mainly known abroad. But, even in regard to that branch of his literary endeavours, time has long since largely dissipated his early fame. In the lasting literature of the world, More is only remembered as the author of the *Utopia*, wherein he lives for all time, not so much as a man of letters, but in that imaginative rôle, which contrasts so vividly with other parts in his repertory, of social reformer and advocate of reason. In English literary history his voluminous work in English prose deserves grateful, if smaller, remembrance. Despite the many crudities of his utterance, he first indicated that native English prose might serve the purpose of great literature as effectively as Latin prose, which had hitherto held the field among all men of cultivated intelligence. There is an added paradox in the revelation that one who was the apostle in England at once of the cosmopolitan culture of the classical Renaissance and of the mediæval dogmatism of the Roman Catholic Church should also be a strenuous

More's literary repute abroad.

champion of the literary usage of his vernacular tongue. But paradox streaks all facets of More's career.

Few careers are more memorable for their pathos than More's. Fewer still are more paradoxical. In that regard he was a true child of an era of ferment and undisciplined enthusiasm, which checked orderli- ness of conduct or aspiration. Sir Thomas More's variety of aim, of ambition, has indeed few parallels even in the epoch of the Renaissance. Looking at him from one side we detect only a religious enthusiast, cheerfully sacrific- ing his life for his convictions—a man whose religious creed, in defence of which he faced death, abounded in what seems, in the dry light of reason, to be superstition. Yet survey- ing More from another side we find ourselves in the presence of one endowed with the finest enlightenment of the Renais- sance, a man whose outlook on life was in advance of his generation; possessed too of such quickness of wit, such imaginative activity, such sureness of intellectual insight, that he could lay bare with pen all the defects, all the abuses, which worn-out conventions and lifeless traditions had imposed on the free and beneficent development of human endeavour and human society. That the man, who, by an airy effort of the imagination, devised the new and revolutionary ideal of *Utopia*, should end his days on the scaffold as a martyr to ancient beliefs which shackled man's intellect and denied freedom to man's thought is one of history's perplexing ironies. Sir Thomas More's career propounds a riddle which it is easier to enunciate than to solve.

The para- doxes of his career.

III

SIR PHILIP SIDNEY

'A combination and a form indeed,
Where every god did seem to set his seal,
To give the world assurance of a man.'

SHAKESPEARE, *Hamlet*, III. iv. 55-57.

[BIBLIOGRAPHY.—The earliest attempt at a biography of Sir Philip
Sidney was made by his intimate friend, Fulke Greville, Lord
Brooke, in the *Life of the Renowned Sir Philip Sidney*, which
was first published in 1652. It is a rambling character sketch,
intermingled with much irrelevant discussion of English foreign
policy. The fullest modern biography is by Mr. H. R. Fox-
Bourne, which was first published in 1862, and afterwards revised
for re-issue in the 'Heroes of the Nations' series, 1891. Sidney's
Arcadia, together with his chief literary works, appeared in 1598,
and the volume was many times reprinted down to 1721. An
abridgment of the *Arcadia*, edited by J. Hain Friswell, appeared
in 1867. An attractive reprint of Sidney's *Astrophel and Stella*
was edited by Mr. A. W. Pollard in 1888, and that collection of
poems is included in *Elizabethan Sonnets* (1904), edited by the
present writer in Messrs. Constable's 'English Garner.' The
Apologie for Poetrie has been well edited by Prof. Albert S.
Cook, of Yale (1901, Boston, U.S.A.)]

I

THE course of Sir Philip Sidney's life greatly differed from
that of More's. Sidney held by patrimony a place in the

Sidney's
high birth.

social hierarchy which was outside More's experience. A grandson of a Duke, a nephew of Earls,
he belonged by birth to the English aristocracy, to the
governing classes of England. To some measure of distinction he was born. The professions of arms, of diplomacy,
of politics, opened to him automatically without his personal

effort. The circumstance of his lineage moulded the form and pressure of his career.

From other springs flowed his innermost ambitions. The spirit of the Renaissance imbued his intellectual being more consistently than it imbued More's. The natural affinities of Sidney's mind were from first to last with great literature and art, not with the turmoil of war, or politics, or creeds. The Muse of poetry who scorns the hollow pomp of rank laid chief claim to his allegiance. But he was a curious and persistent inquirer into many fashions of beauty besides the poetic. One part of his energies was devoted to a prose romance, which he designed on a great scale ; another part to prose criticism of a reasoned enlightenment that was unprecedented in England. To all manifestations of the new spirit of the age he was sensitive. But there were contrary influences, bred of his inherited environment, there were feudal and mediæval traditions, which disputed the sway over him of the new forces of culture. The development of his poetic and literary endowments was checked by rival political and military preoccupations. Even if death had spared him until his faculties were fully ripened, he seemed destined to distribute his activities over too wide a field for any of them to bear the richest fruit. He ranks with the heroes who have promised more than they have performed, with the pathetic sharers ' of unfulfilled renown.'

Intellectual ambitions.

II

Nineteen years after More's tragic death, and ten years before the birth of Shakespeare, Sir Philip Sidney came into the world. His short life of thirty-two years covers the central period in the history of the English Renaissance, which reached its first triumph in More's *Utopia* and its final glory in Shake-

The central period of the Renaissance.

spearean drama. Sidney died while Shakespeare was yet unknown to fame, when the dramatist's fortunes were in the balance, before his literary work was begun.

Interests with which literature had little in common distracted the mental energies of the nation between the dates of More's execution and of Sidney's birth. The religious reformation had been carried to a conclusion by coercive enactments, which outraged the consciences of too many subjects of the king to give immediate assurance of finality. The strong-willed monarch, Henry VIII., had died, amid signs that justified doubt of the permanence of the country's new religious polity. Disease soon laid its hands on the feeble constitution of the boy, who, succeeding to Henry's throne as Edward VI., upheld there with youthful eagerness and extravagance the cause of the Reformation. Factions of ambitious noblemen robbed the Court of respect, and jeopardised the Government's power. The air rang with confused threats of rebellion. The succession to the throne was disputed on the boy-king's premature death. It was no time for the peaceful worship of the Muses. Political and religious strife oppressed the England of Sir Philip Sidney's infancy, and the circumstances of his birth set him in the forefront of the struggle.

National strife.

Sidney was a native of Kent, born at Penshurst, in an old mansion of great beauty and historic interest which, dating from the fifteenth century, still stands. His father, Sir Henry Sidney, was a politician who had long been busily engaged in politics, mainly in the ungrateful task of governing Ireland. His mother was a daughter of the ambitious nobleman, the Duke of Northumberland, who endeavoured to place his daughter-in-law (of a nobler family than his own), Lady Jane Grey, upon the throne of England after the death of the boy-king Edward VI. The plot failed

Sidney's birth.

and Henry VIII.'s eldest daughter, Mary, who shared More's enthusiasm for the papacy and his horror of Protestantism, became Queen in accordance with law. The failure of the Duke's ambitious schemes led to his death on the scaffold. Queen Mary's accession preceded Sidney's birth by a few months, and the tragedy of his grandfather's execution darkened his entry into life.

The two critical events—the failure of the Duke of Northumberland's scheme of usurpation, and Queen Mary's revival of a Catholic sovereignty—were vividly recalled at Philip's baptism. His godmother His baptism. was his grandmother, the widowed Duchess of Northumberland. His godfather was the new Catholic Queen's lately married husband, Philip of Spain, the sour fanatic, who shortly afterwards became King Philip II. It was an inauspicious conjunction of sponsors. Both were identified with doomed forces of reaction. The ancient régime of Spain, which King Philip represented, was already on its downward grade. The widowed Duchess was the survivor of a lawless and selfish political faction, which had defied political justice and the general welfare. Shadows fell across the child's baptismal font. A cloud of melancholy burdened the minds of those who tended him in infancy, and his childish thoughts soon took a serious hue.

But before his childhood ended, the gloom that hung about his country and his family's prospects was lightened. The superstitious Queen Mary, having restored to her country its old religion, died prematurely, and her Queen Elizabeth's accession. work was quickly undone by her sister and successor, Queen Elizabeth. Fortune at length smiled again on the English throne, and the new sovereign won by her resolute temper, her self-possession and her patriotism, her people's regard and love. Slowly but surely the paths of peace were secured. The spirit of the nation was relieved of the griefs of religious and civil conflict. The Muses flourished in England as never before.

On Sidney's domestic circle, too, a new era of hope dawned. His mother's brother, the ill-fated Duke of Northumberland's younger son, Robert Dudley, Earl of Leicester, became Queen Elizabeth's favoured courtier, and, by a strange turn of fortune's wheel, wielded, despite his father's disgrace and death, immense political influence. Throughout Sidney's adult life his uncle, Leicester, who, although unprincipled and self-indulgent, had affection for his kindred, was the most powerful figure in English public life. Such advantages as come of a near kinsman's great place in the political world lay at Sidney's disposal in boyhood and early manhood.

Sidney's uncle, the Earl of Leicester.

III

The boy was at first brought up at Penshurst, but was soon taken further west, to Ludlow Castle. At the time his father, in the interval of two terms of government in Ireland, was President of the principality of Wales, which was then separately governed by a high officer of state. Ludlow Castle, then a noble palace, now a magnificent ruin, was his official residence. Owing to his father's residence in the western side of England, the boy Philip was sent to school at Shrewsbury, which was just coming into fame as a leading public school.

At Shrewsbury school.

On the same day there entered Shrewsbury school another boy of good family, who also attained great reputation in literature and politics, Fulke Greville, afterwards Lord Brooke. Greville was a poet at heart, although involved and mystical in utterance. He was Sidney's life-

Fulke Greville.

long friend, and subsequently his biographer. Greville died forty-two years after his friend, but the memory of their association sank so deep in his mind and heart that, despite all the other honours which he won in mature life, he had it inscribed on his tomb that he was 'Friend to Sir Philip Sidney.'

Sidney was a serious and thoughtful boy. Of his youth his companion, Greville, wrote:—'I will report no other wonder than this, that, though I lived with him and knew him from a child, yet I never knew him other than a man, with such staidness of mind, lovely and familiar gravity, as carried grace and reverence above greater years ; his talk ever of knowledge, and his very play tending to enrich his mind, so that even his teachers found something in him to observe and learn above that which they had usually read or taught.   Which eminence by nature and industry made his worthy father style Sir Philip in my hearing, though I unseen, *lumen familiæ suæ* (light of his household).'   Gravity of demeanour characterised Sidney at all periods of his life.

Sidney's serious youth.

From childhood Sidney was a lover of learning.   At eleven years old he could write letters in French and Latin ; and his father gave him while a lad advice on the moral conduct of life which seemed to fit one of far maturer years.   The precocious spirit of the Renaissance made men of boys, and youths went to the University in the sixteenth century at a far earlier age than now.   At fourteen Philip left Shrewsbury school for the University of Oxford—for the great foundation of Christ Church, to which at an earlier epoch More had wended his way.   At Oxford Sidney eagerly absorbed much classical learning, and gathered many new friends.   His tutor was fascinated by his studious ardour, and he, too, like

At Oxford.

Sidney's friend Greville, left directions for the fact that Sidney had been his pupil to be recorded on his tombstone. As at school so at college Greville was Sidney's most constant companion. The Protestant faith, which Queen Elizabeth had re-established, was now the dominant religion, and Sidney, at school and college, warmly embraced the doctrines of the Reformation. But religious observances which dated from the older papal régime were still in vogue in England, and from one of them Philip as an undergraduate sought relief. His health was delicate. His influential uncle, the Earl of Leicester, was well alive to his promise, and he obtained a licence of the Archbishop of Canterbury for the boy to eat flesh in Lent, 'because he was subject to sickness.'

The circumstance that Sidney was the Earl of Leicester's nephew placed many other special privileges within his reach. It opened to him the road to the Court, and gained for him personal introduction to the great statesmen of the time. Queen Elizabeth's astute Lord Treasurer and Prime Minister, Sir William Cecil, afterwards Lord Burghley, came through Leicester to know of Sidney in his youth, and while at Oxford Philip spent a vacation with the statesman's family, who then lived near London, at Hampton Court. The experienced minister—like all who met Philip—acknowledged infinite attraction in the youth. 'I do love him,' he said, 'as he were my own,' and he was moved by parental sentiment to suggest means whereby the lad might become 'his own.' He proposed to Philip's father, after the manner of parents of that time, a marriage between his elder daughter and the boy. Marriages in the higher ranks of society were in those days rarely arranged by the persons chiefly concerned. Parents acted as principals throughout the negotiations. Fathers and mothers

Lord Burghley's favour.

were always anxious to marry off daughters as soon as they left the nursery. Sons might wait a little longer. The girl in the present case was only thirteen. Philip was two years older. Money was the pivot on which such matrimonial compacts turned. But Sir Henry Sidney could not afford to make much pecuniary provision for his son. The Earl of Leicester did what he could to forward the auspicious project. He undertook to provide his nephew, Philip, with an income of near £300 a year on the day of his marriage with the Prime Minister's daughter, and promised something like three times that amount at a subsequent period. The discussion went far between the parents, but the scheme was ultimately wrecked on pecuniary rocks. The girl's father wavered, and, on further consideration, thought it well to seek a suitor who was richer in his own right. Sidney was rejected. The young lady married a wealthier young nobleman, the Earl of Oxford, between whom and Sidney no love was lost thenceforth. The Earl of Oxford was a poet and a lover of poetry, but the new culture left no impress on his manners. Boorish and sullen tempered, Lord Burghley's new son-in-law assimilated the crude vices of the Renaissance. His nature rejected its urbanities.

Epidemic disease, in days when cleanliness was reckoned a supererogatory virtue, devastated at frequent intervals England and Europe. An outbreak of the plague at Oxford cut short Philip's career there. Students were scattered in all directions. At seventeen Sidney left the University. He did not return to it. His education was pursued thereafter in a wider sphere.

The plague at Oxford.

IV

A year later Sidney obtained permission from the Queen to travel abroad, for a further period of two years. Thereby he gained a more extended knowledge of life and letters than was accessible at home. The value of foreign travel

Foreign travel.

as a means of education was never better understood, in spite of rudimentary means of locomotion, than by the upper classes of Elizabethan England. All who drank deep of the new culture had seen ' the wonders of the world abroad.' Sidney's keen-witted uncle, Leicester, recognised that his nephew, despite his promise, was as yet 'young and raw.' The French Court was already famed for its courtesy. Thither his uncle sent him with a letter of introduction to the English Ambassador there, Sir Francis Walsingham. Walsingham, a politician of rare acumen, and a man of cultivated taste, had fashioned himself on the model of Machiavelli, the Florentine. Intercourse with him was well qualified to sharpen a pensive youth's intellect.

Sidney's foreign tour was only destined to begin in France. It was to extend to both the east and south of Europe.

In Paris.

His Parisian experiences, as events proved, were calculated to widen his views of life and deepen his serious temper more effectually than to polish his manners or to foster in him social graces. Sidney stayed three months at the English Embassy in Paris. He went to the French Court, and was well received by the Protestant leaders, the leaders of the Huguenots, a resolute minority of the French people, who were pledged to convert France at all hazards into a Protestant country. Ronsard was the living master of French poetry, and Sidney readily yielded himself to the fascination of the delicate harmonies and classical imagery of the Frenchman's muse. But while Philip was still forming his first impressions of the French capital, Paris and the world suffered a great shock. The forces of civilisation seemed in an instant paralysed. The massacre of the Protestants in Paris by the French

Government—or the leaders of the Catholic majority—on St.
Bartholomew's Day (23rd August 1572) is one of *The St.*
those crimes of history of which none can read *Bartho-lomew*
without a shudder. For the time it gave new *Massacre.*
life to the worst traditions of barbarism. Sidney was safe at
the embassy, and ran no personal risk while the fiendish
work was in progress. But his proximity to this Catholic
carnival of blood inflamed his hatred of the cause to which
it ministered, and intensified his Protestant ardour. Until
his death every persecuted Huguenot could reckon in him a
devoted friend.

When the news of the great crime reached England,
Sidney's friends were alarmed for his safety. Lord Burghley
and Lord Leicester bade Walsingham procure
passports for the youth to leave France for *Departure for*
Germany. Religious turmoil—the strife of Pro- *Germany.*
testant and Catholic—infected Germany as well as France,
but the scale in Germany seemed turning in the Protestant
direction, and there was small likelihood there of danger to
a Protestant traveller.

In Germany learning of the severest type was, then as
now, sedulously cultivated. Sidney soon reached Frankfort.
There he lodged with Andrew Wechel, a learned
printer in Hebrew and Greek, and gathered under *The meet-ing with*
his roof the latest fruit of Renaissance scholarship. *Languet.*
Printing—still a comparatively new art—was a learned and
a scholarly profession, and German printers had earned a
high repute for disinterested encouragement of classical
proficiency. A fellow-lodger at this learned printer's house
was Hubert Languet, a Huguenot controversialist and
scholar. Languet, a quiet thoughtful student, was fifty-four
years old, no less than thirty-five years Sidney's senior.
But, despite the disparity of age, Sidney's heart went out

at once to the exile from France for conscience' sake. The Frenchman on his side was attracted by the sympathetic bearing of the young traveller, and there sprang up between them a lasting and attractive friendship. Languet, Sidney said afterwards, taught him all he knew of literature and religion.

From Frankfort Sidney went on to Vienna, the capital of Austria, and the home of the ruler of the Holy Roman Empire. There the Renaissance was held in check by mediæval tradition and prejudice, and Sidney's first stay there was short. For the moment Vienna was a mere halting-place in his progress towards what was the land of promise for all enlightened wayfarers. He passed quickly to the true home of the Renaissance—to Italy, where all the artistic, literary, and scientific impulses of contemporary culture were still aglow with the fire of the new spirit.

At Vienna.

Most of his time was spent in Venice. That city of the sea seemed to him to owe its existence to the rod of an enchanter, and cast on him the spell of her artistic and intellectual triumphs in their glistening freshness. At Venice Sidney studied with characteristic versatility the newest developments of astronomy and music. He read much history and current Italian literature. He steeped himself in the affectations of the disciples of the dead Petrarch, and eagerly absorbed the rich verse of the living Tasso. He was entertained magnificently by Venetian merchants. But above all he came to know the great Italian painters, Tintoretto and Paolo Veronese, in whom Venetian pictorial art, if not the pictorial art of the world, came nearest perfection. In all directions Sidney came to close quarters with contemporary culture of the most finished kind.

At Venice.

The sensual levities of Venetian society made no appeal to Sidney, who still took life in a solemn spirit. He avoided

the pleasures of youth. His friends thought him almost too
serious, too sad and thoughtful for a young man of Seriousness
twenty or twenty-one. Sidney admitted that he of temper.
was 'more sober than my age or business requires,' and he
endured patiently the sarcasms of those to whom zeal for
things of the mind was always a synonym for dulness and
boredom. Although he was a good horseman, he was never
a sportsman, and the story is told by a friend, Sir John
Harington, that of the noble and fashionable recreations of
hawking and hunting, Sidney was wont to say that next to
hunting, he liked hawking worst. The falconers and hunters,
Harington proceeded, would be even with him, and would
say that bookish fellows such as he could judge of no sports
but those within the verge of the fair fields of Helicon,
Pindus, and Parnassus. It was no brilliant jest, but the
anecdote testifies to the exceptional refinement of temper
and the independence of social convention that Sidney
acquired early and enjoyed in permanence.

Not that Sidney had keen eyes and ears only for what
was passing about him in spheres of literature and art.
• Every serious interest that weighed with intelligent men
found some echo in his being. He was fast Protestant
gathering political convictions on his foreign tour ; zeal.
he was watching narrowly the strife of Protestant and
Catholic, and his nascent enthusiasm for the future of the
Protestant religion in Europe, which he identified with the
free development of human thought, mounted high.

As the nephew of the Queen of England's favourite,
Leicester, Sidney could count on a respectful hearing, when
he enunciated political opinions. Occult English Diplomatic
diplomacy honeycombed continental courts, and employ-
those in close touch at home with the English ment.
sovereign were credited with an exaggerated power over

her, which it was to the advantage of foreign potentates to conciliate. Sidney, as his continental tour lengthened, and the attractions of his personality attained wider recognition, was held to reflect something of his uncle's influence and his country's glory. When he returned to Vienna from Venice, there was talk of his offering himself as a candidate for a European throne—the vacant throne of Poland—which was filled by electoral vote. The suggestion came to nothing, but it illustrated the spreading faith in his fitness for political responsibilities. Finally, in his anxiety to perfect his political experience, he accepted an offer of employment as Secretary at the English Legation in Vienna. Despite his antipathy to sport, he yielded to friendly advice, and learned, in the Austrian capital, horsemanship—all the intricate graces of the equestrian art—of the Emperor's esquire of the stables.

Sidney's friends in England were growing alarmed at his long absence on the Continent of Europe. They had not yet fully understood him. They feared that he might be converted to Catholicism, which in Austria had mastered the Protestant revolt, or that he might be corrupted by the fantastic vice of Italy. At his friends' instance, when three years—a goodly part of his short life—had ended, he made his way home. On the journey he greatly extended his intercourse with scholars who were settled in Germany. At Heidelberg he met the greatest of scholar-printers, Henri Étienne or Stephens. Stephens, whose name is honoured by all who honour scholarship, afterwards dedicated to Sidney an edition—an *editio princeps*—of a late Greek historian, Herodian. Sidney returned home under the sway of the purest influences that dominated the art, literature, and scholarship of the Continental Renaissance. His moral sense had triumphed over the current temptations to sensual

End of the foreign tour.

indulgence. His Protestantism was untainted. Only that which was of good repute had lent sustenance to his mind or heart.

v

Settled in England, Sidney, like all young men of good family, was formally presented to his sovereign. As nephew of the Court favourite, Leicester, he was heartily welcomed by the Queen, and was admitted to the select circle of her attendants. Attached to the Court, he largely occupied his time in its splendid recreations. He was at Kenilworth in 1576 when his uncle Leicester gave that elaborate and fantastic enter- tainment in honour of the Queen's visit, which fills a glow- ing page in Elizabethan history. It is reasonable to conjec- ture that in the crowd of neighbouring peasants who came to gaze at the gorgeous spectacles—the decorations, the triumphal arches, the masques, the songs, the fireworks— was John Shakespeare, from Stratford-on-Avon, a dozen miles off, and that John brought with him his eldest son William,—the poet and dramatist whose fame was com- pletely to eclipse that of any of the great lords and ladies in the retinue of their sovereign. Reminiscences of the great fête, with its magnificent pageantry, are traceable in a spirited speech of the dramatist's *A Midsummer Night's Dream.* They are actual incidents in the scenic and musical devices at Kenilworth which Oberon describes in his picture of

> ' A mermaid on a dolphin's back,
> [Uttering] such dulcet and harmonious breath,
> That the rude sea grew civil at her song.'

But if Sidney's uncle sought by his splendid shows in- extricably to entangle the Queen's affections, he failed. ' Young Cupid's fiery shaft' missed its aim ;

> ' And the imperial votaress passed on
> In maiden meditation, fancy free.'

[marginal notes: At Court. At Kenilworth.]

From Kenilworth Sidney went on a visit with his sovereign to another great house, Chartley Castle, the owner of which, the first Earl of Essex, was Leicester's successor as the Queen's host. The visit exerted important influence on Philip's future. There he first met the Earl's daughter Penelope, who, although then only a girl of twelve, was soon to excite in him a deep, if not passionate, interest. It was, however, her father, the Earl of Essex, who, like so many other eminent men and women, first fell under Sidney's spell. The Earl delighted in the young man's sympathetic society, and invited him to accompany him to Ireland, whither he went to fill a high official post. Sidney's father was once again Lord Deputy of Ireland, and Sidney was glad of the opportunity of visiting his family. Together he and his new friend crossed the Irish Channel. But the journey had an unhappy outcome. The Earl of Essex was taken ill at Dublin and died immediately after he had landed. His last words were unqualified love and admiration for Philip. ' I wish him well—so well that, if God move their hearts, I wish that he might match with my daughter. I call him son—he is so wise, virtuous, and godly. If he go on in the course he hath begun, he will be as famous and worthy a gentleman as ever England bred.'

Penelope Devereux.

The Earl's dying wish that he should marry his daughter bore wayward fruit; it was fraught with consequences for which the Earl had not looked. Philip was now a serious youth of twenty-two; Penelope was only fourteen. Like her brother, the new Earl of Essex, who was to succeed the Earl of Leicester in Queen Elizabeth's favour, and then, after much storm and strife, to sacrifice his life to pique and uncontrollable temper, Penelope Devereux was impetuous and precocious. She was gifted

'Astrophel and Stella.'

with a coquettish disposition, which was of doubtful augury for the happiness of herself and her admirers. Encouraged by her dead father's hopes, she sought Philip's admiration. He made kindly response. Passion did not enslave him. A gentle attachment sprang up between them, and Sidney turned it to literary account. In accordance with the fashion of the day he began addressing to Penelope a series of sonnets, in which he called himself 'Astrophel' and the young girl 'Stella.' Nothing came of this courtship except the sonnets. Penelope soon married another. Sidney, a few years later, also married another. But 'Astrophel,' with full approval of his sister and subsequently of his wife, never ceased to cultivate a platonic and literary friendship with the daughter of his dead friend, the Earl of Essex, both while she was a maid and after she became another's wife. He continued to address poetry to 'Stella' till near his death.

The sonnet-sequence called 'Astrophel and Stella,' which owed its being to Sidney's faculty for friendship, *Sidney's* was probably Sidney's earliest sustained attempt *sonnets.* at literature. The collection illustrates with exceptional clearness the influence that the Renaissance literature of France and Italy had exerted on him during his recent travels. By these sonnets, too, he signally developed a tract of literature, which had hitherto yielded in England a barren harvest.

Though Dante was an admirable sonnetteer, it was his successor, Petrarch, in the fourteenth century, whose example gave the sonnet its lasting vogue in Europe. The far-famed collection of sonnets which Petrarch addressed to his lady-love Láura generated, not only in his own country *History* but also in France and Spain, a spirit of imitation *of the* and adaptation which was exceptionally active *Sonnet.* while Sidney was on his travels. Early in the sixteenth

century two of Henry VIII.'s courtiers, Sir Thomas Wyatt
and the Earl of Surrey, had made some effort to familiarise
the English people with Petrarch's work, by rendering portions of it into the English tongue. But the effort ceased
with their death. Subsequently, in Sidney's youth, the
vogue of the Petrarchan sonnet spread to France. The
contemporary poets, Ronsard, Du Bellay, and their associates, wrote thousands of sonnets on the Italian model. It
was in France that Sidney practically discovered the sonnet
for England anew. He, like two other poets of his own
generation, Thomas Watson and Edmund Spenser, who
essayed sonnetteering about the same time, gained his first
knowledge of the sonnet from the recent French development of it, with which his visit to Paris familiarised him,
rather than from the original Italian source, of which he
drank later. Not that Sidney did not quickly pass from
the examples of France to the parent efforts of Italy,
but it was France, as the undertone of his sonnets proves,
that gave the first spur to Sidney's sonnetteering energy.
The influence of Ronsard is at least as conspicuous as that
of Petrarch, and of Petrarch's sixteenth-century disciples
in Italy. But, in whatever proportions the inspiration is to
be precisely distributed between France and Italy, nearly
all of it came from the Continent of Europe. Sidney's
endeavour quickly acquired in England an extended vogue,
and thereby Sidney helped to draw Elizabethan poetry into
the broad currents of continental culture.

The sonnet of sixteenth-century Europe was steeped in
the Platonic idealism which Petrarch had first conspicuously
Platonic   enlisted in the service of poetry. Earthly beauty
idealism.   was the reflection of an eternal celestial type, and
the personal experiences of the sonnetteer were subordinated
to the final aim of celebrating the praises of the immortal

pattern or idea of incorporeal beauty. The path of the
sonnetteer as defined by the Petrarchists—disciples of
Petrarch in Italy and France—was bounded by a series of
conventional conceits, which gave little scope to the writer's
original invention. Genuine affairs of the heart, the uncontrollable fever of passion, could have only remote and
shadowy concern with the misty idealism and hyperbolical
fancies of which the sonnet had to be woven. Sidney's
addresses to 'Stella' follow with fidelity Petrarch's arche-
typal celebration of his love for Laura. Petrarchan idealism
permeates his imagination. The far-fetched course, which
the exposition of his amorous experience pursues, is defined
by his reading in the poetry of Petrarch, and of Petrarch's
French and Italian pupils. His hopes and fears, his apo-
strophes to the river Thames, to sleep, to the nightingale,
to the moon, and to his lady-love's eyes, sound many a
sweet and sympathetic note, but most of them echo the
foreign voices. At times Sidney's lines are endowed with
a finer music than English ears can detect in the original
harmonies, but he nearly always moves in the circle of
sentiment and idea which foreign effort had consecrated
to the sonnet. To the end he was loyal to his masters,
and he closes his addresses to 'Stella' in Petrarch's most
characteristic key. In his concluding sonnet he adapts
with rare felicity the Italian poet's solemn and impressive
renunciation of love's empire :—

> 'Leave me, O love, which reachest but to dust,
>   And thou, my mind, aspire to higher things.'

Perfect sincerity and sympathy distinguish Sidney's final act
of homage to the greatest of his poetic masters.

None of Sidney's poetic fellow-countrymen assimilated
more thoroughly the manner or matter of their poetic tutors.

In metrical respects especially, Sidney showed as a sonnetteer far greater loyalty to foreign models than any of the
Elizabethan sonnetteers who succeeded him.
The metre
of the   Almost all his successors, while they endeavoured
sonnets.   to reproduce the foreign imagery and ideas, ignored foreign rules of prosody. Sidney sought to reproduce
the foreign metres as well as the foreign imagery and ideas.
In gradually unfolding the single idea which the true
sonnet develops, he knew the value of quatrains and tercets
linked together by interlaced rhymes. He saw the danger
of incoherence or abruptness in the accepted English habit
of terminating the poem by a couplet, in which the rhymes
were unconnected with those preceding it. Five rhymes,
variously distributed (not seven rhymes, after the later
English rule), sufficed for the foreign sonnet, and Sidney
proved that a close student of foreign literature could work
out an English sonnet under like restriction without loss of
energy.

Sidney's sonnets were in his lifetime circulated only in
manuscript. They were first published five years after his
death. Whether in manuscript or in print they
Influence
of his   met with an extraordinarily enthusiastic recep-
sonnets.   tion, and stimulated sonnetteering activity in
Elizabethan England to an extent which has had no parallel
at later epochs. 'Stella,' Sidney's poetic heroine, received
in England for a generation homage resembling that which
was accorded in Italy to Laura, Petrarch's poetic heroine,
whose lineaments she reflected. . Apart from considerations
of poetic merit, Sidney's sonnets form an imposing land-
mark in the annals of English literature, by virtue of the
popularity they conferred on the practise of penning long
series or sequences of sonnets of love. Their progeny is
legion. In all ranks of the literary hierarchy their issue

abounded. Sidney's efforts were the moving cause of
Spenser's collection of ' Amoretti,' and it is more important
to record that to their example stands conspicuously indebted the great sonnetteering achievement of Shakespeare himself.

VI

The composition of Sidney's sonnets was pursued amid the
practical work of life.   It was never his ambition nor his
intention to become a professional poet and man
of letters.   His devotion to literature shed its   No professional
glow over all his interests.   But his most active   poet.
energies were absorbed by other than literary endeavours.
'The truth is,' wrote his friend Greville, 'his end was not
writing, even while he wrote, nor his knowledge moulded
for tables and schools,—but both his wit and understanding
bent upon his heart, to make himself and others, not in
words or opinion, but in life and action, good and great.'

Like all young men of his rank and prospects, Sidney
proposed to devote the main part of his career to the public
service.   An early opportunity of gratifying his   Political
wish seemed to offer.   Early in 1577, while he   ambitions.
was no more than twenty-three, an active political career
appeared to await his will.   He was entrusted with a diplomatic mission, which, although it was of an elementary
type, put no small strain on his youthful faculties.   He was
bidden carry messages of congratulation from Queen Elizabeth to two foreign sovereigns, both of whom had just
succeeded to their thrones, the Elector Palatine at Heidelberg, and the new Emperor Rudolph ii. at Prague.

Sidney threw himself into his work with vigour and
enthusiasm—with more vigour indeed than was habitual to
the hardened politician.   He would do more than the mere

bloodless work which diplomacy required of him. He would break a lance for his personal principles as well as carry out his sovereign's commands. He endeavoured to influence the policy and aspirations of the rulers of the countries that he visited. It was indiscretion on the part of an ambassador which was likely to breed trouble.

In Heidelberg, the capital city of the Elector Palatine's Protestant state, the people were divided between Lutherans and Calvinists, and the two parties were at deadly enmity with one another. Sidney urged on both sides the need of reconciliation, but neither approved with any warmth the interference of a foreigner. Throughout Germany he urged on rulers the formation of a great Protestant league to stem the spread of Catholic doctrine. At the Catholic Court of Vienna where he had already accepted frequent hospitalities and was held in high esteem, he slightly changed his tone. While he sought to consolidate and unify the Protestant views of Europe, he desired to sow dissension among the Catholic powers. He lectured the newly crowned Emperor on the iniquities of Spain and Rome, and urged on him the duty of forming another league, a great league of nations to resist Spanish and Romish tyranny. He was listened to civilly, if not with serious attention.

At Heidelberg and Vienna.

A more grateful experience befell him before he returned home. On his way back to England he was ordered by the Queen's Government to visit Antwerp, that city which had been the parent of More's *Utopia*, in order to congratulate the Protestant prince and general, William the Silent, Prince of Orange, on the birth of a son. It was not only his own cultured fellow-countrymen nor the poets and artists of foreign lands who felt the spell of Sidney's character   The great Dutch leader, the taciturn

At Antwerp.

master of the supreme arts of strategy in peace and war, was captivated by the young Englishman's fervour and intelligence. Sidney exerted on him all the fascination which Lord Burghley and the Earl of Essex had acknowledged. The Prince of Orange, who was reputed never to speak a needless word, declared that the Queen of England had in Sidney one of the greatest and ripest counsellors that could be found in Europe.

Despite some characteristic display of youthful impetuosity which escaped Prince William's notice, the tour greatly added to Sidney's reputation. The Queen's Secretary, Walsingham, wrote to Sidney's father in Ireland on the young man's return : 'There hath not been any gentleman, I am sure, these many years, that hath gone through so honourable a charge with as good commendations as he.' *His success.*

Sidney's energy and activity were now untamable. 'Life and action' were now all in all to him. He put no limits to the possibilities of his achievement. He believed himself capable of solving the most perplexing of political problems. His father, who was a liberal and tolerant statesman, was distracted by the difficulties inseparable from Irish rule. With the self-confidence that came of the laudations of the great, Sidney thought to aid him by writing in detail on the perennial problem. He had faith in the justice of his father's methods of government, which were called in question by selfish timeservers in high places. Philip pointed to the dangers of the arrogant pretensions of the Anglo-Irish nobility, immigrants from England, who dominated the native population. He recommended equality of taxation. He showed a reasonable interest in the native Irish which few other Elizabethans admitted, and avowed small sympathy with the Irish landlord, deference *His views on Ireland.*

to whose selfish claims habitually guided the home policy. But Sidney was preaching to deaf ears, and was merely jeopardising his chances of advancement.

VII

No regular work in the service of the state was offered Sidney. Without official occupation at Court, he had no opportunity there of bending his wit and under-

Varied occupations.

standing to the exploits of ' life and action ' for which he was yearning. He was impelled to seek compensation in those intellectual interests, which his temperament, despite his professions to the contrary, would never allow him to forgo entirely. For the enter-tainment of the Queen, when she was paying another visit to his uncle Leicester, he wrote a crude masque of conven-tional adulation, called ' The Lady of the May.' The slender effort abounds in classical conceits, and seeks to satirise classical pedantry. It gives no promise of dramatic faculty. The little piece has, however, historic value, because Shakespeare read it, and partly assimilated it in his *Love's Labour's Lost*. In other directions Sidney gave fuller scope to his cultured intelligence. He sought friends amongst poets, painters, musicians, and engineers (or mechanicians), and he showed stimulating sympathy with their work and ambition. It was with men of letters that he found himself most at home, and with the greatest Elizabethan poet of all who were the fore-runners of Shakespeare he formed, by a fortunate chance, at a midmost point of his adult career, a memorable friendship, which increases the dignity and interest of his own career.

Sidney was often at his uncle Leicester's house in London, and there Edmund Spenser, the poet and moralist of the *Faerie Queene*, was employed for a time in a secretarial

capacity. The two men met, and a warm affection at once
sprang up between them. Spenser was Sidney's
senior by two years; when they became acquainted
with one another in 1578, Sidney was twenty-
four, Spenser was twenty-six. It was the younger man whom
the elder at first hailed as master: Spenser was anxious
to rank as Sidney's admiring disciple. But the means
he took to announce this relationship put each man in his
rightful place. Spenser's first published work—that book
which heralded the great Elizabethan era of literature—
the *Shepheards Calender*, is distinguished by a dedication to
Sidney, 'the president,' Spenser calls him, 'of nobleness
and chivalry.' The patron recognised that he thereby
received more honour than he could confer. Of all reputa-
tions the one that Sidney most valued was that of association
with the noblest figure in the literature of his day.

> Friendship with Spenser.

Other men of letters, prominent among whom was the
courtier poet, Sir Edward Dyer, joined Sidney and Spenser
in social intercourse at Leicester House. The
nights were passed in eager literary debate. The
company formed itself into a literary club, all
members of which were fired with literary zeal—with zeal
for creating an English literature that should compete with
the best that the Continent had yet produced. A like ambition had fired a band of Frenchmen of the previous generation, when returning from travel in Italy. A like ambition
had led to the formation in France of that little regiment of
cultured lyric poets which christened itself 'La Pléiade.'
As in France so in England, the poetic pioneers lay under
the spell of the great classical literature, knowledge of which
had lately reached them from Italy. The future of literature
depended, they erroneously believed, on the closeness with
which it fashioned itself on classical models. Classical style,

> The liter-
> ary club
> of 'The
> Areopagus.'

classical expression, was the philosopher's stone which could convert the dross of the vernacular into literary gold. At the club, which met at Leicester House, and bore the classical title of 'The Areopagus,' the members were dazzled for the time by this perilous theory. They committed themselves to the heretical belief that rhyme and accent, the natural concomitants of English verse, were vulgar and unrefined. It was incumbent on the new poets if they would attain lasting glory to acclimatise in English poetry the Latin metre of quantity, which the genius of Virgil and Horace had ennobled.

The principle which underlay this endeavour was misconceived, and only required to be practically applied to be convicted of impotence. Modern literature might well assimilate classical ideas, but classical prosody or syntax had no juster place in a modern language than a Greek chiton or a Roman toga in a modern wardrobe. Sidney, like fellow-members of the Club, experimented in English

Classical metres. sapphics and hexameters and elegiacs, but the uncouth results brought home to genuine lovers of poetry that the movement was marching in a wrong direction. When, after a year's trial, Sidney's literary club was dissolved, English poetry was proving beyond risk of doubt, that accent and rhyme were its only instruments of work, and that the classical fashions of prosody or syntax were barbarisms outside the ancient languages of Rome or Greece. Versatility of interest was characteristic of Sidney and his friends. It had suddenly led them into error, but it led them out again with almost equal celerity.

Hereditary rank combined with his individual tastes and character to facilitate Sidney's assumption of a leader's place in the intellectual society of London. At the same time Sidney steadily maintained his interest in the literary efforts of continental Europe. Insularity was foreign to

the literary spirit of the Elizabethan age. Especially did
Sidney and his associates cherish that fraternal feeling which
binds together literary workers of all races and
countries. His breadth of intellectual sympathy
comes into peculiar prominence in the reports

Intercourse
with
Bruno.

of the reception which he and his friends accorded to the
Italian philosopher, Giordano Bruno, on his visit to London
in 1584. At the house of his friend, Fulke Greville, Sidney
and Bruno often met. Together they discussed moral, meta-
physical, mathematical and natural scientific speculations.
The Italian poured into Sidney's eager ears the reason for
Galileo's new belief that the earth moves round the sun.
No teacher could have found a more receptive pupil. Bruno
proved his regard for Sidney's sympathetic attention by
dedicating to him two of his best known speculative works,
and thus linked his name with the most advanced thought of
the Renaissance. Not that Sidney meekly accepted Bruno's
opinions. Sidney's faith in Christianity was not easily shaken.
With Christianity Bruno had small concern. His philosophy
was the philosophy of doubt. Like the Utopians of Sir
Thomas More, Bruno was a vague Pantheist, to whom the
truths of orthodox Christianity did not appeal. A fearless
thinker, he was ultimately burnt with revolting brutality
as a heretic at Rome in 1600. Religious toleration came
naturally to Sidney's active and inquisitive mind. He gave
Bruno's religious opinions courteous consideration. They
deeply interested him. But he did not adopt them. He
zealously cultivated independence of mind and, as if to prove
his equable temper, at the same time as he was debating the
bases of religion with Bruno, he was translating a perfectly
orthodox treatise on the Christian religion by a distinguished
French Protestant friend, De Mornay. When De Mornay
visited London, Sidney was no less profuse in hospitality to

him than to Bruno. Every man of intellectual tastes attracted him, but he was steadfast to his own conviction, and was not hastily led away by novel speculation, even if he were fascinated by the charm of exposition which hovered on its inventor's lips.

VIII

To another form of literary endeavour Sidney's attention was diverted somewhat against his will. English Drama was still in its infancy. Comedy had not yet emerged from the shell of horseplay and burlesque and rusticity; genuine humour or genuine romance was to develop later. Tragedy was still a bombastic presentment of blood and battle, of barbarous and sordid crime. But the embryonic Drama was encouraged by men of enlightenment, and by none so warmly as by the cultured leaders of the aristocracy. To the leisured classes any new form of recreation is welcome, and the drama could adapt itself to all gradations of literary taste among its patrons. The acting profession in England was first organised under the protection of the nobility. Like other great noblemen, Sidney's uncle Leicester took under his patronage a band of men who went about the country engaged in rudimentary dramatic performances. The company of actors called itself the Earl of Leicester's men or his servants. It ultimately developed into that best of all organised bands of Elizabethan actors, which was glorified by Shakespeare's membership. Sidney interested himself in the company of players which was under the patronage of his uncle. He stood godfather to the son of one of its leaders, a very famous comic actor, Richard Tarleton—one of the earliest English actors whose name has escaped oblivion. But there was nothing individual in Sidney's attitude to actors. His attitude was the conventional one of his class.

Sidney and the Drama.

Despite the favour of the great, the prospects of the Drama in England in those days of infancy were critical and uncertain. It was a new development in England Puritan and had little but its novelty to recommend it. attacks. Its artistic future was unforeseen. Its earliest manifestation, too, excited the fears and animosity of the growing Puritan sentiment of the country. To the delight in Art which the Renaissance encouraged, the Puritan feeling, when once roused, was mortally opposed. Puritanism was in fact a reactionary movement against the delights in things of the sense which the study of ancient literature fostered. Puritanism was impatient of the current culture. It viewed all recreation with distrust, and detected in most forms of amusement signs of sin. Especially did the Drama, the most recent outcome of the Renaissance of paganism, rouse ugly suspicions in the Puritan minds. Its lawfulness in a Christian commonwealth was doubted. Controversy arose as to whether or no the Drama was an emanation of the devil: whether or no the theatre was to be tolerated by members of Christ's Church.

The Puritan attack was bitter and persistent. The Puritan champions sought recruits from all ranks of society and were anxious to divert from the new-born theatre the Stephen favour of the nobility. Their fanaticism lent Gosson them strength. Their methods were none too seeks Sidney's scrupulous. Sidney was known to be of serious support. temper; he was held in esteem in fashionable society. His countenance was worth the winning for any cause. Accordingly one of the most outspoken of the Puritan controversialists—one of the warmest foes of the budding Drama—endeavoured, by a device that had nothing but boldness to excuse it, to press Sidney's influence into his service. Without asking Sidney's leave, Stephen Gosson, who had once been himself a writer of plays and now wrote with the fury of an apostate, dedicated to Sidney a virulent invective, or libel, on plays, players, and dramatists, which he called *The School of Abuse.* He affected to take for granted Sidney's sympathy. To him he dedicated his diatribe, and paraded his name in the preface of the book as an illiberal foe of dramatic literature.

The misrepresentation of Sidney's sentiment was unblushing. Sidney's soul rebelled against the obscurantist views to which the pamphleteer committed him. One might have as justly dedicated to Sir Thomas More a Lutheran tract and credited him with enthusiasm for the doctrines of Luther. No truce was possible between Sidney and one who failed to see in the Drama which Greeks and Romans had especially dignified an honoured branch of literature. Sidney retaliated with spirit. Turning the tables on the offending author, he set to work on an enlightened defence of the Drama. The essay which he called *An Apologie for Poetrie*, embodied his firmest convictions on the value to life of literature and works of imagination.

Sidney's resentment.

Sidney's retort to Gosson went far beyond its immediate purpose. He did much more than expound the worth of the Drama. The Drama was for him one of many manifestations of poetry. It was to the defence of the whole poetic art that he bent his energies. In an opening paragraph he calls himself a 'piece of a logician,' and it is a logical mode of argument that he pursues. Nowhere is the fine quality of Sidney's intellect seen to better advantage. Nowhere else does he illustrate with equal liberality the breadth of his literary sympathies or his instinct for scholarship. He had studied not only the critical philosophy of Aristotle, together with Plato's general

The Apologie for Poetrie.

discussions of the merits and defects of poetry, but had steeped himself in the elaborate criticism of the Renaissance scholars, Minturno and Julius Cæsar Scaliger, who had in their treatises, named respectively ' De Poeta ' and ' Poetice,' attempted, in the middle of the sixteenth century, to codify anew the principles and practices of poetry.

Despite the extent and variety of his sources of learning, Sidney retained full mastery of his authorities, and welds them together with convincing effect. The catholicity of his literary taste preserved him from pedantry. A popular ballad sung with heartiness roused him as with a trumpet, while the gorgeous eloquence of Pindar could do no more. Sidney wrote with lucidity. His style is coloured by his enthusiasm for all that elevates the mind of man. Nearly two centuries and a half later, Shelley, in emulation of Sidney, wrote another *Defence of Poetry*, where the poet's creed was again defined in language of singular beauty. No higher testimony to Sidney's suggestive force or influence can be offered than the fact that his tract should have engendered in Shelley's brain offspring of so rare a charm.

Freedom from pedantry.

Sidney's central proposition, to which all sections of the treatise converge, is that poetry is the noblest of all the works of man. Philosophy and history are for the most part mere handmaidens of poetry, which is the supreme teacher, and ranks as a creative agent beside Nature herself. To the ordinary matter-of-fact intellect of every age such a claim on behalf of poetry is barely intelligible. That poetry is a ' deep thing, a teaching thing, the most surely and wisely elevating of human things,' is an assertion that sounds whimsical in the ears of the multitude of all epochs. It represents a faith whose adherents in every era have been few. Sidney gave reasons for it with

The worth of poetry.

exceptional sincerity and logical force.   In Elizabethan
England the tendency to accept the belief was perhaps
more widely disseminated than at any other period of
English history.   Certainly Sidney's words seem to have
fallen on willing ears, and widened the ranks of the faithful.

In details Sidney's *Apologie for Poetrie* lies open to
criticism.   He underrated the value of poetic expression
Confusion   and poetic form.   Poetry embraced for him every
between
poetry and exercise of the imagination.   Matter was for him
prose.   more valuable than manner.   'Verse,' he wrote,
'is but an ornament, and no cause to poetry'; prose might
consequently be as effective a vehicle of poetry as metrical
composition.   Though his main contention that poetry is
the supreme teacher is not materially affected by the misconception, Sidney here falls a victim to a confusion of
terms.   The place of expression in poetry is overestimated
when it is argued that it counts alone.   But expression is the
main factor.   The functions of poetry and prose lie, too, for
the most part, aloof from one another.   Neither theory nor
practice justifies a statement of their identity, even though
on occasion they may traverse the same ground.   Things of
the mind are the fittest topic of prose which seeks to supply
knowledge.   Things of the emotions are the fittest topic
of poetry which seeks to stimulate feeling.   Prose is under
no obligation to appeal to aught beside the intellect; poetry
is under a primary obligation to appeal to the emotions and
to the sense of sound.

In one other respect Sidney disappoints us.   After he has
enumerated and defined with real insight the
Misunder-
standings   various known classes of poetic effort, he offers
about
English   an estimate of the past, present, and future posi-
poetry.   tion of English poetry.   His commendations of
Chaucer, Surrey, and his friend Spenser, satisfy a reasonable

standard of criticism. But his insight fails him in his comments on the literary prospects of the English Drama. Reverence for Aristotle's laws, as they were developed by the classicists of the Renaissance, shackles his judgment. He ridicules the failure to observe the primeval unity of action or the later classical unities of place and time. He warmly denounces endeavours to echo in a single play the voices of comedy and tragedy. Tragi-comedy he anathematises. An obstinate conservatism mingled with his liberal sympathies and led him at times to confuse progress with anarchy. Sidney wrote before Elizabethan effort had proved the capacity of forms of dramatic art of which classical writers had not dreamed.

But if Sidney's views of the Drama were halting and reactionary, he regained his clearness of vision in the concluding pages of his great *Apologie*. His final Enlightened condemnation of strained conceits in lyrical poetry conclusions. —although a fault from which his own verse is not always free—is wise and enlightened. He perceived that the English tongue was, if efficiently handled, comparable with Greek, and was far more pliant than Latin, in the power of giving harmonious life to poetic ideas. If he underrated the poetic promise of his age, his eloquent appeal to his fellow-countrymen at the end of his *Apologie,* to disown the 'earth-creeping mind' that 'cannot lift itself up to look into the sky of poetry,' proved for many a stirring call to arms. He took leave of his readers like a herald summoning to the poetic lists all the mighty combatants with whom the Elizabethan era was yet to be identified.

IX

But Sidney was soon summoned from these altitudes. Controversies in public and Court life were competing with

literary debates for Sidney's attention. The Queen's favour
was always difficult to keep. Her favourite, Leicester,
Difficulties Sidney's uncle, forfeited it for a time when the
at Court.   news reached her of his secret marriage with that
Countess of Essex who was mother of Sidney's Penelope,
his poetic idol, 'Stella.' The Queen's wrath, when roused,
always expended itself over a wide area, and it now involved
all Leicester's family, including his nephew.

There was much in Court life to alienate Sidney's genuine
sympathies. Many of his fellow-courtiers were difficult companions. The ill-mannered Earl of Oxford always regarded
Quarrels   Sidney with dislike and ridiculed his aspirations.
with   The Earl's wife was that daughter of the Prime
courtiers.   Minister Burghley whose hand in girlhood had
been at first offered by her father to Sidney himself.
Childish quarrels between Sidney and the Earl were
frequent. Once, at the Queen's palace at Whitehall, while
Sidney was playing tennis, the Earl insolently insisted on
joining uninvited in the game. Sidney raised objections.
The Earl bade all the players leave the court. Sidney
protested. The Earl called him 'a puppy.' Sidney retorted,
truthfully if not very felicitously 'Puppies are got by
dogs, and children by men,' and then with greater point
challenged the unmannerly nobleman to a duel. The dispute reached the Queen's ears. She forbade the encounter,
and with great injustice ordered Sidney to apologise for an
insult which he had directed at a man of higher rank than
himself. Sidney declined, and the Queen's wrath against
him increased. He was in no yielding mood, and sought
no reconciliation.

In the Queen's personal and political conduct there
was at the moment much to offend Sidney's innermost
convictions. He was resolved to forfeit altogether his

position at Court rather than acquiesce in silence. The Queen was contemplating marriage with the King of France's brother. On grounds of patriotism and of Protestantism he begged her to throw over a Frenchman and a Catholic. There was no lack of plainness or of boldness in this address to his prince. The result was inevitable. He was promptly excluded from the royal presence.

Sidney's intellectual friends had long regretted the waste of his abilities which idle lounging about the Court entailed, and they viewed his taste of the royal anger without dejection. He, too, left the Court with a sense of relief. Preferment that should be commensurate with his character and abilities had long seemed a hopeless quest; vanity now appeared the only goal of a courtier's life. He could escape from it, with the knowledge that solace for his disappointments awaited him in the society of a beloved comrade, his sister, the Countess of Pembroke, whose tastes were singularly like his own. At her husband's country-house in Wiltshire he was always a welcome guest, and there could cut himself off with a light heart from the mean and paltry pursuit of the royal countenance. In this period of enforced retirement he engaged with the Countess in literary recreation of an exacting kind. For her and his own amusement he wrote a romance. He called it the Countess of Pembroke's *Arcadia*. It was the latest and most ambitious of all his literary endeavours, and gave him a world-wide repute.

In retirement.

Sidney affected to set no value on the work, which exile from the central scene of the country's activities had given him the opportunity of essaying. He undertook it, he said, merely to fill up an idle hour and to amuse his sister. 'Now, it is done only for you, only to you:' he modestly told her 'if you keep it to yourself, or to such friends, who will weigh errors in the balance of good-

The Arcadia.

will, I hope, for the father's sake, it will be pardoned, perchance made much of, though in itself it have deformities. For indeed, for severer eyes it is not, being but a trifle, and that triflingly handled.'

The work is far more serious than the deprecatory preface suggests. Sidney's pen must have travelled with lightning speed. Whatever views may be entertained of the literary merits of his book, it amazes one by its varied learning, its wealth of episode and its exceptional length. It was eulogised in its own day by Sidney's friend, Gabriel Harvey, as a 'gallant legendary, full of pleasurable accidents and profitable discourses; for three things especially very notable—for amorous courting (he was young in years), for sage counselling (he was ripe in judgment), and for valorous fighting (his sovereign profession was arms)—and delightful pastime by way of pastoral exercises may pass for the fourth.' [1] The commendation is pitched in too amiable a key. The *Arcadia* is a jumble of discordant elements; but, despite its manifold defects, it proves its author to have caught a distant glimpse of the true art of fiction.

The romance was acknowledged on its production to be a laborious act of homage to a long series of foreign literary influences. In his description of character and often in his style of narration he was thought to have assimilated the tone of the Latin historians Livy, Tacitus and the rest, and the modern chroniclers, Philippe de Comines and Guicciardini. The *Arcadia* is a compound of an endless number of simples, all of which are of foreign importation. Sidney proves in it more than in his sonnets or his critical tract his loyalty to foreign models and the catholicity of taste which he brought to the study of them.

The corner stone of the edifice must be sought in a

Foreign models.

----

[1] *Pierces Supererogation*, etc.

pastoral romance of Italy. A Neapolitan, Sanazzaro, seems to have been the first in modern Europe to apply the geographical Greek name of Arcadia to an imaginary realm of pastoral simplicity, where love alone held sway. Sanazzaro, who wrote very early in the 16th century, was only in part a creator. He was an enthusiastic disciple of Virgil, and he had read Theocritus. His leading aim was to develop in Italian prose the pastoral temper of these classical poets. But he brought to his work the new humanism of the Renaissance and broadened the interests and outlook of pastoral literature. His Italian *Arcadia* set an example which was eagerly followed by all sons of the Renaissance of whatever nationality. In Spain one George de Montemayor developed forty years later Sanazzaro's pastoral idealism in his fiction of *Diana Inamorada*, and the Spanish story gained a vogue only second to its Italian original. Sidney was proud to reckon himself a disciple of Montemayor the Spaniard, as well as of Sanazzaro the Neapolitan.

But it was not exclusively on the foundations laid by Italian or Spaniard that Sidney's ample romantic fiction was based. Two other currents merged in its main stream. Sidney knew much of late Greek literary effort which produced, in the third century of the Christian era, the earliest specimen of prose fiction. It was the Græco-Syrian Heliodorus, in his ' Aethiopian Tales,' who first wrote a prose novel of amorous intrigue. Heliodorus's novels became popular in translation in every western country, and Sidney familiarised himself with them. But his literary horizon was not bounded either by the ancient literature of Greece or by the contemporary adaptations of classical literary energy. Feudalism had its literary exponents. Mediæval France and Spain were rich in tales of chivalry and feudal adventure. The tedious narrative, for example, of *Amadis of Gaul*, which was mainly responsible for the mental perversion of Don Quixote, fired the Middle Ages with a genuine enthusiasm. That enthusiasm communicated itself to Sidney.

To each of these sources—the pastoral romances of the Renaissance of Italy and Spain, the Greek novel, and the mediæval tales of chivalry—Sidney's *Arcadia* is almost equally indebted. But his idiosyncrasy was not wholly submerged. Possibly Sidney originally thought to depict with philosophic calm in his retirement from the Court the life of shepherds and shepherdesses, and thereby illustrate the contrast between the simplicity of nature and the complex ambitions of princes and princesses. But the theme rang hollow to one who had studied closely life and literature, who sought above all things to be sincere. To credit rusticity which he knew to be coarse, ignorant, and sensual, with unalloyed innocence was little short of fraud. To confine himself solely to pastoral incident, however realistically treated, was to court tameness. On his pastoral ground-plan, therefore, he grafted chivalric warfare of a mediæval pattern, and intrigue in the late Greek spirit.

The mingling of pastoral with chivalry and intrigue.

Chivalric adventure is treated by Sidney for the most part with directness and intelligibility. At the outset of his *Arcadia*, two princely friends, Musidorus of Macedon and Pyrocles of Thessaly, who enjoy equal renown for military prowess, are separated in a shipwreck, and find asylum in different lands. Each is entertained by the king of the country which harbours him, and is set at the head of an army. The two forces meet in battle. Neither commander recognises in the other his old friend, until they meet to decide the final issues of the strife in a hand-to-hand combat. Peace follows the generals' recognition of one another. The two friends are free to embark together on a fantastic quest of love in Arcadia. Each seeks the hand of an Arcadian princess, and they willingly involve themselves in the domestic and dynastic struggles which distract the Arcadian court and country.

Sidney developed the design with bold incoherence. The exigences of love compel his heroes to disguise themselves. Musidorus, the lover of the Arcadian Princess Pamela, assumes the part of a shepherd, calling himself Dorus; while Pyrocles, the lover of the Arcadian Princess Philoclea, with greater boldness, metamorphoses himself into a woman; he arrays himself as an Amazon, and takes the feminine name of Zelmane. Out of this strange disguise is evolved a thread of story which winds itself intricately through nearly the whole of the romance. The Amazonian hero spreads unexpected havoc in the Arcadian court by attracting the affections of both the Princess's parents—of Basilius, the old king of Arcady, who believes him to be a woman; and of Synesia, the lascivious old queen, who perceives his true sex.

The involutions and digressions of the plot are too numerous to permit full description. The extravagances grow more perplexing as the story develops. Arcadian realms exhibit in Sidney's pages few traditional features. The call of realism was in Sidney's ears the call of honesty, and his peasants divested themselves of ideal features for the ugly contours of fact. His shepherds and shepherdesses have long passed the age of innocent tranquillity. Their land is a prey to dragons and wild beasts, and their hearts are gnawed by human passions. Sidney had, too, a sense of the need of variety in fiction. New characters are constantly entering to distort and postpone the natural *dénouement* of events. The work is merged in a succession of detached episodes and ceases to be an organic tale. Parts are much more valuable than the whole. Arguments of coarseness and refinement enjoy a bewildering

The complex intrigue.

contiguity.   At one moment Platonic idealism sways the
scene, and the spiritual significance of love and beauty
overshadows their physical and material aspects.   At the
next moment we plunge into a turbid flood of abnormal
passion.   The exalted thought and aspiration of the Renaissance season Sidney's pages, but they do not exclude the
grosser features of the movement.   There are chapters
which almost justify Milton's sour censure of the whole book
as 'a vain and amatorious poem.'[1]

The *Arcadia* is a prose tale and Milton only applied to it
the title of poem figuratively.   But one important
characteristic of the *Arcadia* is its frequent introduction of interludes of verse which, although they appeal

The verse.

---

[1] The text of the *Arcadia* suffers from the author's casual methods of
composition.   Much of it survives in an unrevised shape.   He seems to have
himself prepared for press the first two books, and the opening section of the
third—about a half of the whole.   This portion of the romance was printed
in 1590, and ended abruptly in the middle of a sentence.   Subsequently
there was discovered a very rough draft of portions of a long continuation,
forming the conclusion of the third book, with the succeeding fourth and
fifth books.   This supplement survived in 'several loose sheets (being never
after reviewed or so much as seen altogether by himself) without any certain
disposition or perfect order.'   With a second edition of the authentic text
these unrevised sheets were printed in 1593.   Sidney's sister, the Countess
of Pembroke, supplied the recovered books with 'the best coherences that
could be gathered out of those scattered papers,' but no attempt was made
to fill an obvious hiatus in the middle of the third book at the point where
the original edition ended and the rough draft opened.   Nor did the editor
or publisher venture to bring the unfinished romance to any conclusion.
What close was designed for the story by the author was 'only known to his
own spirit.'   The editors of later editions, bolder than their predecessors,
sought to remedy such defects.   The gap in the third book was in 1621 filled
by a 'little essay' from the pen of a well-known Scottish poet, Sir William
Alexander, Earl of Stirling.   Finally, in 1628 a more adventurous spirit,
Richard Beling, or Bellings, a young barrister of Lincoln's Inn, endeavoured
to terminate the story in a wholly original sixth book.   It is with these addi-
tions that subsequent re-issues of the *Arcadia* were invariably embellished.
Other efforts were made to supplement Sidney's unfinished romance.   One by
Gervase Markham, an industrious literary hack, came out as early as 1607.
Another, by 'a young gentlewoman,' Mrs. A. Weames, was published in
1651.   The neglect of these fragmentary contributions by publishers of the
full work, calls for no regret.

more directly to the historian of literature than to its
æsthetic critic, must be closely examined by students of
Sidney's work. Shepherds come upon the stage and sing
songs for the delectation of the Arcadian King, and
actors in the story at times express their emotions lyric-
ally. Occasionally Sidney's verse in the *Arcadia* seeks to
adapt to the English language classical metres, after the
rules that the club of 'Areopagus' sought to impose on
his pen. The sapphics and hexameters of the *Arcadia* are
no less strained and grotesque than are earlier efforts in
the like direction. They afford convincing proof of the
hopeless pedantry of the literary principles to which
Sidney for a time did homage, but which he afterwards
recanted. Sidney's metrical dexterity is seen to advantage,
however, in his endeavours to acclimatise contemporary
forms of foreign verse. In his imitation of the sestina and
terza rima of contemporary Italy he shows felicity and
freedom of expression. He escapes from that servile adherence to rules of prosody which is ruinous to poetic invention.
Sidney's affinity with the spirit of Italian poetry is seen to
be greater than his affinity with the spirit of classical poetry.

No quite unqualified commendation can be bestowed
on the prose style of his romance. It lacks the directness
which distinguishes the *Apologie for Poetrie*. It *The prose*
fails to give much support to Drayton's conten- *style.*
tion that Sidney rid the English tongue of conceits and
affectations. His metaphors are often far-fetched, and he
overloads his page with weak and conventional epithets.
The vice of diffuseness infects both matter and manner.
But delightful oases of perspicuous narrative and description
of persons and places are to be found, although the search
may involve some labour.

The unchecked luxuriance of Sidney's pen, and absence

of well-wrought plan did injustice to the genuine insight
into life and the descriptive power which belonged
to him. Signs, however, are discernible amid all
the tangle that, with the exercise of due restraint, he might
have attained mastery of fiction alike in style and subject-
matter.

Want of
coherence.

x

It was difficult for Sidney, whatever the attractions that the
life of contemplation and literary labour had to offer him,
complacently to surrender Court favour, and with it
political office, altogether. He knew the meaning
of money difficulties; tailors and bootmakers often
pressed him for payment. They were not easy to appease.
The notion of seeking a livelihood from his pen was foreign to
all his conceptions of life. From the Queen and her Ministers
he could alone hope for remunerative employment. He
therefore deemed it prudent to seek a reconciliation. Quarrels
with Queen Elizabeth were rarely incurable. A solemn undertaking to abstain from further political argument which
involved the Queen, opened to Sidney an easy road to peace.

Reconcili-
ation with
the Queen.

His uncle Leicester interested himself anew in his fortunes,
and transferred to him a small administrative office which he
himself had held, that of Steward to the Bishop of
Winchester. He succeeded his father, too, as
Member of Parliament for Kent. In Parliament he joined
with eagerness in the deliberations of a Committee which
recommended strenuous measures against Catholics and
slanderers of the Queen. But in the House of Commons he
made little mark. The slow methods of the assembly's
procedure, and its absorption in details which lacked large
significance, oppressed Sidney's spirit. He was ill-adapted to
an arena where success came more readily to tactful reticence
and apathy than to exuberant eloquence and enthusiasm.

Official
promotion.

In 1583 he was knighted, and assumed his world-famous designation of Sir Philip Sidney. But it is one of history's little ironies than it was not for any personal merit   Knight-
that he received the title of honour. English   hood.
people like titles, although it be the exception, and not the rule, for them to reward notable personal merit. In Sir Philip's case it happened that a friend whom he had met abroad, Prince John Casimir, brother of the Elector Palatine, had been nominated by Queen Elizabeth to the dignity of a Knight of the Garter. Unable to attend the investiture himself the prince had requested his friend Sidney to act as his proxy. Such a position could only be filled by one who was himself of the standing of a knight-bachelor, the lowest of all the orders of knighthood. Consequently in compliment to the foreign prince, the Queen conferred knighthood on the prince's representative. It was a happy accident by which Sidney was enrolled among English knights. It was not designed as a recognition of his worth; it conferred no special honour on him; but it renewed the dignity of an ancient order of chivalry, and it lends a picturesque colour to the closing scene of his career.

For a year Sidney's course of life ran somewhat more smoothly. Once again he sought scope for political ambitions. He obtained more remunerative official   Joint-
employment. He was offered a post in the mili-   Master of
tary administration of the country. He was   Ordnance.
appointed Joint-Master of the Ordnance with another uncle, the Earl of Warwick, Leicester's elder brother.

The need of a regular income was the more pressing because Sidney was about to enter the married state. His old friend, the Queen's Secretary, Sir Francis
Walsingham, who, when English ambassador, was   Marriage.
his host at Paris in the year of the St. Bartholomew's

Massacre, chose him for his son-in-law, for the husband of
his daughter Frances, a girl of only fourteen.   Sidney was
twenty-nine years old, more than twice her age, and there
seems good reason to regard the union as a marriage *de
convenance*.   The astute Secretary of State, who had always
cherished an affectionate interest in Sidney, thought that the
young man might yet fill with credit high political office, and
his kinship with Leicester gave him hope of a rich inherit-
ance.   The arrangement was not, however, concluded without
difficulty.   Sidney's father declared that ' his present biting
necessity' rendered monetary aid from him out of the question.   Leicester was not immediately helpful, and other
obstacles to the early solemnisation of the nuptial ceremony
presented themselves.   The Queen was never ready to
assent quickly to her courtiers' marriages.   For two months
she withheld her assent.   Then she suddenly yielded, and
showed no trace of resentment.   The marriage took place in
the autumn of 1583.   It was the first scene of the last act
in Sidney's life.   He had barely three years to live.

Sidney took up his residence with his wife's parents near
London, at Barn Elms.   His course of life underwent little

Relations
with Lady
Rich.
other change.   His literary relations with his old
friend Penelope Devereux, who two years before
had become the wife of Lord Rich, were not
interrupted.   He continued to write sonnets to her, and
their loyal friendship remained the admiration of fashionable society.   None the less Sidney stirred in his girl-wife a
genuine affection, and nothing in his association with Lady
Rich seems to have prejudiced her happiness.

Sidney's married life, after its first transports were over,
increased rather than diminished his dissatisfaction with his
prospects at home.   A complete change of scene and of
effort crossed his mind.   He thought of trying his fortune

in a new field of energy. The passion for exploration, for founding English colonies in the newly discovered Continent of America, which had mastered the minds of so many contemporaries, suddenly absorbed him. His active intellect was drawn within the whirlpool of that new enthusiasm. At first he merely took a few shares in an expedition in search of the North-West Passage, but his hopes ran high as he scanned the details of the project. He believed that gold, and all that gold might bring, was to be found in abundance in the hazy continent of the north. But to take a vicarious part in adventure ill sorted with his nature. He resolved to join in person Sir Humphrey Gilbert, who was about to set forth on that eventful expedition to Newfoundland from which he never returned. Sidney was finally induced to stay behind. He was thus preserved from the fate of Gilbert who was wrecked on the voyage home.

The call of the New World.

But Sidney's imagination dwelt on the possibilities which control of a new and untrodden world implied. Designs of dazzling scope vaguely shaped themselves in his brain: he would gain control of the greater part of the new continent and make of it a purified Arcadia such as fiction could hardly comprehend. Accordingly, he sought and obtained letters patent to hold for himself and colonise at will the unknown world. No less than three million acres of undiscovered land in America were soon set at his disposal. The document announcing the grant is well fitted to be enrolled in the courts of Faerie. Sir Philip was 'licensed and authorised to discover, search, find out, view, and inhabit certain parts of America not yet discovered, and out of those countries, by him, his heirs, factors, or assigns to have and enjoy, to him his heirs and assigns for ever, such and so much quantity of ground as should amount to the

Grant to Sidney of American lands.

number of thirty hundred thousand acres of ground and wood, with all commodities, jurisdiction, and royalties, both by sea and land, with full power and authority that it should and might be lawful for the said Sir Philip Sidney, his heirs and assigns, at all times thereafter to have, take, and lead in the said voyage, to travel thitherwards or to inhabit there with him or them, and every or any of them, such and so many of her Majesty's subjects as should willingly accompany him or them, or any or every of them, with sufficient shipping and munition for their transportations.

History seemed obeying the laws that govern fiction. Sidney was building, on a basis of legal technicalities, a castle in the air. The scheme suffered the fate of all speculations in unverified conditions. Little followed the generous grant. But Sidney steadily fixed his eyes for the time on the Atlantic horizon. He was greatly moved by Sir Walter Ralegh's plans for the exploration of the land that Ralegh named 'Virginia.' Sidney sat on a committee of the House of Commons which was appointed to adjust the shadowy boundaries of the first projected settlement of Englishmen in that country. The committee's deliberations had no practical effect. Sidney was destined to come to no closer quarters with the fanciful property, of which the law, working for once in strange agreement with the vagaries of the imagination, had made him master.

XI

The short remainder of Sidney's life was passed in new surroundings. It was on the field of battle that he closed

The last scene.

his brief pilgrimage on earth. Hostility to Catholic Spain had combined with his imaginative energy greatly to stimulate his interest in the American schemes. Advancing life and closer study of current

politics strengthened the conviction that Spain, unless
her career were checked, was England's fated Hostility
to Spain.
conqueror in every sphere. The cause alike
of Protestantism, of enlightenment, and of trade was
menaced by Spanish predominance. A general attack on
the Empire of Spain was essential to England's security.
With characteristic impetuosity he turned from his American
speculations and surveyed the Spanish peril. He was
tiring of the contemplative life. He was bent on trying
his fortune in an enterprise of action. An opportunity
for active conflict with Spain seemed to be forced on
England's conscience which could hardly suffer neglect.
Spain was making a determined effort to drive Protestantism
from the stronghold that it had acquired in the Low
Countries. Sidney's old admirer, William of Orange, had,
in 1584, been murdered there at Spanish instigation, a
martyr to the cause of Protestant freedom. It was England's
duty, Sidney now argued, vigorously to avenge that outrage.
The more direct the onslaught on Spain the better. Spain
should be attacked in all her citadels; the Low Countries
should be over-run ; raids should be made on Spanish ports ;
her rich trade with South America should be persistently
intercepted and ultimately crushed.

Such a design, as soon as his mind had formulated it,
absorbed all Sidney's being. But it met with faint encouragement in the quarter whence authority to carry it into
execution could alone come. The Queen was averse to a
direct challenge of Spain. She was not fond of The atti-
tude of
the Queen.
spending money. She deprecated the cost of open
war. But Sidney and his friends were resolute.
They would not let the question sleep. The nation ranged
itself on their side. At length, yielding to popular clamour,
the Queen agreed, under conditions which indemnified her for

loss of money, to send strictly limited help to the Protestant States of the Low Country. She would assist them in a qualified way to repel the assault of Spain. She would lend them money and would send an army, the cost of which they were to defray. With a policy so meagre in conception and so poor in spirit Sidney had small sympathy. But it was all that it was possible to hope for, and with it he had to rest content. At any rate, wherever and however the blow was to be struck against Spain, he was resolved to lend a hand. That resolve cost him his life.

The command of the English force for the Low Countries was bestowed on Sidney's uncle Leicester; and the Queen Governor reluctantly yielded to persuasion and conferred of Flushing. on Sidney a subordinate post in the expedition. He was appointed Governor of Flushing, one of the cities which the Queen occupied by way of security for the expense which she was incurring. In the middle of November, 1585, Sidney left Gravesend to take up his command. It was to be his first and last experience of battle.

The campaign was from the outset a doubtful success. The Queen refused to provide adequate supplies. Leicester Difficulties proved an indolent commander. Harmonious co-of the operation with their Dutch allies was not easy for campaign. the English. Sidney soon perceived how desperate the situation was. He wrote hastily to his father-in-law Walsingham, who shared in a guarded way his political enthusiasm, urging him to impress the Queen with the need of a larger equipment. He had not the tact to improve the situation by any counsel or action of his own on the spot. He persuaded his uncle to make him Colonel of a native Dutch regiment of horse, an appointment which deeply offended a rival native Dutch candidate. The Queen, to Sidney's chagrin, judged the rival's grievance to be just.

Sidney showed infinite daring when opportunity offered, but good judgment was wanting. There was wisdom in his uncle's warning against his facing risks in active service. Direction was given him to keep to his post in Flushing.

At length Leicester, yielding to the entreaties of his colleagues and his nephew, decided to abandon Fabian tactics and to come to close quarters with the *The attack* enemy. The great fortress of Zutphen, which *on Zutphen.* was in Spanish hands, was to be attacked. As soon as the news reached Sidney, he joined Leicester's army of assault as a knight-errant; his own regiment was far away at Deventer. He presented himself in Leicester's camp upon his own initiative.

On the 21st September 1586 the English army learned that a troop of Spaniards, convoying provisions to Zutphen, was to reach the town at daybreak next morning. *The fatal* Five hundred horsemen of the English army were *wound.* ordered to intercept the approaching force. Without waiting for orders, Sidney determined to join in the encounter. He left his tent very early in the morning of the 22nd, and meeting a friend who had omitted to put on leg-armour, he rashly disdained the advantage of better equipment, and quixotically lightened his own protective garb. Fog hung about the country. The little English force soon found itself by mistake under the walls of the town, and threatened alike in front and at the rear. A force of three thousand Spanish horsemen almost encircled them. They were between two fires—between the Spanish army within the town and the Spanish army which was seeking to enter it. The Englishmen twice charged the reinforcements approaching Zutphen, but were forced to retreat under the town walls. At the second charge Sidney's horse was killed under him. Remounting another, he foolhardily thrust his way through the enemy's

ranks.   Then, perceiving his isolation, he turned back to
rejoin his friends, and was struck as he retreated by a bullet
on the left thigh a little above the knee.   He managed to
keep his saddle until he reached the camp, a mile and a half
distant.   What followed is one of the classical anecdotes of
history, and was thus put on record by Sidney's friend
Greville :—' Being thirsty with excess of bleeding, he called
for drink, which was presently brought him ; but as he
was putting the bottle to his mouth, he saw a poor
soldier carried along, who had eaten his last at the same
feast, ghastly casting up his eyes at the bottle, which Sir
Philip perceiving, took it from his head before he drank, and
delivered it to the poor man, with these words, "Thy necessity is greater than mine."   And when he had pledged this
poor soldier he was presently carried (by barge) to Arnheim.'

Sidney's wife hurried from England to his bedside at
Arnheim, and after twenty-six days' suffering he died.   In
Sidney's
death. his last hours he asked that the *Arcadia*, which
had hitherto only circulated in manuscript, might
be burnt, but found in literary study and composition solace
in his final sufferings.   The States General—the Dutch
Government—begged the honour of according the hero
burial within their own dominions, but the request was
refused, and some months later he was buried in great state
in that old St. Paul's Cathedral—the church of the nation
—which was burnt down in the great fire of 1666.

Rarely has a man been more sympathetically mourned.
Months afterwards Londoners refused to wear gay apparel.
National
mourning. The Queen, though she shrewdly complained that
Sidney invited death by his rashness, was over-
whelmed with grief.   Students of both Oxford and Cambridge Universities published ample collections of elegies in
honour of one who served with equal zeal Mars and Apollo.

Fully two hundred poems were written in his memory at the time. Of these by far the finest is Spenser's pathetic lament 'Astrophel, a Pastoral Elegy,' where the personal fascination of his character receives especially touching recognition :—

> 'He grew up fast in goodness and in grace,
> And doubly fair wox both in mind and face,
> Which daily more and more he did augment,
> With gentle usage and demeanour mild :
> That all mens hearts with secret ravishment
> He stole away, and weetingly beguiled.
> Ne spite itself, that all good things doth spill,
> Found aught in him, that she could say was ill.'
>
> 'Astrophel,' I. 17.

XII

Sidney's career was, to employ his own words, 'meetly furnished of beautiful parts.' It displayed 'many things tasting of a noble birth and worthy of a noble mind.' Yet his achievements, whether in life or literature, barely justify the passionate eulogy which they won from contemporaries. In none of his endeavours did he win a supreme triumph. His friend, Gabriel Harvey, after eulogising his ripe judgment in many callings, somewhat conventionally declared that 'his sovereign profession was arms.' There is small ground for the statement. Sidney's fame owes more to the fascination of his chivalric personality and quick intelligence, and to the pathos of his early death, than to his greatness in any profession, whether in war or politics or poetry.

In practical life his purpose was transparently honest. He showed a boy-like impatience of the temporising habit of contemporary statesmanship, but there was a lack of balance in his constitution which gave small assurance of ability to control men or to mould the course of events. The catastrophe at Zutphen tempts one to exclaim :

> ' 'Twas not a life,
> 'Twas but a piece of childhood thrown away.'

To literature he exhibited an eager and an ardent devotion. The true spirit of poetry touched his being, but he rarely abandoned himself to its finest frenzies. It was on experiments in forms of literary art, which foreign masters had taught him, that he expended most of his energy. Only in detached lyrics, which may be attributed to his latest years, did he free himself from the restraints of study and authority. Only once and again as in his great dirge beginning :

His literary work.

> ' Ring out your bells !   Let mourning shows be spread,
> For love is dead,'

did he wing his flight fearlessly in the purest air of the poetic firmament.   Elsewhere his learning tends to obscure his innate faculty.   Despite his poetic enthusiasm and passionate idealism, there is scarcely a sonnet in the famous sequence inscribed by Astrophel to Stella which does not illustrate an ' alacrity in sinking.'

But no demerits were recognised in Sidney by his contemporaries.   He was, in the obsolete terminology of his admiring friend, Gabriel Harvey, ' the secretary of eloquence, the breath of the Muses, the honey bee of the daintiest flowers of wit and art, the pith of moral and intellectual virtues, the arm of Bellona in the field, the tongue of Suada in the chamber, the spirit of practice in esse, and the paragon of excellency in print.' [1]   His literary work, no less than his life, magnetised the age.   His example fired scores of

---

[1] *Pierces Supererogation*, etc.

Elizabethans to pen long sequences of sonnets in that idealistic tone of his, which itself reflected the temper
of Petrarch and Ronsard.   His massive romance of
Arcadia appealed to contemporary taste despite
its confusions, and was quickly parent of a long line of
efforts in fiction which exaggerated its defects.   Elizabethan dramatists attempted to adapt episodes of Sidney's
fiction to the stage.   Shakespeare himself based on Sidney's
tale of 'an unkind king' the incident of Gloucester and
his sons in *King Lear*.   It was not only at home that his
writings won the honour of imitation.   The fame of the
Arcadia spread to foreign countries.   Seventeenth-century
France welcomed it in translations as warmly as the original
was welcomed in England.

    It was indeed by very slow degrees that the *Arcadia* was
dethroned either at home or abroad.   In the eighteenth
century it had its votaries still.   Richardson borrowed the
name of Pamela from one of Sidney's princesses.   Cowper
hailed with delight 'those Arcadian scenes' sung by 'a
warbler of poetic prose.'   But the revolt against the predominance of Sidney's romance could not then be long
delayed.   English fiction of ordered insight was coming into
being.   The *Arcadia*, which defied so much of the reality
of life, could not breathe the true atmosphere, and it was
relegated to obscurity.   Historically it remains a monument
of deep interest to literary students, but its chief attraction is
now that of a curious effigy ; the breath of life has fled from it.

    Yet, despite the ephemeral character of the major part of
Sidney's labours, the final impression that his brief career
left on the imagination of his countrymen was
lasting.   He still lives in the national memory as
the Marcellus—the earliest Marcellus of English
literature.   After two centuries the poet Shelley gave voice

to a faith, almost universal among Englishmen, that his
varied deeds, his gentle nature, and his early death had
robed him in 'dazzling immortality.'   In Shelley's ethereal
fancy—

> 'Sidney, as he fought
> And as he fell, and as he livèd and loved,
> Sublimely mild, a spirit without spot,'

was among the first of the inheritors of unfulfilled renown to
welcome to their thrones in the empyrean the youngest of
the princes of poetry, John Keats.

SIR WALTER RALEGH
AT THE AGE OF 34.

From the portrait attributed to Federigo Zuccaro in the National Portrait Gallery.

I V

SIR WALTER RALEGH

'O what a noble mind is here o'erthrown !
The courtier's, soldier's, scholar's eye, tongue, sword,
The expectancy and rose of the fair state . . .
The observed of all observers, quite, quite down !'
SHAKESPEARE, *Hamlet*, Act. III., Sc. i., 159-162.

[BIBLIOGRAPHY.—By far the best biography of Ralegh is *Sir Walter Ralegh; a biography* by Mr. William Stebbing, Oxford 1891. His letters may be studied in the second of the two volumes of the 'Life,' by Edward Edwards, 1868. The chief collection of his works in prose and verse was published at Oxford in eight volumes in 1829. The best edition of his poetry is 'The Poems of Sir Walter Raleigh and other courtly poets, collected and authenticated, by John Hannah, D.C.L. (Aldine Edition), London, 1885.' The most characteristic of his shorter prose writings, his *Discovery of Guiana*, is published in Cassells' National Library (No. 67).]

I

THE primary cause of colonial expansion lies in the natural ambition of the healthy human intellect to extend its range of vision and knowledge. Curiosity, the inquisitive desire to come to close quarters with what is out of sight, primarily accounts for the passion for travel and for exploration whence colonial movements spring. Intellectual activity is the primary cause of the colonising instinct.

Primary cause of colonial expansion.

But the colonising, the exploring spirit, when once it has come into being, is invariably stimulated and kept alive by at least three secondary causes, which are sometimes mistaken for the primary. In them good and bad are much tangled. 'The web of our life,'

Three secondary causes.

115

says Shakespeare, ' is of a mingled yarn, good and ill together.' Of a very mingled yarn is the web of which colonial effort is woven.

The intellectual desire to know more about the world than is possible to one who is content to pass his life in his native district or land is commonly stimulated, in the first place, by the hope of improving one's material condition, by the expectation of making more money than were likely otherwise. Evil lurks in this expectation; it easily degenerates into greed of gain, into the passion for gold.

Greed of gain.

The desire for foreign exploration, too, is invigorated by impatience of that restraint which law or custom imposes on an old country, by the hope of greater liberty and personal independence. This hope may tempt to moral ruin; it may issue in the practice of licentious lawlessness.

Passion for liberty.

Then there emerges a third motive—the love of mastery, the love of exercising authority over peoples of inferior civilisation or physical development. The love of mastery is capable alike of benefiting and of injuring humanity. If it be exercised prudently, it may serve to bring races, which would otherwise be excluded, within the pale of a higher civilisation; but if it be exercised imprudently, it sinks to tyranny and cruelty.

Love of mastery.

The passion for mastery, the passion for gold, and the passion for freedom, have all stimulated colonising energy with mingled results. When the three passions are restrained by the moral sense, colonising energy works for the world's advantage; the good preponderates. Wherever the moral sense proves too weak to control the three perilous passions, colonising energy connotes much moral and physical evil.

II

Great colonising effort, which has its primary source in intellectual curiosity, is an invariable characteristic of eras like the era of the Renaissance, when man's intellect is working, whether for good or ill, with exceptional energy. The Greeks and Romans were great colonisers at the most enlightened epochs of their history. In modern Europe voyages of discovery were made by sailors of the Italian Republics, of the Spanish peninsula, and of France, when the spirit of the Renaissance was winging amongst them its highest flight.

Great colonising epochs.

At first the maritime explorers of Southern Europe confined their efforts to the coast of Africa, especially to the west coast. Then they passed to the East—to India, at first by way of the Red Sea, and afterwards round the Cape of Good Hope, and through the Indian Ocean. Nothing yet was known of the Western Hemisphere. It was a sanguine hope of reaching India by a new and direct route through western seas that led to the great discovery of the Continent of America.

The Western Hemisphere.

Columbus, its discoverer, was a native of the Italian Republic of Genoa, a city distinguished by the feverish energy with which its inhabitants welcomed new ideas that were likely to increase men's material prosperity. It was in August 1492—when sailing under the patronage of the greatest sovereigns that filled the throne of Spain, Ferdinand and Isabella, on what he believed would prove a new route to the Indies — that Columbus struck land in what he called, and in what we still call, the West Indies. He made two voyages to the West Indies before he passed further west

Columbus's discovery 1492.

and touched the mainland, which turned out to be South America.

England, under the intellectual stimulus of the Renaissance, was not behind Spain in the exploration of the

England and the New World.

Western Seas. Colonial expansion loomed on England's horizon when the English Renaissance was coming to birth at the end of the fifteenth century. Like Spain, England owed its first glimpse of the New World to the courage of an Italian sailor.

At the time that Columbus sighted South America, John Cabot, also a native of energetic Genoa, had been long settled at Bristol in England, and was now a pilot of that port. No sooner had Columbus sighted South America than Cabot sighted North America. Columbus and Cabot flourished at the end of the fifteenth century—in Sir Thomas More's youth. The work which they inaugurated was steadily carried forward throughout the sixteenth century, and its progress was watched with a restless ecstasy.

The division of labour in exploring the new continent, which was faintly indicated by the two directions which

North and South America.

Cabot and Columbus took respectively to North and South, was broadly adopted in the century that followed by sailors starting respectively from English and Spanish ports. Spaniards continued to push forward their explorations in South America, or in the extreme south of the northern continent. Englishmen by no means left South America undisturbed, but they won their greatest victories for the future in the northern division of the new continent. Spain and England were throughout the sixteenth century strenuous rivals as colonisers of the Western Hemisphere. In the end, South America became for the most part a Spanish settlement; North America became for the most part an English settlement.

The knowledge that a New World was opening to the Old, proved from the first a sharper spur to the imagination in England than in any country of Europe. It contributed there, more notably than elsewhere, to the formation among enlightened men of a new ideal of life; it gave birth to the notion that humanity had it in its power to begin at will existence afresh, could free itself in due season from the imperfections of the Old World. *America and new ideals.* Within very few years of the discovery of America, Sir Thomas More described, as we have seen, that ideal state which he located in the new hemisphere, that ideal state upon which he bestowed the new name of 'Utopia.' Sir Thomas More's romance of *Utopia* is not merely a literary masterpiece; it is also a convincing testimony to the stirring effects on English genius of the discovery of an unknown, an untrodden world.

But the discovery of America brought of necessity in its train to England, no less than to other countries, the less elevated sentiments which always dog the advances of exploration. The spirit of English exploration was not for long uncoloured by greed of gain. Licence and oppression darkened its development. But the vague immensity of the opportunities opened by *Material-istic influences.* the sudden expansion of the earthly planet filled Englishmen with a 'wild surmise' which, if it could not kill, could check the growth of active evil. England's colonial aspirations of the sixteenth century never wholly lost their first savour of idealism.

In Elizabethan England a touch of philosophy tinged the spirit of adventure through all ranks of the nation. Men were ambitious, Shakespeare tells us, to see the wonders of the world abroad in *The spirit of adventure.* order to enlarge their mental horizons. They lavished their

fortunes and their energies in discovering islands far away,
in the interests of truth.   The intellectual stir which moved
his being impelled Sir Philip Sidney, the finest type of the
many-sided culture of the day, to organise colonial exploration, although he died too young to engage in it actively.
The unrest which drove men to cross the ocean and seek
settlement in territory that no European foot had trodden
was identified with resplendent virtue.   Such was the burden
of Drayton's ode 'To the Virginian Voyage':—

> 'You brave heroic minds,
> Worthy your country's name,
> That honour still pursue,
> Whilst loitering hinds
> Lurk here at home with shame,
> Go, and subdue.
> Britons, you stay too long;
> Quickly aboard bestow you,
> And with a merry gale
> Swell your stretched sail,
> With vows as strong
> As the winds that blow you.'

Englishmen of mettle were expected to seek at all hazards
earth's paradise in America.   Not only was the New World
credited with unprecedented fertility, but the laws of nature
were believed to keep alive there a golden age in per-
petuity.

These fine aspirations were never wholly extinguished,
although there lurked behind them the hope that an age of
gold in a more material and literal sense than
philosophers conceived might ultimately reward
the adventurers.   The Elizabethans were worldly-
minded enough to judge idealism alone an unsafe foundation on which to rear a colonial empire.   'For I am not
so simple,' said an early advocate of colonial enterprise who
fully recognised in idealism a practical safeguard against

Imaginary age of Gold.

its degradation, ' I am not so simple to think that any other
motive than wealth will ever erect in the New World a
commonwealth, or draw a company from their ease and
humour at home to settle [in colonial plantations].'

The popular play called *Eastward Ho !* published early in
the seventeenth century, reviewed at the close of the epoch
of the English Renaissance all the prevailing incitements to
colonial expansion.   The language is curiously reminiscent
of a passage in Sir Thomas More's *Utopia,* and illustrates
the permanence of the hold that idealism in the sphere of
colonial experiment maintained in the face of all challenges
over the mind of sixteenth-century Englishmen.

In the play an ironical estimate was given of the wealth
that was expected to lie at the disposal of all-comers to the
New World.   Infinite treasure was stated to lie at the feet
of any one who cared to come and pick it up.   Gold was
alleged by the dramatist to be more plentiful in America than
copper in Europe; the natives used household utensils of
pure gold; the chains which hung on the posts in the streets
were of massive gold ; prisoners were fettered in gold ; and
' for rubies and diamonds,' declares the satiric playwright,
' the Americans go forth on holidays and gather them by the
seashore, to hang on their children's coats, and stick in their
caps, as commonly as our children in England wear saffron
gilt brooches and groats with holes in them.'

At the same time the dramatist recognised that the
passion for moral perfection remained an efficient factor in
colonising enterprise.   He claimed for the new   Moral
country that public morality had reached there a   ideals.
pitch never known in England.   No office was procurable
except through merit; corruption in high places was un-
heard of.   The New World offered infinite scope for the
realisation of perfection in human affairs.

III

The mingled motive of sixteenth-century colonial enterprise is best capable of realisation in the career of a typical

Ralegh a
type of
Elizabethan
versatility.

Elizabethan—Sir Walter Ralegh. The character
and achievements of Ralegh, alike in their defects
and merits, sound more forcibly than those of
any other the whole gamut of Renaissance feeling and
aspiration in Elizabethan England. His versatile exploits
in action and in contemplation—in life and literature—are
a microcosm of the virtues and the vices which the Renaissance bred in the Elizabethan mind and heart.

Ralegh as a boy was an enthusiast for the sea. He was a
native of Devonshire, whence many sailors have come. Sir

Sir Francis
Drake.

Francis Drake, the greatest of Elizabethan maritime explorers, was also a Devonshire man. It
was he who first reached the Isthmus of Panama, and, first
of Englishmen to look on the Pacific Sea beyond, besought
Almighty God of His kindness to give him life and leave to
sail an English ship once in that sea. That hope he realised
six years later when he crossed the Pacific, touched at Java,
and came home by way of the Cape of Good Hope. Drake's
circumnavigation of the globe was the mightiest exploit of
any English explorer of the Elizabethan era.

Only second to Drake as a maritime explorer was Sir
Humphrey Gilbert, also a Devonshire man, who in 1583 in

Ralegh's
half-
brother,
Sir
Humphrey
Gilbert.

the name of Queen Elizabeth took possession of
Newfoundland, the oldest British colony. This
Sir Humphrey Gilbert was Ralegh's elder half-
brother, for they were sons of the same mother, who
married twice. Her first husband, Sir Humphrey's
father, was Otho Gilbert, who lived near Dartmouth.
Her second husband, who was Ralegh's father, was a

country gentleman living near Budleigh Salterton, where Ralegh was born about 1552, some two years before Sir Philip Sidney.

Gilbert was Ralegh's senior by thirteen years, and like him Ralegh obtained his first knowledge of the sea on the beach of his native place. The broad Devonshire accent, in which he always spoke, he probably learnt from Devonshire sailors. His intellect was from youth exceptionally alert. Vigorous as was always his love of outdoor life, it never absorbed him. With it there went a passion for books, an admirable combination, the worth of which was never better illustrated than in the life and letters of the Renaissance. *Infancy and Education.*

After spending a little time at Oxford, and also studying law in London—study that did not serve him in life very profitably—Ralegh followed the fashion among young Elizabethans and went abroad to enjoy experience of military service.

IV

Englishmen were then of a more aggressive temper than they think themselves to be now. The new Protestant religion, which rejected the ancient domination of the Papacy, had created a militant spiritual energy in the country. That spiritual energy, combining with the new physical and intellectual activity bred of the general awakening of the Renaissance, made it almost a point of conscience for a young Elizabethan Protestant in vigorous health to measure swords with the rival Catholic power of Spain. As Sir Philip Sidney realised, Spain and England had divided interests at every point. Spain had been first in the field in the exploration of the New World, and was resolved to spend its energy in maintaining exclu- *The rivalry with Spain.*

sive mastery of its new dominion. Spain was the foremost champion of the religious ideals of Rome. Pacific persuasion and argument were not among the proselytising weapons in her religious armoury. She was bént on crushing Protestantism by force of arms. She lent her aid to the French Government to destroy the Protestant movement in France

Spain and Holland. which the Huguenots had organised there. She embarked on a long and costly struggle in her own territory of the Low Countries in Holland to suppress the Dutch champions of the Reformed religion, whose zeal for active resistance was scarcely ever equalled by a Protestant people.

Naturally Ralegh at an early age sought an opportunity of engaging in the fray. He found his earliest military

Ralegh in France. experiences in fighting in the ranks of the Huguenots in France. Then he crossed the French territory on the North to offer his sword to the Dutch Protestants, who were struggling to free themselves from Spanish tyranny and Spanish superstition in the Low Countries.

But it was in the New World that Spain was making the most imposing advance. Spanish pretensions in Europe

His first conflict with Spain. could only be effectually checked if the tide of Spanish colonisation of the New World were promptly stemmed. Ralegh was filled to overflowing with the national jealousy of Spain, and with contempt for what he deemed her religious obscurantism. His curiosity was stirred by rumours of the wonders across the seas, where Spain claimed sole dominion. Consequently his eager gaze was soon fixed on the New Continent.

At twenty-six, after gaining experience of both peace and war in Europe, he joined his half-brother, Sir Humphrey Gilbert, in a first expedition at sea, on a voyage of discovery.

He went as far as the West Indies. With the Spaniards who had already settled there inevitable blows were exchanged. But Ralegh's first conflict with the arch enemy was a drawn battle. He was merely prospecting the ground, and the venture bore no immediate fruit.

During a succeeding season he exhausted some of his superabundant energy in a conflict nearer home. In Ireland, England was engaged in her unending struggle with the native population. On Ralegh's return In Ireland. from the West Indies he enlisted, with a view to filling an idle hour, in the Irish wars. The situation was not hopeful, and his mind was too busy with larger projects to lead him to grapple with it seriously. Ireland appeared to him to be ' a lost land,' ' a common woe, rather than a commonwealth.' But its regeneration seemed no work for his own hand. He gained, however, a great material advantage from his casual intervention in the affairs of the country. There was granted to him a great tract of confiscated land in the South of Ireland, some forty thousand acres in what are now the counties Waterford and Cork. The princely estate stretched for many miles inland from the coast at Youghal along the picturesque banks on both sides of the river Blackwater in Munster.

The soil was for the most part wild land overgrown with long grass and brambles, but Ralegh acquired with the demesne a famous house and garden near Youghal which was known as Myrtle Grove, and he afterwards built a larger mansion at Lismore. There he spent much leisure later, and both houses are of high biographic interest. It was not, however, the puzzling problems of Irish politics which occupied Ralegh's attention, while he dwelt on Irish soil. He formed no opinions of his own on Irish questions. He accepted the conventional English view. For the native population he cherished the English planters' customary scorn. He did not hesitate to recommend their removal by means of 'practices,' which were indistinguishable from plots of assassination. But politics were not the interests which he cultivated in the distracted country. He devoted his energies there to the pacific pursuits of poetry and of gardening, and to social intercourse with congenial visitors.

v

The passion for colonisation, for colonisation of territory further afield than Munster, was the dominant influence on Ralegh's mind. It was his half-brother Gilbert's discovery of Newfoundland, and the grant to Gilbert of permission to take, in the Queen's name, possession of an almost infinite area of unknown land on the North American Continent, that led to the episode which gave Ralegh his chief claim

Gilbert's to renown in the history of the English Colonies.
death, 1583. Gilbert's ship was wrecked; he was drowned on returning from Newfoundland, and the Queen was thereupon induced to transfer to Ralegh most of the privileges she had granted to his half-brother. The opportunity was one of dazzling promise. Ralegh at once fitted out an expedition to undertake the exploration which Gilbert's death had interrupted.

But Ralegh had meanwhile become a favourite of the Queen.[1] He had exerted on her all his charm of manner

[1] The well-known story that Ralegh first won the Queen's favour by placing his cloak over a muddy pool in her path is not traceable to any earlier writer than Fuller, who in his *Worthies*, first published in 1662, wrote: 'Captain Raleigh coming out of Ireland to the English court in good habit (his clothes being then a considerable part of his estate) found the queen walking, till meeting with a plashy place, she seemed to scruple going thereon. Presently Raleigh cast and spread his new plush cloak on the ground; whereon the queen trod gently, rewarding him afterwards with many suits, for his so free and seasonable tender of so fair a foot cloth. Thus an advantageous admission into the first notice of a prince is more than

and of speech.   He had practised to the full those arts
familiar to all the courts of the Renaissance which gave a
courtier's adulation of his prince the tone of
amorous passion.   In the absence of 'his Love's
Queen' or of 'the Goddess of his life' Ralegh
declared himself, with every figurative extravagance, to live
in purgatory or in hell ; in her presence alone was he in
paradise.   Elizabeth rejoiced in the lover-like attentions that
Ralegh paid her.   She affected to take him at his word.   His
flatteries were interpreted more literally than he could have
wished.   She refused to permit her self-styled lover to leave
her side.   He was ordered to fix his residence at the court.
Reluctantly Ralegh yielded to the command of his exacting
mistress.   The expedition that he fitted out to North
America left without him.

    Ralegh's agents, after a six weeks' sail, landed on what is
now North Carolina, probably on the island of Roanoke.
The reports of the mariners were highly favourable.
A settlement, they declared, might readily be
made.   At length Englishmen might inhabit the New
World.   The notion presented itself to Ralegh's mind to
invite the Queen's permission to bestow on this newly
discovered territory, which was to be the corner-stone of a
British colonial empire, a name that should commemorate his
fealty to the virgin Queen, the name of ' Virginia.'   It was a
compliment that the Queen well appreciated at her favourite's
hand.   It gave her a lease of fame which the soil of England
alone could not secure for her.   For many years afterwards
all the seaboard from Florida to Newfoundland was to bear
that designation of Virginia.   It was a designation which
linked the first clear promise of the colonisation by English-

Ralegh and Queen Elizabeth.

Virginia.

half a degree to preferment.'   The incident was carefully elaborated by Sir
Walter Scott in his novel *Kenilworth*, chap. xv.

men of the North American Continent with the name of the
greatest of English queens.

Ralegh's project of planting a great English colony in
North America had arisen in many other minds before it
took root in his. He had heard, while fighting with the
Huguenots in France, of their hopes of founding in North
America a New France, where they should be free from
the persecution of the Roman Catholic Government. He
had studied the ambitious designs of Coligny, the leader of
the French Huguenots, and the tragic failure which marked
the first attempt of Frenchmen to colonise North America.
It was probably this knowledge that fired Ralegh's ambition
to make of Virginia a New England. In that hope he did
not himself succeed, but his failure was due to no lack of zeal.

Grenville's Two years after he had received the report of
expedition. his first expedition, he sent out his cousin, Sir
Richard Grenville, with a band of colonists whom he intended
to settle permanently in his country of Virginia. But difficulties arose which baffled his agent's powers. There were
desperate quarrels between the settlers and natives. Food
was scanty. The forces of nature conquered the settlers.
Most of them were rescued from peril of death and carried
home a year later by Sir Francis Drake. Ralegh was not
daunted by such disasters. He refused to abandon his aim.
Further batches of colonists were sent out by him in later
years at his expense. The results of these expeditions did
not, however, bring him appreciably nearer success. Mystery
overhangs the fate of some of these earliest English settlers
in America, Ralegh's pioneers of the British empire. They
were either slain or absorbed past recognition by the native
peoples. In 1587, one band of Ralegh's emigrants, consisting
of eighty-nine men, seventeen women, and two children,
were left in Virginia, while their leaders came home for

supplies, but when these emissaries arrived again in the new continent, the settlers had all disappeared. What became of them has never been known.

Ralegh was never in his life in Virginia. He was never near its coast-line. His project, the fruit of idealism, was not pursued with much regard for practical realisation. Ralegh's The difficulty of settling a new country with relations with Europeans he hardly appreciated. He is reckoned Virginia. to have spent forty thousand pounds in money of his own day —about a quarter of a million pounds of our own currency— in his efforts to colonise Virginia. So long as he was a free man his enthusiasm for his scheme never waned, and he faced his pecuniary losses with cheerfulness. Despite his failures and disappointments, his costly and persistent efforts to colonise Virginia are the starting-point of the history of English colonisation. To him more than to any other man belongs the credit of indicating the road to the formation of a greater England beyond the seas.

Two subsidiary results of those early expeditions to Virginia which Ralegh organised, illustrate the minor modifications of an old country's material economy that may The potato spring from colonial enterprise. His sailors brought and back two new products which were highly benefi- tobacco. cial to Great Britain and Ireland, especially to Ireland. Englishmen and Irishmen owe to Ralegh's exertions their practical acquaintance with the potato and with tobacco. The potato he planted on his estates in Ireland, and it has proved of no mean service alike to that country and to England. Tobacco he learnt to smoke, and taught the art to others.

Tobacco-smoking, which revolutionised the habits, at any rate, of the masculine portion of European society, is one of the striking results of the first experiments in colonial

expansion. The magical rapidity with which the habit of
smoking spread, especially in Elizabethan England,
Spread of was a singular instance of the adaptability of Eliza-
tobacco-
smoking. bethan society to new fashions. The practice of
tobacco-smoking became at a bound a well-nigh universal
habit. Camden, the historian of the epoch, wrote a very few
years after the return of Ralegh's agents from Virginia
that since their home-coming 'that Indian plant called
Tobacco, or Nicotiana, is grown so frequent in use, and
of such price, that many, nay, the most part, with an
unsatiable desire do take of it, drawing into their mouth the
smoke thereof, which is of a strong scent, through a pipe
made of earth, and venting of it again through their nose;
some for wantonness, or rather fashion sake, or other for
health sake. Insomuch that Tobacco shops are set up in
greater number than either Alehouses or Taverns.'[1]

VI

In more imposing ways Ralegh's early endeavours bore
fruit while he lived. Early in the seventeenth century
Captain Captain John Smith, a born traveller, considered
John
Smith in somewhat more fully and more cautiously than
Virginia. Ralegh the colonising problem, and reached a
workable solution. In 1606 Smith took out to Virginia 105
emigrants, to the banks of the James river in Virginia. His
colonists met, like Ralegh's colonists, with perilous vicissitudes, but the experiment had permanent results. Before
Ralegh's death he had the satisfaction of learning that another
leader's colonising energy had triumphed over the obstacles
that dismayed himself, and the seed that he had planted
had fructified.

Smith was a harder-headed man of the world than

[1] Camden, *Annales*, 1625, Bk. 3, p. 107.

Ralegh.   Idealism was not absent from his temperament, but it was of coarser texture, and was capable of answering to a heavier strain.   It was stoutly backed by a rough practical sense.   He took the *Colonial philosophy of Ralegh's disciples.* work of colonising to be a profession or handicraft worthy of any amount of energy.   He preached the useful lesson that settlers in a new country must work laboriously with their hands.   His views echo those of his far-seeing contemporary, Bacon, who compressed into his Essay on Plantations the finest practical wisdom about colonisation that is likely to be met with.   There must be no drones among colonists is the view of Bacon and Captain John Smith ; the scum of the people should never be permitted to engage in colonial enterprise ; there should not be too much moiling underground in search of mines ; there should be no endeavour to win profit hastily and inconsiderately ; the native races should be treated justly and graciously.   ' Do not *Bacon's views.* entertain savages,' Bacon wrote, ' with trifles and gingles, but show them grace and justice, taking reasonable precautions against their attacks, but not seeking the favour of any one tribe amongst them by inciting it to attack another tribe.'   Above all, it was the duty of a mother-country to promote the permanence and the prosperity of every colonial settlement which had been formed with her approval.   ' It is the sinfullest thing in the world to forsake or destitute a plantation once in forwardness.   For, beside the dishonour, it is the guiltiness of blood of many commiserable persons.'

It was colonisation conceived on these great lines that Captain John Smith, Ralegh's disciple, carried out in practice with a fair measure of success.   His *Captain John Smith's views.* idealism was not of the tender kind which enfeebled his working methods, but it flashed forth with brilliant force in the prophetic energy with which he

preached the value of a colonial outlet to the surplus population of an old country. ' What so truly suits with honour
and honesty as the discovering of things unknown, erecting
towns, peopling countries, informing the ignorant, reform-
ing things unjust, teaching virtue, and to gain our native
mother-country a kingdom to attend her, to find employment for those that are idle because they know not what
to do ? '

VII

The rivalry between Spain and England which was largely
the result of the simultaneous endeavour to colonise the
newly-discovered countries reached its climax in
1588, when Spain made a mighty effort to crush
English colonial enterprise at its fountain-head by
equipping a great fleet to conquer and annex the island of
Britain itself. Ralegh naturally took part in resisting the
great expedition of the Spanish Armada, and contributed to
the defeat of that magnificently insolent effort. He does
not seem to have taken a very prominent part in active
hostilities, but he did useful work ; he helped to organise
the victory. When the danger was past he was anxious to
pursue the offensive with the utmost vigour and to forward
attacks on Spain in all parts of the world. Her dominion
of the Western oceans must be broken if England was to
secure a colonial empire. Others for the moment took more
active part than Ralegh in giving effect to the policy of
aggression. But in 1592 an expedition under his control
captured a great Spanish vessel homeward bound from the
East Indies with a cargo of the estimated value of upwards
of half a million sterling.

Ralegh had ventured his own money on the expedition,
and was awarded a share of the plunder, but it was some-

thing less than that to which he thought himself entitled, and
he did not dissemble his annoyance.   Ralegh was masterful
and assertive in intercourse with professional colleagues of his own rank.   His colonising idealism   Ralegh's
                                                        hopes of
was not proof against the strain of idly watching   gain.
others reap from active participation in the great struggle
with Spain a larger personal reward than himself.   Desire
for wealth grew upon him as the passions of youth cooled,
and the hope that some of the profits which Spain had
acquired from her settlements in the New World might fill
his own coffers besieged his brain.   Anxiety to make out
of an energetic pursuit of colonisation a mighty fortune,
was coming into conflict with the elevated aspirations of
early days.   The vehement struggle of vice and virtue for
mastery over men's souls, which characterised the Elizabethan age in a greater degree than any other age, was
seeking a battle-ground in Ralegh's spirit.

Ralegh shared that versatility of interest and capacity
which infected the enlightenment of the era.   Like his
great contemporaries, his energy never allowed   Intellectual
him to confine his aims to any one branch of   pursuits
                                                 and
effort.   Interest in literature and philosophy was   sympathies.
intertwined with his interest in the practical affairs of life, and
he had at command many avenues of escape from life's sordid
temptations.   The range of his speculative instinct was not
limited by the material world.   It was not enough for him
to discover new countries or new wealth.   He was ambitious
to discover new truths of religion, of philosophy, of poetry.
No man cherished a more enthusiastic or more disinterested
affection for those who excelled in intellectual pursuits.   No
man was more generous in praise of contemporary poets, or
better proved in word and deed his sympathy with the
noblest aspirations of contemporary literature.   From the

early days of his career in Ireland he was the intimate associate of Spenser, who held civil office there, and lived in his neighbourhood. Spenser, the great poet and moralist, who in his age was second in genius only to the master poet, Shakespeare, was proud of the friendship. With character-

His poetry.
istic ambition to master all branches of intellec-tual energy, Ralegh emulated his friend and neighbour in writing poetry. His success was paradoxically great. His poetry breathes a lyric fervour which is not out of harmony with his disposition, but its frequent tone of placid meditation seems far removed from the stormy temper of his life. The most irrepressible of talkers, when speech was injurious to his own interests, he preached in verse more than once the virtues of silence :

> ' Passions are likened best to flood and streams ;
>   The shallow murmur, but the deep are dumb ;
> So when affections yield discourse, it seems
>   The bottom is but shallow whence they come.
> They that are rich in words, in words discover
> That they are poor in that which makes a lover.'

Amid the rush and turmoil of politics and of warfare which absorbed the major part of his activity, Ralegh never for long abandoned

> ' Those clear wells
>   Where sweetness dwells,'

—the sweetness of philosophy, poetry, history, and all the pacific arts that can engage the mind of man. Poetry was only one of many interests in the literary sphere. He loved to gather round him the boldest intellects of his day and, regardless of consequences, frankly to discuss with them the mysteries of existence. Marlowe, the founder of English tragedy, the tutor of Shakespeare, was his frequent com-panion. They debated together the evidences of Christi-

anity, and reached the perilous conclusion that they were
founded on sand. He was a member, too, of one of the
earliest societies or clubs of Antiquaries in England, and
surveyed the progress of civilisation in England from very
early times. He caught light and heat from intercourse
with all classes of men to whom things of the mind appealed.
To him, tradition assigns the first invention of those famous
meetings of men of letters which long dignified
the 'Mermaid' Tavern in Bread Street in the   Meetings
                                                 at the
City of London. Credible tradition asserts that 'Mermaid.'
those meetings were attended by Shakespeare, Ben Jonson,
and all the literary masters of the time; that there stimulating wit was freer than air. Genius encountered genius,
each in its gayest humour. The spoken words were

> ' So nimble, and so full of subtle flame,
> As if that every one from whence they came
> Had meant to put his whole wit in a jest,
> And had resolved to live a fool the rest
> Of his dull life.'

No part of Ralegh's life could be dull. All parts of it were
full of ' subtle flame.' But that flame was destined to burn
itself out far away from the haunts of his comrades of the pen.

VIII

Ralegh's versatility, the free unfettered play of his fertile
thought, distinguishes him even among Elizabethan Englishmen, and lends his biography the strangest mingling of light
and shadow. His tireless speculative ambition manifested
itself in the most imposing practical way when he was about
forty years old. Self-contradiction was inherent in his acts.
Despite his reverence for the triumphs of the intellect, the
affairs of the world were ever under his eager observation.
Ripening experience deepened the conviction that gold

was the pivot on which human affairs mainly revolved, and that he who commanded untold sources of wealth could gratify all human desires. The opportunity of making such a conquest suddenly seemed to present itself to Ralegh. His poetic imagination made him credulous. He resolved on a pilgrimage to a fabulous city, where endless treasure awaited the victorious invader.

Reports had been spread in Spain of the existence of a city of fabulous wealth in South America to which had been given the Spanish name of 'El Dorado.' Its location was vaguely defined. It was stated to be in the troublous country that we now know as Venezuela, which is itself part of the wider territory called by geographers Guiana. The rumour fired Ralegh's brain. The ambition to investigate its truth proved irresistible. Hurriedly he sent out an agent to inquire into the story on what was thought to be the spot, but the messenger brought him no information of importance. Vicarious inquiry proved of no avail. At length in 1595 Ralegh went out himself. He infected his friends with his own sanguine expectation. He succeeded in enlisting the sympathy or material support of the chief ministers of state. He obtained a commission from the Queen permitting him to wage war if necessary upon the Spaniard and the native American in South America. No risk was too great to be run in such a quest. The exploit which was to provide endless peril and excitement was the turning-point of Ralegh's career.

Without delay Ralegh reached Trinidad, a Spanish settlement. From the first active hostilities had to be faced. Little resistance was offered, however, at Trinidad, and Ralegh took prisoner the Spanish governor, who proved a most amiable gentleman. The governor freely told Ralegh all he knew of this reputed city or mine of gold on the mainland. A Spanish explorer a few years ago had, it appeared, lived among the natives of Guiana for seven months, and on his death-bed bore witness to a limitless promise of gold near the banks of the great river Orinoco and its tributaries which watered the territory of Guiana.

In April 1595 Ralegh, with a little flotilla of ten boats bearing one hundred men, and provisions for a month, started on his voyage up the river. The equipment was far from adequate for the stirring enterprise. 'Our vessels,' Ralegh wrote, 'were no other than wherries, one little barge, a small cockboat, and a bad galliota, which we framed in haste for that purpose at Trinidad, and those little boats had nine or ten men apiece with victuals and arms.' They had to row against the stream, which flowed with extraordinary fury; the banks were often covered with thick wood, and floating timber was an ever present danger. Debarcation for prospecting purposes was attended with the gravest risks. The swiftness of the current often rendered swimming or wading impossible.

The hardships which Ralegh and his companions faced hardly admit of exaggeration. Almost every day they were 'melted with heat in rowing and marching, and suddenly wet again with great showers. They ate of all sorts of corrupt fruit and made meals of fresh fish without season.' They lodged in the open air every night. Not in the filthiest prison in England could be found men in a more 'unsavory and loathsome' condition than were Ralegh and his friends while they ran their race for the golden prize. But their spirits never drooped. Their hopes ran high to the end. Ralegh was able in his most desperate straits to note in detail the aspects of nature and the varied scenery that met his gaze. Despite the inhospitable river

Hardships.

banks, nature smiled on much of the country beyond. After climbing one notable hill, 'there appeared,' Ralegh wrote with attractive vivacity, ' some ten or twelve water-

The natural scenery.
falls in sight, every one as high above the other as a church tower, which fell with that fury, that the rebound of waters made it seem as if had been all covered over with a great shower of rain ; and in some places we took it at the first for a smoke that had risen over some great town. For mine own part, I was well persuaded from thence to have returned, being a very ill footman ; but the rest were all so desirous to go near the said strange thunder of waters, as they drew me on by little and little, till we came into the next valley, where we might better discern the same. I never saw a more beautiful country, nor more lively prospects, hills so raised here and there over the valleys, the river winding into divers branches, the plains adjoining without bush or stubble, all fair green grass, the ground of hard sand, easy to march on either for horse or foot, the deer crossing in every path, the birds towards the evening singing on every tree with a thousand several tunes, cranes and herons of white, crimson, and carnation, perching on the river's side, the air fresh, with a gentle easterly wind ; and every stone that we stopped to take up promised either gold or silver by his complexion.'

But Ralegh and his friends had mistaken their route, and were bent on what proved a fool's errand. The golden fleece was unattainable. The promise of the stones on the shores was imperfectly fulfilled. After proceeding four hundred and forty miles up the difficult river, further progress was found impossible. Then Ralegh and his companions went down with the current back to the sea. The ' white spar ' on the river bank, in which appeared to be signs of gold, was all that the travellers brought home. Metallurgists

to whom he submitted them, on revisiting London, declared
the appearance true.[1]

There is no doubt that Ralegh came near making a great
discovery. Little question exists that a great gold mine
lay in Venezuela, not far from the furthest point
of his voyage up the river Orinoco. Many years
later, during the nineteenth century, a gold mine
Within reach of gold.
was discovered within the range of Ralegh's exploration, and
has since been worked to great profit. But the El Dorado
which Ralegh thought to grasp had eluded him. It remained for him a dream. Not that he ever wavered in his
confident belief that the city of gold existed and was yet
to be won. He retired for the time with the resolve to
make new advances hereafter. He left behind, with a
tribe of friendly natives, ' one Francis Sparrow (a servant of
Captain Gifford), who was desirous to tarry, and could
describe a country with his pen, and a boy of mine, Hugh
Goodwin, to learn the language.'

Affairs at home prevented Ralegh's early return to South
America. A new Spanish settlement soon blocked the
entrance to the river Orinoco, and the region he had entered
was put beyond his reach. A last desperate attempt to

---

[1] Scoffers freely asserted that the ' white spar,' many tons of which Ralegh
brought home with him, was nothing else than ' marcasite ' or iron-pyrites.
In the letter to the reader with which be prefaced his *Discovery of Guiana*
Ralegh categorically denied the allegation. He wrote hopefully, ' In London it was first assayed by Master Westwood, a refiner dwelling in Wood
Street, and it held after the rate of 12,000 or 13,000 pounds a ton. Another
sort was afterwards tried by Master Bulmar and Master Dimoke, assay-
master, and it held after the rate of 23,000 pounds a ton. There was
some of it again tried by Master Palmer, comptroller of the mint, and
Master Dimoke in Goldsmith's hall, and it was held after at the rate of
26,900 pounds a ton. There was also at the same time, and by the same
persons, a trial made of the dust of the said mine, which held eight pounds
six ounces weight of gold in the hundred ; there was likewise at the same
time, a trial made of an image of copper made in Guiana which held a third
part gold, besides divers trials made in the country, and by others in London.'

force a second passage up the Orinoco brought, as events turned out, Ralegh to the scaffold. He had soared to heights at which he could not sustain his flight.

One result of Ralegh's first experience of the banks of the Orinoco demands a recognition, which requires no apology. His narrative of the expedition—*The Discovery of Guiana*—ranks with the most vivid pictures of travel. No reader, be he naturalist or geographer or ethnologist, or mere lover of stirring adventure, will turn to the fascinating pages without delight. Literary faculty in a traveller is always refreshing. Few books of travel are more exhilarating or invigorating than this story by Ralegh of his hazardous voyage.

When Ralegh came back to England from the Orinoco he flung himself with undaunted energy into further conflict with Spain. There were rumours of a new Spanish invasion of England, which it was deemed essential to divert by attacking Spain in her own citadels. Two great expeditions were devised, and in both Ralegh took an active part. He was with the fleet which attacked Cadiz in 1596. Again next year he joined in a strenuous effort to intercept Spanish treasure ships off the Azores. Ralegh worked ill under discipline, and, chiefly owing to his quarrels with his fellow-commanders, the attempt on the islands of the Atlantic failed. Fortune had never been liberal in the bestowal of her favours on him. At best she had extended to him a cold neutrality. Little of the glory or the gain that came of the last two challenges to Spain fell to Ralegh. Thenceforth the fickle goddess assumed an attitude of menace, which could not be mistaken. She became his active and persistent foe.

Further conflict with Spain.

IX

Ralegh's later years were dogged by disaster. With the death of Queen Elizabeth begins the story of his ruin. She had proved no constant mistress and had at times driven him from her presence. His marriage in 1592 had excited more than the usual measure of royal resentment. But Queen Elizabeth was not obdurate in her wrath. Her favour was never forfeited irrevocably. Ralegh long held the court office of captain of the guard. In her latest years there was renewal of his sovereign's old show of regard for him. She liked to converse with him in private; and the envious declared that she 'took him for a kind of oracle.' To the last he addressed her in those adulatory strains which she loved. During all her reign, adversity had mingled in his lot with prosperity, but prosperity delusively seemed at the close to sway the scales.

A bitter spirit of faction divided Queen Elizabeth's advisers against themselves. Ralegh's hot-temper and impatience of subordination made him an easy mark for the hatred and uncharitableness which the factious atmosphere fostered. The outspoken language which was habitual to him was violently resented by rival claimants to the Queen's favour. With one of these, the Earl of Essex, who was even more self-confident and impetuous than himself, he maintained an implacable feud until the Earl's death on the scaffold. Ralegh had come into conflict with Lord Howard of Effingham, the great admiral of the Armada, and an influential member of the Howard family. The admiral's numerous kindred regarded him with aversion. Sir Robert Cecil, the principal Secretary of State in Queen Elizabeth's last years, who held in his hand all the threads of England's policy, although more outwardly complacent,

Ralegh and Court factions.

cherished suspicion of Ralegh.   It was only royal favour that had hitherto rendered innocuous the shafts of his foes. Now that that favour was withdrawn Ralegh was to find that he had sown the wind and was to reap the whirlwind. Fortune, wrote a contemporary, 'picked him out of purpose . . . to use as her tennis ball'; having tossed him up from nothingness to a point within hail of greatness she then unconcernedly tossed him down again.

Between Ralegh and his new sovereign, James I., little sympathy subsisted.   They knew little of one another.   To Ralegh's personal enemies at Court James owed the easy road which led him to the English throne.   Ralegh on purely personal grounds, which court schisms fully account for, abstained from showing enthusiasm for James's accession.   He fully recognised the justice of the Scottish monarch's title to the English crown₁   But he had not pledged himself like his private foes in a preliminary correspondence to support the new King actively.   By that preliminary correspondence the King set great store.   He was not prepossessed in favour of any of Elizabeth's courtiers who had failed before Elizabeth's death to avow in writing profoundest sympathy with his cause.

The accession of James I.

As soon as James became King of England, Ralegh's position at Court was seen to be insecure.   His enemies were favourably placed for avenging any imagined indignity which his influence with the late sovereign had enabled him to inflict on them.   He lay at the mercy of factions which were markedly hostile to himself and held the ear of the new sovereign.   There was no likelihood that the new wearer of the crown would exert himself to protect him from assault.

At first a comparatively petty disgrace was put on him. He was unceremoniously superseded in his court office of captain of the guard, a post which had brought him into much personal contact with the late sovereign. He naturally resented the affront and showed irritation among his friends. The king's allies found ready means of increasing their own importance and improving their prospects of advancement by drawing to light of day and exaggerating any hasty expression of doubt respecting James's legal title to the English crown of which they could find evidence. Dishonest agents easily distorted an inconsiderate word of dissatisfaction with the political situation into deliberate treason. An intricate charge of this character was rapidly devised against Ralegh by his factious foes, and almost without warning he was brought within peril of his life. He was accused on vague hearsay of having joined in a plot to surprise the king's person with a view to his abduction or assassination. It was alleged that he was conspiring to set up another on the throne, to wit, the king's distant cousin, Arabella Stuart. Ralegh was put under arrest. Thoroughly exasperated by the victory which his enemies had won over him, he for the first time in his life lost nerve. He made an abortive attempt at suicide. This rash act was held by his persecutors to attest his guilt. When he was brought to trial at Winchester—the plague in London had compelled the Court's migration—all legal forms were pressed against him. In the result he was condemned to a traitor's death (17 Nov. 1603). His estates were forfeited, and such offices as he still retained were taken from him.

Fabricated charges of treason.

Sentence of death.

For three weeks Ralegh lay in Winchester Castle in almost daily expectation of the executioner's dread summons. He sought consolation in literature, and in letters and in poems addressed to his wife he sought to reconcile himself to his fate. He made no complaint of his

The respite.

perverse lot. He had drunk deep of life and was not averse
in his passion for new experience to taste death. But James
faltered at the last and hesitated to sign the death-warrant.
A month after the trial Ralegh was informed that he was
reprieved of the capital punishment. He was to be kept a
prisoner in the Tower of London. He was not pardoned,
nor was his sentence commuted to any fixed term of confinement. As long as he was alive, it was tacitly assumed by
those in high places that liberty would be denied him. It
was difficult for one of Ralegh's energy to reconcile himself
to the situation. Bondage was for him barely thinkable.
Long years of waiting could not vanquish the assured hope
that freedom would again be his, and he would carry further
the projects that were as yet only half begun.

x

Ralegh's intellectual activity was invincible, and there he
found the main preservative against the numbing despair
In the   with which the prison's galling tedium menaced
Tower.   him. He was allowed some special privileges.
At first, his lot was alleviated by the companionship of his
wife and sons. Within the precincts of the Tower and its
garden he was apparently free to move about at will. But
he concentrated all his mental strength while in confinement
on study—study of exceptionally varied kinds. Literature
and science divided his allegiance. In a laboratory or still-
house which he was allowed to occupy in the garden of the
Scientific   Tower he carried on a long series of chemical ex-
curiosity.   periments. Many of his scientific investigations
proved successful; he condensed fresh water from salt, an
art which has only been practised generally during the past
century. He compounded new drugs against various dis-
orders; these became popular and were credited with great

efficacy. Chemistry, medicine, philosophy, all appealed to his catholic curiosity. Nevertheless his main intellectual energy was absorbed by literature. The grandeur of human life and aspiration impressed him in his enforced retirement from the world more deeply than when he was himself a free actor on the stage. He designed a noble contribution to English prose literature, his *History of the World*. He set himself the heavy task of surveying minutely and exactly human endeavours in the early days of human experience. He sought to write a history of the five great empires of the East—of Egypt, Babylon, Assyria, Persia, and Macedonia. Only a fragment of the work was completed; it broke off abruptly one hundred and thirty years before the Christian era, with the conquest of Macedon by Rome. But Ralegh's achievement is a lasting memorial of his genius and of the elevated aspect of his career.

History of the World.

Ralegh did not approach a study of history in a strictly critical spirit, and his massive accumulations of facts, which he collected from six or seven hundred volumes in many tongues, have long been superannuated. But he showed enlightenment in many an unexpected direction. He betrayed a lively appreciation of the need of studying geography together with history, and he knew the value of chronological accuracy. His active imagination made him a master of historic portraiture, and historical personages like Artaxerxes, Queen Jezebel, Demetrius, Pyrrhus, or Epaminondas, are drawn with a master's pencil.

Ralegh's methods were discursive. He often digressed from the ancient to the modern world. The insight which illumined his account of the heroes of a remote past was suffered now and again to play quite irrelevantly about the personalities of recent rulers of his own land. He was content to speak the truth as far as it was

Censure of Henry VIII.

known, without fear of consequences. Of Henry VIII. he writes uncompromisingly, thus : ' If all the pictures and patterns of a merciless prince were lost in the world, they might all again be painted to the life out of the story of this king. For how many servants did he advance in haste (but for what virtue no man could suspect), and with the change of his fancy ruined again, no man knowing for what offence ! . . . What laws and wills did he devise, to establish this kingdom in his own issues ? using his sharpest weapons to cut off and cut down those branches which sprang from the same root that himself did. And in the end (notwithstanding these his so many irreligious provisions) it pleased God to take away all his own without increase ; though, for themselves in their several kinds, all princes of eminent virtue.' The father of his late royal mistress could hardly have been more caustically limned.

It was Ralegh's intense love of the present which frequently turned his narrative by devious paths far from his rightful topics of the past. He cannot resist the temptation of commenting freely on matters within his personal cognisance as they rose to his mind in the silence of his prison cell. Despite the consequent irregularity of plan, his strange irrelevances endow the *History* in the sight of posterity with most of its freshness and originality. The mass of his material may be condemned as dryasdust, but the breath of living experience preserves substantial fragments of it from decay. A perennial interest attaches to Ralegh's suggestive treatment of philosophic questions, such as the origin of law. Remarks on the tactics of the Spaniards in the Armada, on the capture of Fayal in the Azores, on the courage of Elizabethan Englishmen, on the tenacity of Spaniards, on England's relations with Ireland, may be inappropriate to their Babylonian or Persian

Criticism of current events.

surroundings, but they reflect the first-hand knowledge of an observer of infinite mental resource, who never failed to express his own opinions with sincerity and dignity.   His style, although often involved, is free from conceits, and keeps pace as a rule with the majesty of his design.

The general design and style of Ralegh's *History of the World* are indeed more noteworthy than any details of its scheme or execution.   The design is instinct with magnanimous insight into the springs of human action.   Throughout it breathes a serious moral purpose.   It illustrates the sureness with which ruin overtakes 'great conquerors and other troublers of the world' who neglect law whether human or divine.   It is homage paid to the corner-stone of civilised society by one who knew at once how to keep and how to break laws of both God and man. There is an inevitable touch of irony in Ralegh's large-hearted sermon.   After showing how limitless is man's ambition and how rotten is its fruit unless it be restrained by respect for justice, Ralegh turns aside in his concluding pages to salute human greatness, however it may be achieved, as an empty dream.   He closes his book with a sublime apostrophe to Death the destroyer, who is after all the sole arbiter of mortal man's destiny.

The moral purpose of the enterprise.

XI

But despite all his characteristic alertness of mind, Ralegh, while a prisoner in the Tower, was always looking forward hopefully to the day of his release.   His mind often reverted to that land of gold, the exploration of which he had just missed completing eight or nine years before.   The ambition to repeat the experiment grew on him.   James I.'s Queen, and her son and heir Henry Prince

Hopes of freedom.

of Wales, had always regarded Ralegh as the victim of injustice, and sympathised with his aspirations for liberty. They listened encouragingly to his pleas for a new expedition to America. Ralegh was not ready to neglect the opportunity their favour offered him. From them he turned to petition the Privy Council and the King himself. He would refuse no condition, if his prayer was granted. He offered to risk his head if he went once more to the Orinoco and failed in his search. At length, after five years of pertinacious petitioning, the King yielded, perhaps at the instigation of his new favourite George Villiers, afterwards Duke of Buckingham, who anticipated profit from his complacence. Ralegh was released from the Tower after thirteen years' imprisonment (19th March 1616), on the condition that he should make a new voyage to Guiana and secure the country's gold mines. At first Ralegh was ordered to live at his own house in the custody of a keeper, but this restriction was removed next year and he was at liberty to make his preparations as he would.

The projected return to Guiana.

Ralegh was sixty-five years old, and although his spirit mounted high his health was breaking. Out of prison, he was a desolate old man without means or friends. There was no possibility of his planning to a successful issue a new quest of El Dorado. The project had to reckon, too, with powerful foes and critics. When the news of his expedition reached the ears of the Spanish Ambassador in London, he protested that all Guiana was his master's property, and that Ralegh had no right to approach it. It was objected that Ralegh's design was a vulgar act of piracy. Ralegh was unmoved by the argument. He acknowledged no obligation to respect the scruples of onlookers at home or abroad. The assurances given by the Government that he

Spanish protests.

would peacefully respect all rights of Spanish settlers in
Guiana floated about him like the idle wind.

All that Ralegh said or did when preparing to leave
England increased the odds against him. His reputation
sank lower and lower. Dangers and difficulties only rendered
his mood more desperate. He was, like Banquo's murderer,

> 'So weary with disasters, tugged with fortune,
> That he would set his life on any chance
> To mend it or be rid on 't.'

Few men of repute would bear him company. He cared
not who went with him provided he went at all. It was
an ill-omened crew that he collected. He filled his ship
(he afterwards admitted) with the world's scum, with
drunkards and blasphemers, and others whose friends were
only glad to pay money to get them out of the country.

At length he started. But fortune frowned on him more
fiercely than before. The weather was unpropitious. He had
to put in off Cork. At length he weighed anchor for South
America, but on the voyage fell ill of a fever. Arrived off
the river Orinoco, he was successful in an attack on the new
Spanish settlement at its mouth which bore the name of
St. Thomé. Careless of the promises solemnly made on his
behalf by his Government, he rudely despoiled it and set
fire to it; but the doubtful triumph cost him the death of a
companion whom he could ill spare, his elder son, Walter.
Thenceforward absolute failure dogged his steps. His
attempt to ascend the river was quickly defeated by the
activity of the new Spanish settlers. Nothing remained for him but to return home. He had failed
in what he had pledged his head to perform; contrary to conditions he had molested the Spanish settlement.
He reached Plymouth in despair. An attempt at flight to
France failed, and he was sent again to the Tower.

*Failure
of the
expedition.*

One fate alone awaited him. He was already under
sentence of death. By embroiling his country anew with

Disgrace
and death.　Spain, he was held to have revived his old
offence. The English judges declared, harshly and
with doubtful justice, that the old sentence must be carried
out. The circumstance that 'he never had his pardon for his
former treason' was treated as argument which there was no
controverting. Accordingly, on Wednesday 28th October
1618, the ruined man was brought from the Tower to the
bar of the King's Bench. He was asked by the Lord Chief
Justice why he should not suffer 'execution of death,'
according to the judgment of death 'for his treason in the
first year of the king.' He offered protest, but his answer
was deemed by the court to be insufficient. He was taken
back to the prison, and the next day was appointed for the
execution of the old sentence. 'He broke his fast early in
the morning,' according to a contemporary annalist, and,
to the scandal of many, smoked a pipe at the solemn moment
'in order to settle his spirits.' At eight o'clock he was con-
ducted to a scaffold erected in Palace Yard, Westminster,
outside the Houses of Parliament.

Ralegh faced death boldly and without complaining. He
talked cheerfully with those around him and in a speech to
the spectators thanked God that he was allowed 'to die in the
light.' Speaking from written notes he traversed the various
imputations that had been laid upon him, and concluded
with the words, 'I have a long journey to take and must
bid the company farewell.' As his fingers felt the edge
of the axe, he smilingly said to the sheriffs: 'This is a
sharp medicine but it is a sure cure for all diseases.' Then
he bade the reluctant executioner strike, and at two blows
his head fell from his body.

'After life's fitful fever he sleeps well.' The night

before he ascended the scaffold he had penned the simple
lines:

> ' Even such is time, that takes in trust
> Our youth, our joys, our all we have,
> And pays us but with earth and dust ;
> Who, in the dark and silent grave
>
> When we have wandered all our ways,
> Shuts up the story of our days.
> But from this earth, this grave, this dust,
> My God shall raise me up I trust.'

He gave death welcome, when it arrived to claim him,
in the same philosophic spirit that he had apostrophised it,
a few years earlier, on putting the finishing stroke to his
History of the World :—' O eloquent, just, and mighty Death !
. . . thou hast drawn together all the far stretched greatness,
all the pride, cruelty, and ambition of man, and covered it
all over with these two narrow words—*Hic jacet !* '

XII

Ralegh's final labour is the least admirable episode of his
career. It was a buccaneering raid, and admits of no eulogy,
even after we make allowance for the strange   The con-
circumstances in which it was undertaken and   temporary
suffer pity to temper condemnation.   It was a   estimate of
Ralegh.
desperate bid for his personal freedom.   But his failure was
punished with tragic injustice.   His fate excited widespread
lamentation.   The facts seemed to the casual observer to be
capable of more than one interpretation.   His memory was
long venerated as that of a man who sacrificed his life in
an honest, public-spirited, magnanimous endeavour to injure
his country's foes.

Ralegh's character is an inextricable tangle of good and
evil. ' What matter how the head lie ! ' he had said when
placing his neck on the block.   ' What matter how the head

lie so the heart be right?' Many of his countrymen deemed those words his fitting epitaph. But neither Ralegh's heart The good and evil in his character. nor head was often quite in a righteous posture. He was physically as courageous, intellectually as resourceful and versatile, as any man known to history. He was a daring politician, soldier, sailor, traveller, and coloniser. He was a poet of exuberant fancy, a historian of solid industry and insight, and a political philosopher of depth. He ranks with the great writers of English prose. Things of the mind appealed to him equally with things of the senses or the sinews. Many serious-minded men treated his *History of the World* with hardly less respect and veneration than the Bible itself, and it was sedulously pressed in the seventeenth century on the attention of young men, whose minds lacked power of application, as mental ballast of the finest quality.[1] Yet it was mental ballast which Ralegh's own character chiefly lacked. His manifold activity declined restraint. He rebelled against law. His actions were heedless of morality. He was proud, covetous, and unscrupulous.

Yet the influence of his inevitable failures was greater than that of most men's successes. The main failure of his His failure and success. life was more fruitful than any ordinary triumph. His passion for colonial expansion, for the settlement of America by Englishmen, lost in course of time almost every trace of the idealism in which it took rise. Exaggerated hopes of gain, a swollen spirit of aggressiveness, ultimately robbed his endeavours of true titles to respect. His

---

[1] Cromwell the Protector, when he found his eldest son Richard wasting his time and energy in athletic pastime, bade him recreate himself with Sir Walter Ralegh's history. There was advantage, Cromwell deemed, in the work's massive proportions; 'it's a body of history' Cromwell told his heir, 'and will add much more to your understanding than fragments of story.' Carlyle's *Letters and Speeches of Cromwell*, ii. 255.

final effort led to little apparent result beyond the loss of his own head; his fellow-countrymen never gained the mastery of South America; they never obtained exclusive possession of its mines, the desperate cause in which Ralegh flung away his life.   None the less the spur that his apparently barren and ill-conceived exploits gave to English colonising cannot be overestimated.   All over the world Englishmen subsequently worked in his spirit.   But it is his primary attempt to create a new England in the Northern Continent of America which gives him his genuine credentials to fame.   It was an attempt on which he lavished his fortune in the spirit of a dreamer, and at the time it seemed, like so much that Ralegh sought to do, to be made in vain.   Yet it was mainly due to his influence, if not to the work of his hands, that the great English settlements of Virginia and New England came into being, and gave religious and political liberty, spiritual and intellectual energy, a new home, a new scope, wherein to develop to the advantage of the human race.   However sternly the moralist may condemn Ralegh's conduct in the great crises of his career, he must, in justice, admit that the good that Ralegh did lives after him, while the evil was for the most part buried with his bones.   Dark shadows envelop much of his life and death, but there are patches of light which are inextinguishable.

The true founder of Virginia.

V

EDMUND SPENSER

'A sweeter swan than ever sang in Po,
A shriller nightingale than ever blessed
The prouder groves of self admiring Rome !
Blithe was each valley, and each shepherd proud,
While he did chant his rural minstrelsy ;
Attentive was full many a dainty ear ;
Nay, hearers hung upon his melting tongue,
While sweetly of his Faerie Queene he sung,
While to the waters' fall he tun'd her fame,'
The Return from Parnassus, Part II. Act i. Sc. 2.

[BIBLIOGRAPHY.—The memoir by Dean Church in the 'Men of Letters' Series is a useful critical biography in brief compass. The 'Globe' edition of the poet's work, with an introductory memoir by Prof. J. W. Hales, supplies a good text. Of the ten volumes of Dr. Grosart's privately printed edition of the works (1880-2), the first volume is devoted to biography by the general editor, and to critical essays from many competent pens. Of earlier critical editions of Spenser the chief is that by Henry John Todd, which was issued in eight volumes in 1805. A good criticism of Spenser appears in James Russell Lowell's *Essays on the English Poets*.]

I

LITERATURE was a recreation of all men of spirit in the Elizabethan age. It mattered little whether or no they were heirs of great genius. Literature was almost universally the occupation of such leisure as could be snatched from the practical affairs of the world. Statesmen and soldiers, in their hours of ease, courted the Muses with assiduity. These damsels might discourage their advances, but the suitors were persistent. Poetry was

The Elizabethan pursuit of poetry.

154

EDMUND SPENSER.

From the portrait in the possession of the Earl of Kinnoull at Dupplin Castle.

the politest of recreations; verses were delightful 'toys to
busy idle brains.' Queen Elizabeth and her successor
James I. are of the number of English authors in both
poetry and prose. 'To evaporate their thoughts in a
sonnet,' was 'the common way' of almost all nobles and
courtiers, who concentrated their main energies on sport,
politics, and war. At the same time the professional pursuit
of letters—the writing of books for money, the reliance on
the pen for a livelihood—was held to be degrading. Literature was not reckoned to be in any sense a profession fit
for a man of high birth to follow. It was the gorgeous
ornament or plaything of life, and no approved source of
its sustenance.

Not that literary work failed on occasion to prove remunerative. From one branch of Elizabethan literature—
from the drama—there were dazzling profits to be *Profits of*
drawn. An inevitable measure of social prestige *literature.*
attached in the Elizabethan, no less than in other eras, to
substantial property; yet to property that was derived from
the exercise of the pen social prestige could only attach in
Elizabethan society, after the owner had ceased to write for
a living. Shakespeare bore convincing testimony to the
strength of the prevailing mistrust of any professional pursuit
of letters by retiring, at a comparatively early age, from active
work, in order to enjoy, unhampered by the conventional
prejudice, the material fruits of his past energy.

A poet by nature, of intensely æsthetic instinct, Spenser
lacked inherited sources of livelihood; but the social sentiment of the era compelled him to seek a career *Spenser's*
elsewhere than in literature. In a far larger *career.*
and higher sense than his friends Sir Philip Sidney or Sir
Walter Ralegh he was a favoured servant of the Muses. But
he, no more than they, reckoned poetry to be his practical

concern in life. Political service, endeavour to gain remunerative political office, coloured his career as it coloured theirs. He knew the vanity of political ambitions. But opportunities of quiet contemplation apart from the haunts of politicians, opportunities for cultivating in seclusion his great literary genius, were not what he asked of those who had it in their power to fashion his line of life. Unlike his great successor Tennyson, with whom his affinities are many, he deliberately engaged in business which lay outside Parnassian fields. He sought with zeal and persistency political employment and official promotion.

As an officer of state, Spenser achieved small repute or reward. The record of his worldly struggles is sordid and

The contrast with his poetic zeal. insignificant. Often, amid the entanglements and disappointments of political strife, did he give voice to that cry of the Psalmist, which his contemporary, Francis Bacon, pathetically echoed, that his life was passed in a strange land. It was only as a poet that he won happiness or renown. It is only as a supreme poet of the English Renaissance that he lives. Imbued from boyhood with the spirit of the new learning, he was in rarest sympathy with the classics, and with the literature of contemporary Italy and France. An innate delight in the harmonies of language grew with his years. A passion for beauty dominated his thought. Although he was brought up in the new religion of Protestantism and accepted it without demur, doctrinal religion laid her hand lightly on his intellect. It was in an ideal world that he found the objects of his worship. None the less, in order to realise the manner of man Spenser was, and the sturdy links which bound him to his age, his vain political endeavours must find on the biographer's canvas hardly a smaller place than his splendid poetic triumphs.

II

Spenser, who ranks second to Shakespeare among Elizabethan poets, was a native of London. Like Sir Thomas More, he was a native of the capital city of His humble the kingdom, but he came of a substantial family birth. whose home was elsewhere, in Lancashire. He was a distant relative of the noble house of Spencer, many members of which have played an important part in English political history. But, however good Spenser's descent, his father was a London tradesman, a journeyman cloth-maker who was at one time in the service of a wool-dealer.

The poet was born, probably in 1552—the year of Ralegh's birth—in East Smithfield. About his birthplace there glowed in his infancy the fires of religious intoler- His birth- ance—intolerance of that blind and inconsequent place. type which first won Sir Thomas More's allegiance, and then, shifting the quarter from which it blew, drove him to the scaffold.

But when Spenser was six years of age, the sway of unreason was brought to a stand. The fanatic Catholic, Queen Mary, died, and with the accession of Queen Elizabeth to the throne, the spirit of the nation Elizabeth's found a practicable equilibrium. Protestantism accession. with a promise of peace was in the ascendant; Catholicism, although by no means exorcised, was not in a position to pursue open hostilities. Another six years passed, and while the nation was enjoying its first taste of security, Shakespeare was born. But the interval which separated Shakespeare from Spenser was wider than that difference of twelve years in their dates of birth suggests. Shakespeare belonged exclusively to Elizabethan England, which saw the final development of Renaissance culture.

Spenser's memory reached further back and absorbed many an ideal and thought which were nearly obsolete when Shakespeare began to write. The mass of Shakespeare's work belongs to the epoch which followed Spenser's death. Spenser's elder genius flowered and passed away before Shakespeare's younger genius was of full age.

But the two men's outward careers ran at the first on much the same lines. There was a strong resemblance between the circumstances of Spenser's boyhood and of Shakespeare's, which it behoves sceptics of the admitted facts of Shakespeare's biography to study closely. In spite of the claim of Spenser's father to high descent, his walk in life was similar to that of Shakespeare's father. Better educational opportunities were open to a tradesman's son in London than to a tradesman's son in a small village, but their superiority is easily capable of exaggeration. The trade or guild of merchant tailors, with which the elder Spenser was distantly connected, had lately founded a new school in London—the Merchant Taylors' School for sons of tailors. To that school, which still flourishes, Edmund Spenser was sent as a boy, under very like conditions to those which brought Shakespeare to the grammar school of Stratford-on-Avon.

Spenser's youth.

Spenser's headmaster was an enlightened teacher, Richard Mulcaster, who believed in physical as well as intellectual training; who thought girls deserved as good an education as boys; who urged the importance of instruction in music and singing; and who turned a deaf ear to the prayers of cockering mothers and indulgent fathers when appeal was made to him to mitigate the punishment of pupils. Spenser's headmaster had imbibed the spirit of pedagogy as Plato first taught it, and More and Ascham had developed it in the light of the Renaissance.

At Merchant Taylors' School.

But the elder Spenser was not well off, and no special attention was paid his son. The boy's school-days threatened to be short. Happily a merchant had lately left large sums of money to be bestowed on poor London scholars—poor scholars of the schools about London—and under this benefaction Edmund received much-needed assistance. Such charities as that by which Spenser benefited were numerous in Elizabethan England, and charitable funds were largely applied to the noble purpose of assisting poor lads to complete their education. What American merchants are doing now for education in their country more conspicuously than elsewhere, Elizabethan merchants were doing for education in Elizabethan England. It was owing to this enlightened application of wealth that Spenser was enabled to finish his school career.

Promising boys of Elizabethan England, whether rich or poor, were encouraged to pursue their studies at the Universities on leaving school, even if their parents At Cambridge. could not supply them with means of subsistence. The college endowments would carry a poor student through the greater part of an academic career, and might at need be supplemented by private munificence. Spenser went to Cambridge—to Pembroke Hall (or College)—trusting for pecuniary support to the college endowments. He was compelled to enter the College in the lowest rank, the rank of a sizar. Sizars were indigent students who, in consideration of their poverty and in exchange for menial service were given food, drink, and lodging.

At Pembroke Spenser found congenial society. The college had not yet acquired its literary traditions. It was long afterwards that it became the home of the poet Crashaw, and later still of the poet Gray. Spenser himself was the first poet, alike in point of time and of eminence, to associate his name with the foundation. But to contemporary members of the college he owed much. A young Fellow of the College, Gabriel Harvey, an ardent but pedantic student of literature, took deep interest in him and greatly influenced his literary tastes. Harvey reinforced in his pupil a passion for classical learning, which the boy had acquired at school, and encouraged him to pursue a study of French and Italian literature, to which on his own initiative he had already devoted his leisure. A young fellow-sizar, Edward Kirke, also became a warm admirer and stimulating friend.

Gabriel Harvey.

From a lad Spenser was a close student and a wide reader, and gave early promise of poetic eminence. He was attracted not merely by the classics, the orthodox subject of study at school and college, but by French and Italian literature. Almost as a schoolboy he began to translate into English the poetry of France. Before he went to Cambridge he prepared for a London publisher metrical translations of poems by Du Bellay, a scholarly spirit of the Renaissance in France, and he also rendered into seven English sonnets an ode of Petrarch, the great Italian master of the sonnet, from the version of the early French poet Clement Marot. It was through his knowledge of French that the gate to the vast and varied literature of Italy opened to him. Both Petrarch's and Du Bellay's verses described the uncertainties of human life and the fickleness of human fortune. Spenser's renderings were merely inserted by an indulgent publisher as letter-press to be attached to old woodcuts in his possession. Letter-press is a humiliating position for literature to fill, but the youth was content to get his first poetic endeavours into type on any conditions. Spenser's ambition at the time was satisfied when a tedious Dutch treatise of morality appeared in English with his earliest

His earliest verse.

poems irrelevantly introduced as explanations of the pictorial illustrations that adorned the opening pages. The musical temper of Spenser's boyish verse argued well for the future, but no critic at the time discerned its potentiality.

While an undergraduate Spenser suffered alike from poverty and ill-health. Small sums of money were granted to him as a poor scholar from the old bequest His love for which had benefited him at school, and he was Cambridge. often disabled by sickness. He remained however at Cambridge for the exceptionally long period of seven years. He took the degree of Master of Arts in 1576, and then left the University. He always speaks of Cambridge—of ' my mother Cambridge '—with respect. He wrote in a well-known passage of the *Faerie Queene* how the River Ouse which runs near Cambridge

' doth by Huntingdon and Cambridge flit,
My mother Cambridge, whom as with a crown
He [*i.e.* the river] doth adorn and is adorn'd of it
With many a gentle muse and many a learned wit.' [1]

Spenser was himself in due time to adorn his Alma Mater ' as with a crown ' by virtue of his ' gentle muse ' and ' learned wit.'

III

When Spenser's Cambridge life closed, he was no less than twenty-four years old. That was a mature age in those days for a man to be entering on a career, and even then, owing to his feeble constitution, he Disappointseems to have been in no haste to seek a settle- love. ment. The omens were none too favourable. In poor health, without money or prospects, he apparently idled away another year with his kinsfolk, his cousins, in Lancashire.

[1] *Faerie Queene*, Bk. IV., canto xi., stanza xxxiv.

There, having nothing better to do, he fell in love. The object of his affections was, we are told, a gentlewoman, of no mean house, ' endowed with no vulgar or common gifts of nature or manners.' But the lady disdained the poet's suit, and he sought consolation in verse. Antiquaries have tried to discover the precise name of the lady, but, beyond the fact that she was the daughter of a Lancashire yeoman, nothing more needs saying of her.

Spenser's failure in his amorous adventure was, despite the passing grief it caused him, beneficial. It stirred him *Settlement in London.* to fresh exertions alike in poetry and the affairs of the world. He resolved to seek in London greater happiness than Lancashire offered him, and the means of earning an honourable livelihood. Gabriel Harvey, his Cambridge friend, strongly urged on him the prudence of seeking employment in the capital. Harvey prided himself on his influence in high circles. His activity at Cambridge made him known to all visitors of distinction to the University. He knew the Queen's favourite, the Earl of Leicester, the uncle of Sir Philip Sidney, who had it in his power to advance any aspirant to fortune. To Leicester Harvey gave Spenser an introduction. That introduction proved the true starting-point of Spenser's adult career.

Like all Queen Elizabeth's courtiers Leicester had literary tastes. He was favourably impressed by the young poet *The patronage of Leicester.* and offered him secretarial employment. Spenser's duties required him to live at Leicester House, the Earl's great London mansion. Literary sympathies overcame, in Elizabethan England, class distinctions, and Spenser—the impecunious tailor's son—was suddenly thrown into close relations with fashionable London society. Many poor young men of ability and character owed all their opportunities in life to wealthy noblemen of the day. The

friendly union between patron and poet often bred strong
mutual affection and was held to confer honour on both.
Spenser's relations with Leicester were of the typical kind.
They were easy and amiable. The poet felt pride in the
help and favour that the Earl bestowed on him, although
he was not backward in pressing his claims to preferment.
Spenser describes with ungrudging admiration Leicester's
influential place in the State as

> ' A mighty prince, of most renowned race,
> Whom England high in count of honour held,
> And greatest ones did sue to gain his grace ;
> Of greatest ones he greatest in his place,
> Sate in the bosom of his sovereign,
> And "Right and Loyal," did his word maintain.' [1]

Referring to his own relations with his patron, he
exclaimed :

> ' And who so else did goodness by him gain ?
> And who so else his bounteous mind did try ? ' [2]

Leicester stands to Spenser in precisely the same relation as
the Earl of Southampton stands to Shakespeare.

Spenser had at Leicester House much leisure for study.
He wrote poems for his patron. He read largely for himself, presenting books to his friend Harvey, who Secretarial
sent him others in return. But his office was no work.
sinecure. He was sent abroad in behalf of his patron,
usually as the bearer of despatches. In Leicester's service
he paid a first visit to Ireland, and went on official errands
to France, Spain, and Italy, notably to Rome, and even
further afield. Foreign travel nurtured his imagination,
and widened his knowledge of the literary efforts of French
and Italian contemporaries.

Spenser's connection with Leicester brought him the

---

[1] *Ruines of Time*, ll. 184-49.   [2] *Ibid.*, ll. 232-33.

acquaintance of a more attractive personality—Leicester's
Sir Philip Sidney. fascinating nephew, Sir Philip Sidney. The
acquaintance rapidly ripened into a deep and
tender friendship, and exerted an excellent influence,
morally and intellectually, on both young men.

Thus, in 1579, when Spenser was about twenty-seven
years old, Fortune seemed to smile on him. He mixed
Harvey's advice. freely with courtiers and politicians, and was in
close touch with all that was most enlightened
in London society. Amid such environment his poetic
genius acquired new energy and confidence. He was
ambitious to excel in all forms of literary composition, and
he was in doubt which to essay first. He confided his
perplexities to his friend and tutor Harvey. Harvey was a
pedantic and shortsighted counsellor. He was no wise
adviser of one endowed with great original genius which was
best left to seek an independent course. Harvey's passion
for the classics, and his absorption in the study of them,
distorted his judgment. English poetry was in his mind a
branch of classical scholarship. Hitherto the art of poetry
had, in his opinion, been practised to best advantage by
Latin writers. Consequently, English poetry, were it to
attain perfection, ought to imitate Latin verse, alike in
metre and ideas. Harvey's theory was based on a very
obvious misconception. Poetry can only flourish if it be free
to adapt itself to the idiosyncrasy of the poet's mother-
tongue. Accent, not quantity, is alone adaptable to poetry
in the English language. English verse which ignores such
considerations cannot reach the poetic level.

Yet for a time Harvey's views prevailed with Spenser.
The classi-cal fallacy. He defied a great law of nature and of art, and
did violence to his bent, in order to essay the
hopeless task of naturalising in English verse metrical rules

which the English language rejects. In the meetings of
the literary club of the 'Areopagus' which Leicester's friends
and dependents formed at Leicester House, Spenser, Sidney,
and others debated, at Harvey's instance, the application
to English poetry of the classical rules of metrical quantity.
Spenser joined the company in making many experiments
in Latinised English verse, a few of which survive. The
result was an uncouth sort of verbiage, lumbering or wallow-
ing in harsh obscurity. Happily Spenser quickly perceived
that no human power could fit the English language to
classical metres; he saw the weakness of the pedantic
arguments. It was well that he escaped the classicists'
toils. It was needful that he should deliberately reject
false notions of English verse before his genius could gain
an open road.

The first serious poetic efforts that Spenser designed in
his adult years are lost, if they were ever completed.
Soon after he had settled at Leicester House, Poetic ex-
Spenser told his friends he was penning nine periments.
comedies, to be called after the nine Muses, in the manner
of the books of Herodotus's *History.* An account of his
patron's family history and chief ancestors was also occupy-
ing his pen; fragments of this design, perhaps, survive
in the elegy on his patron which he subsequently incorporated in his *Ruines of Time.* He seems to have sketched
a lost prose work called *The English Poet,* an essay on
literary criticism, which, like Sidney's *Apologie for Poetrie,*
was intended to prove poetry (so a friend of Spenser reported) to be 'a divine gift and heavenly instinct not to be
gotten by labour and learning, but adorned with both,
and poured into the wit by a certain enthousiasmos and
celestial inspiration.'[1] Spenser, having cut himself adrift

---

[1] *Cf.* Argument before *The Shepheards Calender,* Eclogue x.

of pedantic classicism, adopted a view no less exalted than that of Shelley of the constituent elements of genuine poetry. Even more important is it to note that Spenser had found the form of poetic endeavour, at this early epoch, which best suited his ethical and artistic temper. His ambitious allegorical epic or moral romance, which he called the *Faerie Queene,* dates from the outset of his literary career. He sent some portion to Harvey as early as the autumn of 1579, at the moment when he was recanting his tutor's classical heresy. Harvey was naturally not impressed by a project which he had not advised, and which ignored or defied his pedantic principles of poetic art. The design was in Harvey's eyes an unwarranted innovation, a deflection from tried and well-trodden paths. Spenser was not encouraged by Harvey to hurry on. The discouragement had some effect. Ten years elapsed before any portion of the poem was sent to press. Spenser was shy and sensitive by nature. He could not ignore critical censure. But happily other friends, of better judgment than Harvey, urged him to persevere.

IV

Spenser's ascent of Parnassus was not greatly prejudiced by Harvey's misleading counsel. Temporarily abandoning the *Faerie Queene,* he turned to work for which precedent was more abundant. He completed and caused to be printed, before the close of 1579 —a year very eventful in his career—a poem which left enlightened critics in no doubt of his powers.

The Shepheards Calender.

Spenser's first extant poem of length, which he called *The Shepheards Calender,* consisted of twelve dialogues or eclogues spoken in dialogue by shepherds, one for every month of the year. The design of the volume

Its foreign models.

followed foreign models of acknowledged repute. Greek
pastoral poetry of Theocritus and Bion was its foundation,
modified by study of Virgil's Eclogues and of many French
and Italian examples of more recent date. Mantuanus and
Sanazzaro among Italian poets, and Clement Marot among
Frenchmen, commanded Spenser's full allegiance. The
title was borrowed from an English translation in current
use of a popular French Almanac known as *Kalendrier des
Bergers*, and the debt to Marot's French eclogues is especially large. The names of the speakers Thenot and Colin
are of Marot's invention, and in two of the eclogues Spenser
confines himself to adaptation of Marot's verse. Everywhere he gives proof of reading and respect for authority.
His friends freely acknowledged that he piously 'followed
the footing' of the excellent poets of Greece, Rome,
France, and Italy.

It was not only abroad that Spenser's genius sought
sustenance. Although he was fascinated by the varied
charms of foreign literary effort, he was not oblivious of the
literary achievement of his own country. English poetry
had not of late progressed at the same rate as the poetry of
Italy or France. But a poetic tradition had come into being
in fourteenth-century England. Spenser was attracted by it,
and he believed himself capable of continuing it. He was
eager to enrol himself under the banner of the greatest of
his English predecessors, of Chaucer. By way of Eulogy of
proving the sincerity of his patriotic allegiance, he Chaucer.
took toll openly of the English poet, even exaggerating the
extent of his indebtedness.[1] His direct eulogy of Chaucer
under the name of Tityrus is a splendid declaration of

---

[1] In Eclogue II. (February) Spenser pretends to quote from Chaucer the
fable of the oak and the briar. The alleged quotation seems to be entirely of
Spenser's invention.

homage on the younger poet's part to the old master of
English poetry.

> ' The God of Shepherds, Tityrus, is dead,
>   Who taught me homely, as I can, to make ;
>   He, whilst he lived, was the sovereign head
>   Of shepherds all that bene with love ytake ;
>   Well couth he wail his woes, and lightly slake
>   The flames which love within his heart had bred,
>   And tell us merry tales to keep us wake,
>   The while our sheep about us safely fed.
>
>   Now dead is he, and lieth wrapt in lead,
>   (O ! why should death on him such outrage show !)
>   And all his passing skill with him is fled
>   The fame whereof doth daily greater grow.
>   But if on me some little drops would flow
>   Of that the spring was in his learned head,
>   I soon would learn these woods to wail my woe,
>   And teach the trees their trickling tears to shed.' [1]

No poem of supreme worth ever crept into the world more
modestly or made larger avowal of obligation to poetry of the
The critical   past than *The Shepheards Calender.*   Spenser, who
apparatus.   merely claimed to be trying his 'tender wings' in
strict accord with precedent, hesitated to announce himself as
the author.   The book was inscribed anonymously on its title-
page to his friend Sir Philip Sidney, and in a little prefatory
poem which he characteristically signed ' Immerito,' he fitly
entitles his patron 'the president of noblesse and chivalry.'
A college friend, Edward Kirke, emphasised the work's dependence on the ancient ways in a dedicatory epistle to the
scholar Gabriel Harvey ; and the same hand liberally scattered
through the volume notes and glosses, which emphasised the
poet's loans from the accepted masters of his craft.   Owing
to Spenser's anxiety to link himself to the latest period—
remote as it was—when English poetry had conspicuously

---

[1] *The Shepheards Calender* June, lines 81-96.

flourished, the vocabulary was deliberately archaic. Foreign examples justified such procedure. Kirke explained that, after the manner of the Greek pastoral poets who affected the rustic Doric dialect, Spenser 'laboured to restore as to their rightful heritage such good and natural English words as had been long time out of use and clean disinherited.'

Kirke's sincere enthusiasm for his author neutralises the prejudice which lovers of poetry commonly cherish against officious editorial comment. He justifies his intervention between reader and author on the somewhat equivocal ground that although Spenser was an imitator, his imitations were often so devised that only 'such as were (like his editor) well scented' in the hunt after foreign originals could 'trace them out.'

But the range of topics of the *The Shepheards Calender* suggests to the least observant reader that there is exaggeration in the editor's repeated denial of the poet's ability to walk alone or to strike out new paths for himself. Spenser naturally pursues the old pastoral roads in discoursing of the pangs of despised love of which he had had his own experience, of the woes of age and of the joys of youth; but there is individuality in his treatment of the well-worn themes, and he does not confine himself to them. In his contrasts between the virtues of Protestantism and the vices of Popery he handles problems of theology which his poetic predecessors had not essayed. The interlocutors are the poet himself and his friends and patron under disguised names, and he does not repress his private sentiments or idiosyncrasies. Of his personal beliefs he makes impressive confession in his tenth eclogue, in which he 'complaineth of the contempt of poetry and the causes thereof.' Theocritus and Mantuanus had already condemned monarchs and statesmen for failure to respect the votaries of 'peerless poesy.' Spenser followed in their wake, but the ardour with which he pleads the poet's cause is his own, and the argument had never before been couched in finer harmonies.

Despite its large dependence on earlier literary effort, the value of the *The Shepheards Calender* lies ultimately not (as

Its true value. its editor would have us believe) in the dexterity of its adaptations, but in the proof it offers of the original calibre of Spenser's poetic genius. Historically important as it is for the student and critic to note and to define what a poet takes from others, of greater importance is it for them to note and to define what a poet makes of his borrowings. In the first place, *The Shepheards Calender* shows a faculty for musical modulation of words, of which only the greatest practisers of the poetic art are capable. It is a peculiar quality of Spenser's power to manipulate the metre so that it moves as the sense dictates, now slowly and solemnly, now quickly and joyfully. In the second place, the thought is clothed in a picturesque simplicity, which is the fruit of the poet's personality. The life and truthfulness of the pictures are the outcome of the poet's individual affinities with the poetic aspects of nature and humanity.

Since the death of Chaucer no poet of a distinction similar to that of Spenser had come to light in England. *The*

Its place in English poetry. *Shepheards Calender* was not without signs of immaturity; the melodies of the verse were interrupted by awkward dissonances and by feeble or discordant phrases. But its merits far outdistanced its defects and it worthily inaugurated a new era of English poetry. It proved beyond risk of denial that there had arisen a poet of genius fit to rank above all preceding English poets save only Chaucer, who died nearly two centuries before. It is to the credit of the age that this great fact, despite editorial endeavours to disguise it, was straightway recognised. ' He may well wear the garland and step before the best of all English poets that I have seen or heard,' wrote one early reader of *The Shepheards Calender*. Drayton, the reputed friend of Shakespeare, declared that ' Master Edmund Spenser had done enough for the immortality of his name had he only given us his *The Shepheards Calender*, a masterpiece if any.' Masterpieces had been scarce in English literature since Chaucer produced his *Canterbury Tales*.

v

Elizabethan poetry brought its makers honourable recognition, but it did not bring them pecuniary reward. Spenser had entered Leicester's service in order to obtain an office which should produce a regular revenue. But, as the months went on, Spenser suffered disappointment at his patron's hands. Leicester was not as zealous in the poet's interest as the poet hoped. The services which he rendered his patron seemed to him to be inadequately recognised. He expected more from his master than board and lodging. His dissatisfaction found vent in a rendering of the poem called ' Virgil's Gnat.'

The poet's complaint of his patron.

' Wronged, yet not daring to express my pain,'

the poet dedicated the apologue to his ' excellent' lord ' the causer of my care.' He likened himself to the gnat, which, in the poem, rouses a sleeping shepherd to repel a serpent's attack by stinging his eyelid, and then is thoughtlessly brushed aside and slain by him whom the insect delivers from peril.

Spenser probably wrote in a moment of temporary annoyance, and exaggerated the injury done him by the Earl.
Official Happily a change of fortune was at hand, and his
promotion. irritation with Leicester passed away. Although there is no reason for regarding the sequence of events as other than accidental, it was within six months of the publication of *The Shepheards Calender*, that the poet was offered a remunerative and responsible post. He accepted the office of secretary to a newly-appointed Lord Deputy of Ireland, and the course of his life was completely changed.

In the summer of 1580 Spenser left England practically for good. Though he thrice revisited his native land,
Migration Ireland was his home for his remaining nineteen
to Ireland. years of life. At the outset he accepted the post in the faith that it would prove a stepping-stone to high political office in England. Permanent exile he never contemplated with complacency. London was his native place and the seat of government, and it was his ambition to enjoy there profitable and dignified employment. But this was not to be, and as the prospect of preferment grew dim, his spirit engendered an irremovable melancholy and discontent. He bewailed his unhappy fate with the long-drawn bitterness of Ovid among the Scythians. He declared himself to be a 'forlorn wight' who was banished to a 'waste,' and there was 'quite forgot.'

Sixteenth-century Ireland had few attractions for an English poet. The country was torn asunder by internecine
The Irish strife. The native Irish were in perpetual revolt
problem. against their English rulers. The Spaniards, anxious to injure England at every point, were ready to fan Irish disaffection, and were always threatening to send ships and men to encourage active rebellion The air was infected

by barbarous cruelty, by suffering and poverty. To Spenser's gentle and beauty-loving nature, violence and pain were abhorrent, but he had no chance of escape from the hateful environment, and familiarity with the sordid scenes had the natural effect of dulling, even in his sensitive brain, the active sense of repulsion to its worst evils. Though he never reconciled himself to the conditions of Irish life or government, and vaguely hoped for mitigation of their horrors, he assimilated the views of the governing class to which he belonged, and became an advocate of the coercion of the natives to whose wrongs he gave no attentive ear.

Self-interest, too, insensibly moulded his political views. Having entered the official circle in Ireland, he eagerly sought opportunities of improving his material fortunes. He yearned for the rewards of political life in England, but he came to realise that if *Early friends in Ireland.* those prizes were beyond his reach, he must accommodate himself to the more limited scope of advancement in Ireland. There he met with moderate success. He was quickly the recipient of many profitable posts in Dublin, which he held together with his secretaryship to the Lord Deputy. He was also granted much land, in accordance with the English policy, which encouraged English settlers in Ireland. Happily, there was some worthier mitigation of his lot. His official colleagues included some congenial companions whose sympathy with his literary ambitions went some way to counteract the griefs of his Irish experience. In Lord Grey, his Chief, the governor of the country, Spenser found one who inspired him with affection and respect. To Lord Grey's nobility of nature the poet paid splendid tribute in his description of Sir Artegal, the knight of justice in the *Faerie Queene* (book IV. canto ii.). A humbler colleague, Lodowick Bryskett, was a zealous lover of literature ; he

occupied a little cottage near Dublin, and often invited
Spenser and others to engage there in literary debate.
There the poet talked with engaging frankness and modesty
of his literary ambitions and plans.

Spenser's temperament was prone to seek the guidance
and countenance of others. It was fortunate that Ireland
did not withhold from him the encouragement which was
needful to stimulate poetic exertion. It was not likely that
the poetic impulse would be conquered by his migration,
but in the absence of sympathetic companions its activity
would doubtless have slackened, and he would have wanted
the confidence to give to the world its fruits. As things
turned out, his enthusiasm for his art increased rather than
diminished in his retirement. Literary composition provided congenial relief from the routine work of his office.
At the entreaty of his friends, he took up again his great
His poetic   work the *Faerie Queene,* with its scene laid in an
exertions.   imaginary fairyland, to which the poetic humour
could carry him from any point of the earth's surface. At
the same time he made many slighter excursions in verse,
of which the most beautiful was his lament for the premature
death of his friend and patron, Sir Philip Sidney. No
sweeter imagery ever adorned an elegy than that to be met
with in Spenser's ' Astrophel, a pastorall Elegie upon the
death of the most noble and valorous knight Sir Philip
Sidney.' His brain could summon at will ethereal visions
which the sordid environment of his Irish career could neither
erase nor blur. He was no careless pleasure-seeking official ;
he did his official work thoroughly, although not brilliantly.
There was strange contrast between the poet's official duties
and the intellectual and spiritual aspirations which filled his
brain while he laboured at the official oar.

VI

After eight years, Spenser left Dublin to take up a new
and more dignified post in the South of Ireland.   He was
made clerk of the Council of Munster, the
southern province, a prosaic office for which   Removal to
                                                 the south
poetic genius was small qualification.   He took of Ireland.
active part in the work of planting or colonising with
Englishmen untenanted land, or land from which native
holders were evicted.   Spenser thought it perfectly just to
evict the natives ; it is doubtful if he saw any crime in
exterminating them.   New tracts of land were given him by
way of encouragement in the neighbourhood of Cork.   He
took up his residence in the old castle of Kilcolman, three
miles from Doneraile, in County Cork.   It was surrounded
by woodland scenery, and the prospect was as soothing to
the human brain as any that a poet could wish.   The house
is now an ivy-covered ruin, while the surrounding scenery
has gained in fulness and in richness of aspect.

But the beauty of nature brought to Spenser in Ireland
little content or happiness.   It was on his management of ' the
world of living men,' not on a placid survey of
' wood and stream and field and hill and ocean '   Quarrels
                                                   with
that his material welfare depended.   He had not neighbours.
the tact and social diplomacy needful for the maintenance
of harmony with his rude, semi-civilised neighbours.   With
the landlords of estates contiguous to his own he was constantly engaged in litigation, and was often under dread of
physical conflict.

Nevertheless, one source of relief from the anxieties and
annoyances of official life was present in County Cork as in
County Dublin.   Fortune again gave him a companion who
could offer him welcome encouragement in the practice of
his poetic art.

When Spenser pitched his tent in the south of Ireland, there was there another English settler who was notably Sir Walter imbued with literary tastes in some way akin to Ralegh. his own. Sir Walter Ralegh was living at his house on the Blackwater in temporary retirement from political storms across the Irish Channel. He quickly made his way to Kilcolman Castle. Spenser was cheered in his desolation by a visitor whose literary enthusiasm was proof against every vicissitude of fortune. With Ralegh's inspiring voice ringing in his ear, Spenser's *Faerie Queene* progressed apace. Spenser recognised, too, Ralegh's own poetic power, and he stirred his neighbour to address himself also to the Muse in friendly rivalry. Of his meetings with Ralegh in the fastnesses of Southern Ireland, and of their poetic contests, Spenser wrote with simple beauty thus :—

> ' A strange shepherd chanced to find me out,
> Whether allured with my pipes delight,
> Whose pleasing sound yshrillèd far about,
> Or thither led by chance, I know not right ;
> Whom, when I askèd from what place he came,
> And how he hight, himself he did ycleepe
> The Shepherd of the Ocean by name,
> And said he came far from the main-sea deep.
> He, sitting me beside in that same shade,
> Provokèd me to play some pleasant fit ;
> And when he heard the music which I made,
> He found himself full greatly pleased at it :
> Yet aemuling[1] my pipe, he took in hond
> My pipe, before that aemuled[2] of many,
> And played thereon ; (for well that skill he cond) ;
> Himself as skilful in that art as any.
> He pip'd, I sung ; and, when he sung, I piped ;
> By change of turns, each making other merry ;
> Neither envying other, nor envied,
> So piped we until we both were weary.'[3]

---

[1] rivalling. [2] rivalled. [3] *Colin Clouts come home againe*, ll. 60-79.

It was at Ralegh's persuasion that Spenser, having completed three books of his *Faerie Queene,* took the resolve to visit London once more. At Ralegh's persuasion London revisited. he sought to arrange for the publication of his ambitious venture. His fame as author of *The Shepheards Calender* still ran high, and a leader of the publishing fraternity, William Ponsonby, was eager to undertake the volume. The negotiation rapidly issued in the appearance of the first three books of Spenser's epic allegory under Ponsonby's auspices early in 1590.

Ralegh, to whom the author addressed a prefatory letter 'expounding his whole intention in the course of this work,' had filled the poet with hope that the highest power in the land, the Queen herself, 'whose grace was great and bounty most rewardful,' would interest herself in so noble an undertaking. With the loyalty characteristic of the time, the poet had made his virgin sovereign a chief heroine of Its dedica- his poem. To her accordingly he dedicated the tion to Queen work in words of dignified brevity. The dedica- Elizabeth. tion ran :—'To the most high, mighty, and magnificent Empress, renowned for piety, virtue, and all gracious government. . . . Her most humble servant, Edmund Spenser, doth in all humility dedicate, present, and consecrate these his labours, to live with the eternity of her fame.' But it was not the Queen alone among great personages who could, if well disposed, benefit his material fortunes and restore him in permanence to his native English soil. The poet was urged by friendly advisers to enlist the interest of all leading men and women in his undertaking. In seventeen prefatory sonnets he saluted as a suppliant for their favour as many high officers or ladies of the Court.

The reception accorded to the first published instalment

of the *Faerie Queene* gave Spenser no ground for regret.

Reception of the *Faerie Queene,* bks. i.-iii.

Among lovers of poetry the book attained instant success. The first three books of the *Faerie Queene* dispelled all surviving doubt that Spenser was, in point of time, the greatest poet (after Chaucer) in the English language ; and there were many who judged the later poet to be in merit the equal if not the superior of the earlier.

In the *Faerie Queene* Spenser broke new ground. It was not of the category to which Spenser's earlier effort *The Shepheards Calender* belonged. Since the earlier volume appeared more than ten years had passed, and Spenser's hand had grown in confidence and

Its advance on *The Shepheards Calender.*

cunning. His thought had matured, his intellectual interests had grown, till they embraced well-nigh the whole expanse of human endeavour. His genius, his poetic capacity, had now ripened. At length a long-sustained effort of exalted aim lay well within his scope. As in the case of *The Shepheards Calender* Spenser deprecated originality of design. With native modesty he announced on the threshold his discipleship to Homer and Virgil, to Ariosto and Tasso. It was an honest and just announcement. Many an episode and much of his diction came from the epic poems of Achilles and Æneas, or of Orlando and Rinaldo. But all his borrowings were fused with his own invention by the fire of his brain, and the final scheme was the original fruit of individual genius. Spenser's main purpose was to teach virtue, to instruct men in the conduct of life, to expound allegorically a system of moral philosophy. But with a lavish hand he shed over his ethical teaching the splendour of great poetry, and it is by virtue of that allurement that his endeavour won its triumph.

VII

Spenser was ill content with mere verbal recognition of the eminence of his poetic achievement. His presence in London was not only planned in order to publish A suitor the *Faerie Queene,* and to enjoy the applause of for office. critics near at hand. It was also designed to win official preferment, to gain a more congenial means of livelihood than was open to him in Ireland, a home ' unmeet for man in whom was aught regardful.' To secure this end he spared no effort. He cared little for his self-respect provided he could strengthen his chances of victory. He submitted to all the tedious and degrading routine which was incumbent on suitors for court office ; he patiently suffered rebuffs and disappointments, delays and the indecision of patrons. Some measure of success rewarded his persistency. Ralegh, who enjoyed for the time Queen Elizabeth's favour, worked hard in his friend's behalf. The Queen was not indifferent to the compliments Spenser had paid her in his great poem. Great ladies were gratified by the poetic eulogies he offered them in occasional verse. In the exalted ranks of society his reputation as an unapproached master of his art grew steadily.

A general willingness manifested itself to respond favourably to the plaintive petitions of a poet so richly endowed. A pension was suggested. The Queen herself, The grant the rumour went, accepted the suggestion with of a pension. alacrity, and calling the attention of her Lord Treasurer, Lord Burghley, to it, bade him be generous. She named a sum which was deemed by her adviser excessive. Finally Spenser was allotted a State-paid income of fifty pounds a year. The amount was large at a time when the purchasing power of money was eight times what it is now, and the bestowal of it promised him such prestige as recognition by the crown invariably confers on a poet, although it did not give Spenser the formal title of poet-laureate.

But Spenser was unsatisfied; he resented and never forgave the attitude of Lord Burghley, who, like most practical statesmen, looked with suspicion on poets when they sought political posts : he had no enthusiasm for amateurs in political office, nor did he approve of the appropriation of public money to the encouragement of literary genius. The net result left Spenser's position unchanged. The pension was not large enough to justify him in abandoning work in Ireland. England offered him no asylum. He recrossed the Irish Channel to resume his office as Clerk of the Council of Munster.

The return to Ireland.

At home in Ireland, Spenser reviewed his fortunes in despair. With feeling he wrote in his poem called *Mother Hubberds Tale* :—

His despair of his fortunes.

> ' Full little knowest thou, that hast not tried,
>   What hell it is, in suing long to bide :
>   To lose good days, that might be better spent ;
>   To waste long nights in pensive discontent ;
>   To speed to-day, to be put back to-morrow ;
>   To feed on hope, to pine with fear and sorrow ;
>   To have thy Prince's grace, yet want her Peers ;
>   To have thy asking, yet wait many years ;
>   To fret thy soul with crosses and with cares ;
>   To eat thy heart through comfortless despairs ;
>   To fawn, to crouch, to wait, to ride, to run,
>   To spend, to give, to want, to be undone.
>   Unhappy wight, born to disastrous end,
>   That doth his life in so long tendance spend !' [1]

On a second poem of the same date and on the same theme he bestowed the ironical title *Colin Clouts come home againe* (Colin Clout was a nick-name which it amused him

[1] Spenser's *Prosopopoia, or Mother Hubberds Tale*, ll. 896-909.

to give himself). *Colin Clout* is as charming and simple an essay in autobiography as fell from any poet's pen. He recalls the details of his recent experience in London with charming *naïveté*, and dwells with generous enthusiasm on the favours and ' sundry good turns,' which he owed to his neighbour Sir Walter Ralegh. He sent the manuscript of *Colin Clout* to Ralegh, and, although it was not printed till 1595, it soon passed from hand to hand. Elsewhere in another occasional poem, *The Ruines of Time*, which mainly lamented the death of his first patron Leicester and of that patron's brother the Earl of Warwick, he avenged himself in a more strident note on Lord Burghley's cynical indifference to his need.

All the leisure that his official duties left him he now devoted to poetry. He committed to verse all his thought. He was no longer reticent, and sent copies of his poems in all directions. Quickly he came before the public as author of another volume of verse possessing high auto- *Complaints* biographical attraction. This was a characteristic 1590. venture of the publisher Ponsonby, and with its actual preparation for the press the poet was not directly concerned. Scattered poems by Spenser were circulating in manuscript from hand to hand. These the publisher, Ponsonby, brought together under the title of *Complaints*, without distinct authority from the author. The book seems to have contained compositions of various dates; some belonged to early years, but the majority were very recent. To the recent work belongs one of Spenser's most characteristic, and most mature poetic efforts, the poem of 'Muiopotmos.' That poem is the airiest of fancies treated with marvellous delicacy and vivacity. It tells the trivial story of a butterfly swept by a gust of wind into a spider's web. But the picturesque portrayal of the butterfly's careless passage

through the air, and of his revellings in all the delights
of nature, breathes the purest spirit of simple and sensuous
poetry.

> 'Over the fields, in his frank lustiness,
> And all the champain o'er, he soared light,
> And all the country wide he did possess,
> Feeding upon their pleasures bounteously,
> That none gainsaid and none did him envy.'

It is difficult to refuse assent to the interpretation of the
poem which detects in the butterfly's joyous career on ' his
aircutting wings,' and his final and fatal entanglement in
the grisly tyrant's den, a figurative reflection of the poet's
own experiences.

VIII

A change was imminent in Spenser's private life. Once
more he contemplated marriage. He paid his addresses to
The poet's   the daughter of a neighbouring landlord. Her
marriage.   father, James Boyle, was the kinsman of a great
magnate of the south of Ireland, Richard Boyle, who was
to be created at a later period Earl of Cork.

It was in accord with the fashion of the time, that
Spenser, under the new sway of the winged god, should
interrupt the poetic labours on which he had already
entered, to pen, in honour of his wished-for bride, a long
His   sequence of sonnets. Spenser's sonnets, which he
Amoretti.   entitled *Amoretti*, do not rank very high among
his poetic compositions. Like those of most of his contemporaries, they reflect his wide reading in the similar work
of French and Italian contemporaries to a larger extent than
his own individuality. Although a personal experience
impelled him to the enterprise, it is only with serious
qualifications that Spenser's sequence of sonnets can be

regarded as autobiographic confessions.[1] In his hands, as
in the hands of Sidney and Daniel, the sonnet was a poetic
instrument whereon he sought to repeat in his mother-
tongue, with very vague reference to his personal circumstances, the notes of amorous feeling and diction which earlier
poets of Italy and France had already made their own. The
sonnet, which was a wholly foreign form of poetry, and came
direct to Elizabethan England from the Continent of Europe,
had an inherent attraction for Spenser throughout his career.
His earliest literary efforts were two small collections of
sonnets, renderings respectively of French sonnets by Du
Bellay and Marot's French translation of an ode of Petrarch.
His *Amoretti* prove that in his maturer years he had
fully maintained his early affection for French and Italian
sonnetteers. He had indeed greatly extended his acquaintance among them. The influence of Petrarch and Du
Bellay was now rivalled by the influence of Tasso and
Desportes.[2] At times Spenser is content with literal

---

[1] Spenser makes only three distinctly autobiographical statements in his
sonnets. Sonnet xxxiii. is addressed by name to his friend Lodowick
Bryskett, and is an apology for the poet's delay in completing his *Faerie
Queene*. In sonnet lx. Spenser states that he is forty-one years old, and
that one year has passed since he came under the influence of the winged
god. Sonnet lxxiv. apostrophises the 'happy letters' which comprise the
name Elizabeth, which he states was borne alike by his mother, his sovereign, and his wife, Elizabeth Boyle.

> 'Ye three Elizabeths ! for ever live,
>   That three such graces did unto me give.'

Here Spenser seems to be following a hint offered him by Tasso, who
addressed a sonnet to three benefactresses ('Tre gran donne') all named
Leonora.—(Tasso, *Rime*, Venice, 1583, vol. i. p. 39.)

[2] See *Elizabethan Sonnets*, vol. i. pp. xcii.-xcix. (introd.), edited by the
present writer. The following is a good example of Spenser's dependence
on Tasso. Nine lines of Tasso's sonnet are literally translated by Spenser :—

> 'Fair is my love, when her fair golden hairs
>   With the loose wind ye waving chance to mark ;
> Fair, when the rose in her red cheeks appears,
>   Or in her eyes the fire of love doth spark. . . .

translation of these two foreign masters; very occasionally
does he altogether escape from their toils.   Where he avoids
literal dependence, he commonly adopts foreign words and
ideas too closely to give his individuality complete freedom.
Only three or four times does he break loose from the
foreign chains and reveal in his sonnet sequence the full
force of his great genius.   For the most part the *Amoretti*
reproduces the hollow prettiness and cloying sweetness of
French and Italian conceits with little of the English poet's
distinctive charm.

But if sincerity and originality are slenderly represented
in the sonnets, neither of these qualities is wanting to the
The *Epi-* great ode which was published with them.   There
thalamion. Spenser with an engaging frankness betrayed the
elation of spirit which came of his courtship and marriage.
In this *Epithalamion*, with which he celebrated his wedding,
his lyrical powers found full scope, and the ode takes rank
with the greatest of English lyrics.   The refined tone does
not ignore any essential facts, but every touch subserves
the purposes of purity and brings into prominence the

> But fairest she, when so she doth display
> The gate with pearls and rubies richly dight;
> Through which her words so wise do make their way,
> To bear the message of her gentle spright.'
> > (Spenser, *Amoretti*, lxxxi.)

> ' Bella è la donna mia, se dal bel crine,
> > L'oro al vento ondeggiare avien, che miri;
> > Bella se volger gli occhi in dolci giri
> > O le rose fiorir tra la sue brine. . . .
> Ma quella, ch'apre un dolce labro, e serra
> > Porta di bei rubin sì dolcemente,
> > E beltà sovra ogn' altra altera, ed alma.
> Porta gentil de la pregion de l'alma,
> > Onde i messi d'amor escon sovente.'
> > (Tasso, *Rime*, Venice, 1585, vol. iii. p. 17 *b*.)

Spenser's fidelity as a translator does not permit him to overlook even
Tasso's pleonastic 'che miri' (line 2), which he renders quite literally by
' ye chance to mark.'

spiritual beauty of the nuptial tie.   Of the fascination of
his bride he writes in lines like these :—

> ' But if ye saw that which no eyes can see,
> The inward beauty of her lively spright,
> Garnished with heavenly gifts of high degree,
> Much more then would you wonder at that sight,
> And stand astonished like to those which red
> Medusa's mazeful head.
> There dwells sweet love, and constant chastity,
> Unspotted faith, and comely womanhood,
> Regard of honour, and mild modesty ;
> There virtue reigns as queen in royal throne,
> And giveth laws alone,
> The which the base affections do obey,
> And yield their services unto her will ;
> Ne thought of thing uncomely ever may
> Thereto approach to tempt her mind to ill.
> Had ye once seen these her celestial treasures,
> And unrevealed pleasures,
> Then would ye wonder, and her praises sing,
> That all the woods should answer, and your echo ring.' [1]

Spenser deferred marriage to so mature an age as forty-
two.   His great achievements in poetry were then completed.   Before his marriage he had finished the
last three completed books of his *Faerie Queene* ; a
fragment of a seventh book survives of uncertain
date, but it probably belongs to the poet's pre-nuptial career.
After his marriage, his first practical business was to revisit
London and superintend the printing of the three last
completed books of his great allegory.

*The Faerie
Queene
continued.*

Five years had passed since his last sojourn in England,
and his welcome was not all that he could wish.   In
diplomatic circles he found himself an object of
suspicion.   James vi., the king of Scotland, himself a poet and a reader of poetry, had lately detected in

*Political
difficulties.*

[1] *Epithalamion*, ll. 185-203.

Duessa, the deceitful witch of Spenser's great poem, an ill-disguised portrait of his own mother, Mary, Queen of Scots. Official complaint had been made to the English Government, and a request preferred for the punishment of the offending poet. The controversy went no further and Spenser was unharmed, but the older politicians complained privately of his indiscretion, and Burghley's cynical scorn seemed justified.

The fashionable nobility, however, only recognised his glorious poetic gifts and their enthusiasm was undiminished. Spenser followed the Court with persistence. He was a visitor at the Queen's palace at Greenwich where Shakespeare had acted in the royal presence two seasons before. Especially promising was the reception accorded him by the Queen's latest favourite, the Earl of Essex, a sincere lover of the arts and of artists, but of too impetuous a temperament to exert genuine influence at Court in behalf of his protégé. Spenser was the Earl's guest at Essex House in the Strand. The mansion was already familiar to the poet, for it had been in earlier years the residence of the Earl of Leicester, the poet's first patron, and Essex's predecessor in the regard of his sovereign. Spenser rejoiced in the renewed hospitality the familiar roof offered him. Of his presence in Essex House, he left a memorial of high literary interest. It was in honour of two noble ladies, daughters of the Earl of Worcester, who were married from Essex House in November 1596, that Spenser penned the latest of his poems and one that embodied the quintessence of his lyric gift. His ' *Prothalamion* or a spousal verse, in honour of the double marriage of two honourable and virtuous ladies,' was hardly a whit inferior to his recent *Epithalamion*. Its far-famed refrain :

The Earl of Essex's patronage.

' Sweet Thames ! run softly, till I end my song,'

sounds indeed a sweeter note than the refrain of answering
woods and ringing echoes in the earlier ode. It leaves an
ineffaceable impression of musical grace and simplicity. It
was Spenser's fit farewell to his Muse.

It was not poetry that occupied Spenser's main attention during this visit to London. Again his chief concern
was the search for more lucrative employment
than Ireland was offering him, and in this quest
he met with smaller encouragement than before.

His prose
tract on
Ireland.

With a view to proving his political sagacity and his fitness for political work, he now indeed abandoned with
his *Prothalamion* poetry altogether.   Much of his time
in London he devoted to describing and criticising the
existing condition of the country of Ireland where his
life was unwillingly passed.   He wrote dialogue-wise a
prose treatise which he called 'A view of the present
state of Ireland.'   It was first circulated in manuscript,
and was not published in Spenser's lifetime.   Despite
many picturesque passages, and an attractive flow of
colloquy, it is not the work that one would expect from
a great poet at the zenith of his powers.   For the most
part Spenser's 'View' is a political pamphlet, showing a
narrow political temper and lack of magnanimity.   The
argument is a mere echo of the hopeless and helpless
prejudices which infected the English governing class.
Despair of Ireland's political and social future is the
dominant note.   ' Marry, see there have been divers good
plots devised and wise counsels cast already about
reformation of that realm ; but they say it is the fatal
destiny of that land, that no purposes, whatsoever are
meant for her good, will prosper or take good effect,
which whether it proceed from the very Genius of the soil,
or influence of the stars, or that Almighty God hath not

yet appointed the time of her reformation, or that he reserveth her in this unquiet state still for some secret scourge, which shall by her come unto England, it is hard to be known, but yet much to be feared.'

The poet failed to recognise any justice in the claims of Irish nationality ; English law was to be forced on Irishmen ;

His pre-judice against the Irish. Irish nationality was to be suppressed (if need be) at the point of the sword. Spenser's avowed want of charity long caused in the native population abhorrence of his name. But while condemning Irish character and customs, Spenser was enlightened enough to perceive defects in English methods of governing Ireland. He deplored the ignorance and degradation of the Protestant clergy there, and the unreadiness of the new settlers to take advantage, by right scientific methods of cultivation, of the natural wealth of the soil. Despite his invincible prejudices, Spenser acknowledged, too, some good qualities in the native Irish. They were skilled and alert horsemen. 'I have heard some great warriors say, that, in all the services which they had seen abroad in foreign countries, they never saw a more comely horseman than the Irish man, nor that cometh on more bravely in his charge : neither is his manner of mounting unseemly, though he wants stirrups, but more ready then with stirrups, for in his getting up his horse is still going, whereby he gaineth way.'

Spenser allows, too, a qualified virtue in the native poetry. Of Irish compositions Spenser asserts that 'they savoured of sweet wit and good invention, but skilled not of the goodly ornaments of Poetry : yet were they sprinkled with some pretty flowers of their own natural device, which gave good grace and comeliness unto them.' Spenser also took an antiquarian interest in the remains of Irish art and civilisation, and contemplated a work on Irish antiquities, of which no trace has been found.

Only the natural beauty of the country excited in him any genuine enthusiasm. 'And sure it is yet a most beautiful and sweet country as any is under heaven, seamed throughout with many goodly rivers, replenished with all sorts of fish; most abundantly sprinkled *The natural beauty of Ireland.* with many sweet islands and goodly lakes like little inland seas that will carry even ships upon their waters; adorned with goodly woods fit for building of houses and ships, so commodiously, as that if some princes in the world had them, they would soon hope to be lords of all the seas, and ere long of all the world; also full of good ports and havens opening upon England and Scotland, as inviting us to come to them, to see what excellent commodities that country can afford; besides the soil itself most fertile, fit to yield all kinds of fruit that shall be committed thereunto. And lastly, the heavens most mild and temperate.'

His 'View of the present state of Ireland' is Spenser's only work in prose, and is his final contribution to literature.

IX

Early in 1597 Spenser returned to Ireland for the last time, and at the moment empty-handed. He was more than usually depressed in spirit. His stay at Court, he wrote, had been fruitless. Sullen care over- *Sheriff of Cork 1598.* whelmed him. Idle hopes flew away like empty shadows. None the less a change was wrought next year in his position in Ireland. He received the appointment of Sheriff of Cork in the autumn of 1598. The prefer- ment was of no enviable kind. It was an anxious and a thankless office to which Spenser was called. The difficulties of Irish government were at the moment reaching a crisis which was likely to involve Sheriffs of the South in personal peril. A great effort was in preparation on the part of the native Irish to throw off the tyrannous yoke of England, and a stout nerve and resolute action were required in all officers of state if the attack were to be successfully repulsed.

The first sign of the storm came in August 1598—a week before Spenser's formal instalment as Sheriff. In that month Ireland in the great leader of the native Irish, the Earl of rebellion. Tyrone, gathered an army together and met English troops at the Yellow Ford, on the Blackwater River, in County Tyrone, inflicting on them a complete defeat. That is the only occasion in English history on which Irishmen, meeting Englishmen in open battle, have proved themselves the conquerors. The old spirit of discontent, thus stimulated, rapidly spread to Spenser's neighbourhood. Tyrone sent some of his Irish soldiers into Munster, the whole province was roused, and County Cork was at their mercy. Panic seized the little English garrisons scattered over the County. Spenser was taken unawares; the castle of Kilcolman was burnt over his head, and he, his wife, and four children fled with great difficulty to Cork. An inaccurate report spread at the time in London that one of his children perished in the flames. Spenser's position resembled that of many an English civilian at the outbreak in India of the Indian Mutiny, but he did not display the heroism or firm courage of those who were to follow him as guardians of the outposts of the British Empire. At Cork all that Spenser did was to send a brief note of the situation to the Queen, entreating her to show those caitiffs the terror of her wrath, and send over a force of ten thousand men, with sufficient cavalry, to extirpate them.

In December the President of Munster, Sir Thomas Norreys, an old friend of the poet, sent him over to London to deliver despatches to the Government. It was his last journey. His health was fatally ruined by the shock of the rebellion, and he reached London only to die. He found shelter in an inn or lodging in King Street, Westminster, and there he died on Saturday, 16th January, 1599. He was in the prime of life—hardly more than forty-seven years old—but his choice spirit could not withstand the buffetings of so desperate a crisis.

His last mission to London.

Rumour ran that Spenser died in Westminster, 'for lack of bread,' in a state of complete destitution. It is said that the Earl of Essex, his host in London of three years back, learned of his distressful condition too late, and that, just before the poet breathed his last, the Earl sent him twenty pieces of silver, which Spenser refused with the grim remark that he had no time to spend them. The story is probably exaggerated. Spenser came to London as a Queen's messenger; he was in the enjoyment of a pension, and though his life was a long struggle with poverty, mainly through unbusinesslike habits, it is unlikely that he was without necessaries on his death-bed. It is more probable that he died of nervous prostration than of starvation.[1]

His death.

At any rate Spenser had friends in London, and they, when he was dead, accorded him a fitting burial. Westminster Abbey, the National Church, where the sovereigns

---

[1] Nevertheless the belief that he had been harshly used long survived. John Weever, in an epigram published in the year of Spenser's death, declared:—

'Spenser is ruined, of our latest time
The fairest ruin, Faeries foulest want.'

The author of the *Return from Parnassus* asserts that in his last hours 'maintenance' was denied him by an ungrateful country. A later disciple, Phineas Fletcher, in his *Purple Island*, wrote of Spenser:—

'Poorly, poor man, he lived; poorly, poor man, he died.'

of the country were wont to find their last earthly home,

His burial. became Spenser's final resting-place. The choice
of such a sepulchre was notable testimony to his
poetical repute. The Abbey had not yet acquired its ' Poets'
Corner' in its southern transept. It was Spenser's interment
which practically inaugurated that noble chamber of death.
Only one great man of letters had been buried there
already. Chaucer had been laid in the southern transept
two hundred years before, not apparently in his capacity of
poet, but as officer of the King's royal household, all
members of which had some vague title to burial near their
royal masters. It was not until the middle of the sixteenth
century, when Chaucer's title to be reckoned the father of
great English poetry was first acknowledged, that an admirer
sought and obtained permission to raise a monument to his
memory near his grave. The episode stirred the imagination
of the Elizabethans, and when death claimed Spenser, who
called Chaucer master, and who was reckoned the true
successor to Chaucer's throne of English poetry, a sentiment
spread abroad that he who was so nearly akin to Chaucer by
force of poetic genius ought of right to sleep near his tomb.
Accordingly in fitting pomp Spenser's remains were interred
beneath the shadow of the elder poet's monument.[1] The
Earl of Essex, the favourite of the Queen, who honoured
Spenser with unqualified enthusiasm, and despite his wayward-
ness in politics never erred in his devotion to the Muses,
defrayed the expenses of the ceremony. Those who
attended the obsequies were well chosen. In the procession

[1] The propriety of the honour thus accorded to Spenser is crudely but
emphatically acknowledged by the author of the *Pilgrimage to Parnassus*,
1600, where the critic of contemporary literature, Ingenioso, after lamenting
the sad circumstances of Spenser's death, adds :—

' But softly may our honour's [*var. lect.* Homer's] ashes rest,
That lie by merry Chaucer's noble chest.'

of mourners walked, we are told, the poets of the day, and
when the coffin was lowered these loving admirers of their
great colleague's work threw into his tomb 'poems and
mournful elegies with the pens that wrote them.' Little
imagination is needed to conjure up among those who paid
homage to Spenser's spirit the glorious figure of Shakespeare,
by whom alone of contemporaries Spenser was outshone.

It was welcome to the Queen herself that Spenser, the
greatest of her poetic panegyrists, should receive due
honour in death.   There is reason to believe that The tomb
she claimed the duty of erecting a monument in Westminster
above his grave.   But the pecuniary misfortunes Abbey.
which had dogged Spenser in life seemed to hover about
him after death.   The royal intention of honouring his
memory was defeated by the dishonesty of a royal servant.
The money which was allotted to the purpose by the Queen
was nefariously misapplied.   Ultimately, twenty-one years
after Spenser's death, a monument was erected at the cost
of a noble patroness of poets, Ann Clifford, Countess of
Dorset.   The inscription ran :—'Here lyes expecting the
second comminge of our Saviour Christ Jesus, the body of
Edmond Spencer, the Prince of Poets in his tyme, whose
divine spirit needs noe other witnesse than the workes
which he left behind him.'   Spenser was rightfully named
prince of the realm of which Shakespeare was king.
Although Shakespeare was not buried at Westminster,
Spenser's tomb was soon encircled by the graves of other
literary heroes of his epoch, and in course of time a
memorial statue of Shakespeare overlooked it.   Three of
Spenser's contemporaries, Francis Beaumont, Michael Drayton, and Ben Jonson, were within a few years interred near
him in the Abbey.

Time dealt unkindly with the fabric of Spenser's monument, and in the eighteenth century it needed renovating 'in durable marble.' But it was Spenser's funeral rites that permanently ensured for literary eminence the loftiest dignity of sepulture that the English nation has to bestow. Great literature was thenceforth held to rank with the greatest achievements wrought in the national service. During the last two centuries few English poets of supreme merit have been denied in death admission to the national sanctuary in the neighbourhood of Spenser's tomb. Those who have been buried elsewhere have been, like Shakespeare, commemorated in Westminster Abbey by sculptured monuments.

x

In practical affairs Spenser's life was a failure. It ended in a somewhat sordid tragedy, which added nothing to his political reputation. His literary work stands on a very different footing. Its steady progress in varied excellences was a ceaseless triumph for art. It won him immortal fame.

Spenser's greatness. Spenser's chief work, the *Faerie Queene*, was the greatest poem that had been written in England since Chaucer died, and remains, when it is brought into comparison with all that English poets have written since, one of the brightest jewels in the crown of English poetry. It is worthy of closest study. Minute inquiry into its form and spirit is essential to every estimate of Spenser's eminence.

In all senses the work is great. The scale on which Spenser planned his epic allegory has indeed no parallel

The amplitude of scale. in ancient or modern literature. All that has reached us is but a quarter of the contemplated whole. Yet the *Faerie Queene* is, in its extant shape, as long as Homer's *Iliad* and *Odyssey* combined with Virgil's *Æneid*. Even epics of more recent date, whose

example Spenser confesses to have emulated, fell far behind
his work in its liberality of scale. In the unfinished form
that it has come down to us, Spenser's epic is more than
twice as long as Dante's *La Divina Commedia,* or Tasso's
Gerusalemme Liberata. Ariosto's *Orlando Furioso,* with which
Spenser was thoroughly familiar, was brought to completion
in somewhat fewer lines. Nor did Spenser's great successors compete with him in length. Milton's *Paradise
Lost,* the greatest of all English epics, fills, when joined to
its sequel *Paradise Regained,* less than a third of Spenser's
space. Had the *Faerie Queene* reached a twenty-fourth
book, as the poet at the outset thought possible, not all
the great epics penned in ancient or modern Europe would,
when piled one upon the other, have reached the gigantic
dimensions of the Elizabethan poem.

The serious temper and erudition of which the enterprise
was the fruit powerfully impress the inquirer at the outset.
It is doubtful if Milton and Gray, who are usually reckoned
the most learned of English poets, excelled Spenser in the
range of their reading, or in the extent to which their poetry
assimilated the fruits of their study. Homer and Assimila-
Theocritus, Virgil and Cicero, Petrarch and Du tive power.
Bellay, mediæval writers of chivalric romance, Tasso and
Ariosto, supply ideas, episodes, and phrases to the *Faerie
Queene.* Early in life Spenser came under the spell of Tasso,
the monarch of contemporary Italian poetry, and gathered
much suggestion from his ample store. But the *Faerie Queene*
owes most to the epic of *Orlando Furioso* by Tasso's predecessor, Ariosto. The chivalric adventures which Spenser's
heroes undergo are often directly imitated from the Italian of
'that most famous Tuscan pen.' Many an incident, together
with the moralising which its details suggest, follows Ariosto
in phraseology too closely to admit any doubt of its source.
Spenser is never a plagiarist. He invests his borrowings

with his own individuality.   But very numerous are the
passages which owed their birth to Ariosto's preceding
invention.   The Italian poet is rich in imagery.   He drank
deep of the Pierian spring.   He is indeed superior to
Spenser in the conciseness and directness of his narrative
power.   But Ariosto has little of the warmth of human
sympathy or moral elevation which dignifies Spenser's effort.
Spenser's tone is far more serious than that of the Italian
master, whose main aim was the telling of an exciting tale.
Ariosto is far inferior to Spenser in the sustained energy
alike of his moral and of his poetic impulse.

The *Faerie Queene* was not designed, like Ariosto's achievement, as a mere piece of art.   It was before all else a moral
The   treatise.   Although it was fashioned on the epic
moral aim.   lines with which constant reading of the work
of Homer and Virgil among the ancients, and more especially of Ariosto and Tasso among the moderns, had made
Spenser familiar, Spenser was not content merely to tell
a story.   According to the poet's own account, he sought
'to represent all the moral virtues, Holiness, Temperance,
Chastity, and the like, assigning to every virtue a knight to
be the pattern and defender of the same ; in whose actions
and feats of arms and chivalry the operations of that
virtue, whereof he is the protector, are to be expressed,
and the vices and unruly appetites that oppose themselves
against the same to be beaten down and overcome.'   Twelve
books, one for each moral virtue, were needed for such an
exposition of ethical philosophy.   But this was only the
first step in the poet's contemplated journey.   The author
looked forward to supplementing this ethical effort by
an exposition of political philosophy, in another twelve
books which would expound the twelve political virtues
that were essential to a perfect ruler of men.   Of the

twenty-four projected books there is a tradition that Spenser wrote twelve, nearly half of which were destroyed in manuscript by the rebels in Ireland. It is certain that only the first six books, with a small portion of the seventh, have reached us.

Spenser's ethical views are not systematically developed, but, considered in their main aspect, they owe an immense debt to the Greek philosopher Plato. Plato's The debt ethical teaching glows in page after page of the to Plato. *Faerie Queene* and of Spenser's shorter poems. The English poet loyally accepts Plato's doctrines that true beauty is only of the mind, that reason is the sole arbiter of man's destiny, that war must be waged on the passions and the bodily senses, that peace and happiness are the fruit of the intellect when it is enfranchised of corporeal infirmity. 'All happy peace and goodly government' are only 'settled in sure establishment'

> ' In a body which doth freely yield
> His parts to reason's rule obedient,
> And letteth her that ought the sceptre wield.' [1]

But it is not merely in his general ethical tone that Spenser acknowledges his discipleship to Plato. Many details of the *Faerie Queene* embody Platonic terminology and Platonic conceptions. In book III. he borrows from Plato the conception of 'the garden of Adonis,'—Nature's nursery—and under that image he presents Plato's theory of the infinite mutability of matter, despite its indestructibility. Infinite shapes of creatures are bred, Spenser points out, 'in that same garden' wherewith the world is replenished,

> ' Yet is the stock not lessened, nor spent,
> But still remains in everlasting store,
> As it at first created was of yore.' [2]

---

[1] Bk. II., canto xi., stanza ii.   Bk. III., canto vi., stanza xxxvi.

In book II. Spenser describes the threefold elements which go to the making of man's soul: right reason (Medina), the passion of wrath (Elissa), and the passion of sensual desire (Perissa). Although the poet here recalls the doctrine of Plato's great disciple, Aristotle, to the effect that virtue is the golden mean between excess and defect, he actually accepts the older Platonic principle that virtue is the mean between two equally active and powerful evil passions. Occasionally Spenser ranges himself with later Greek philosophers, who developed and exaggerated Plato's doctrine of the eternal spirit's supremacy over mutable matter. But Plato is always his foremost teacher, not only in the *Faerie Queene* but in his sonnets, in his rapturous hymns of beauty, and in much else of his occasional poetry.

In fulfilment of his ethical purpose the poet imagined twelve knights, each the champion of one of 'the private moral virtues' of Greek philosophy, who should undertake perilous combats with vice in various shapes. The first and second champions,—respectively, the knight of the Red Cross, or of Holiness, and Sir Guyon, the knight of Temperance,—embody with singular precision Platonic doctrine. The third champion, a more original conception, was a woman, Britomart, the lady-knight of Chastity; the fourth was Cambell, who, joined with Triamond, illustrates the worth of Friendship; the fifth was Artegal, the knight of Justice; the sixth, Sir Calidore, the knight of Courtesy. Spenser intended that his seventh knight should be champion of Constancy, but of that story only a fragment survives. Sir Calidore is the last completed hero in the poet's gallery.

Spenser's Knights of the Virtues.

The allegorised adventures in which Spenser's knights engage are cast for the most part in the true epic mould. Episode after episode reads like chapters of chivalric romance of adventure. Rescues of innocent ladies by the

knights from the persecutions of giant villains constantly
recur.   Fiercely-fought encounters with monsters   Affinities
of hateful mien abound.   Spenser indeed employs   with
chivalric
this machinery of chivalric conflict with a fre-   romance.
quency that leaves the impression of monotony.   The charge
of tediousness which has often been brought against the
Faerie Queene is not easy to repel when it is levelled against
Spenser's descriptions of his valiant heroes' physical perils.[1]

But there is much else in the poem to occupy the reader's
mind.   Spenser's design would have failed to satisfy the
primary laws of epic had he allowed it to hinge alone
on isolated adventures of virtuous knights, of knights
who pursued their career independently of one
another.   From the epic point of view there was   The Queen
and Prince
urgent need of welding together the separate   Arthur.
episodes.   Great as is the place they fill in the story, the
chivalric types of the moral virtues are, consequently, not its
only protagonists.   With a view to investing the whole
theme with homogeneity and unity the poet introduced two
supreme beings, a heroine and a hero, to whom the other
characters are always subsidiary.   Each knight is the subject
of a female monarch, the Faerie Queene, in whose person
flourish all human excellences.   She is the worthy object of
every manner of chivalric adoration, and in her name all
chivalric deeds are wrought.   In this royal quintessence of
virtue Spenser, with courtier-like complacency, idealised his

---

[1] Macaulay's denunciation of the monotony of the poem is well known.
In his essay on Bunyan he writes :—'Of the persons who read the first canto,
not one in ten reaches the end of the first book, and not one in a hundred
perseveres to the end of the poem.   Very few and very weary are those who
are in at the end, at the death of the Blatant Beast.'   This criticism only
seems just with qualifications, and it is impaired by the inaccuracy of its
final words.   The Blatant Beast, which typifies the spirit of malice, does
not die in the sixth and last completed book in which it plays its stirring
part.   The knight of Courtesy, Sir Calidore, makes captive of the monster, but
it ultimately escapes its chains, and in the concluding stanzas is described as
ranging through the world again without restraint.

own sovereign, Queen Elizabeth. But the queen of the poem is not quite isolated in her pre-eminence. The knights owe allegiance to another great prince—to Prince Arthur, in whom the twelve private moral virtues are all combined. Prince Arthur presents Aristotle's philosophical idea of magnanimity, the human realisation of moral perfectibility. This perfect type of mankind was, according to Spenser's design, to intervene actively in the development of the plot. He was to meet with each of the twelve knights when they were hard pressed by their vicious foes, and by his superior powers to rescue each in turn from destruction. Nor were these labours to exhaust the prince's function in the machinery of the poem. He was not merely to act as the providence of the knights. He was allotted a romance of his own. He was in quest of a fated bride, and she was no other than the Faerie Queene.

The ground-plan of the great poem proved somewhat unwieldy. The singleness of scheme at which Spenser aimed in subordinating his virtuous knights to two higher powers, the Faerie Queene and Prince Arthur, was hardly attained. The links which were invented to bind the books together proved hardly strong enough to bear the strain. The poet's 'endeavours after variety' conquer his efforts at unity. Each of the extant books might, despite all the author's efforts, be easily mistaken for an independent poem. The whole work may fairly be described as a series of epic poems very loosely bound one to another. It is scarcely an organic whole. The amplitude of scale on which the work was planned, the munificence of detail which burdens each component part, destroys in the reader the sense of epic unity.

Want of homogeneity.

It was hardly possible to obey strictly all the principles of epic art while serving an allegorical purpose, and from that allegorical purpose Spenser never consciously departs. He announced in his opening invocation to Clio his intention to 'moralise' his song, and he frequently reminds his reader of his resolve. His heroes and heroines are not, as in the writings of Spenser's epic tutors, mere creatures of flesh and blood, in whose material or spiritual fortune the reader's interest is to be excited. In the poet's mind they are always moving abstractions which illustrate the moral laws that sway human affairs. Truth, Falsehood, Hypocrisy, Mammon, Pride, Wantonness, are the actors and actresses on Spenser's stage. The scenery is not inanimate nature, nor dwellings of brick and stone. The curtain rises now on the Bower of Bliss; now on the Cave of Despair; now on the House of Temperance. The poet seeks to present a gigantic panorama of the moral dangers and difficulties that beset human existence.

The allegorical intention.

To manipulate a long-drawn allegory so as to concentrate the reader's attention on its significance, and to keep his interest at all seasons thoroughly alive is a difficult task. The restraints which are imposed by the sustained and prolonged pursuit of analogies between the moral and material worlds are especially oppressive to the spirit of a poet who is gifted with powers of imagination of infinite activity. In his capacity of worker in allegory Spenser falls as far short of perfection as in his capacity of worker in epic. Only one Englishman contrived a wholly successful allegory. Spenser was not he. John Bunyan, in the *Pilgrim's Progress,* alone among Englishmen possessed just that definite measure of imagination which enabled him to convert with absolute sureness personifications of virtues and vices into speaking likenesses of men and women and places. Bunyan's great exercise in the allegorical art is rarely disfigured by inconsistencies or incoherences. His scenes and persons—

Spenser and Bunyan compared.

Christian and Faithful, The House Beautiful and Vanity Fair
—while they are perfectly true to analogy,—are endowed
with intelligible and life-like features. The moral significance is never doubtful, while the whole picture leaves the
impression of a masterpiece of literary fiction.

Spenser's force of imagination was far wider than Bunyan's.
His culture and his power over language were infinitely
greater. But Spenser failed where Bunyan succeeded
through the defect of his qualities, through excess of
capacity, through the diversity of his interests, through the
discursiveness of his imagination. He had little of Bunyan's
singleness of purpose, simplicity of thought and faith, or
faculty of self-suppression. His poetic and intellectual ebul-
lience could not confine itself to the comparatively narrow
and direct path, pursuit of which was essential to perfection
in allegory and won for Bunyan his unique triumph.

Spenser's interests in current life and his æsthetic temperament were, in fact, too alert to allow him to confine his
Influence　　efforts to the search after moral analogies. Strong
of his age.　　as was his moral sense, he was also thrall to his
passion for beauty. Few manifestations of beauty either in
nature or in art, which fell within his cognisance, could he pass
by in silence. He had drunk deep, too, of the ideals peculiar
to his own epoch. He was a close observer of the leading
events and personages of Elizabethan history, and in defiance
of the laws of allegory he wove into the web of his poetry many
personal impressions of contemporary personages and movements, which had no just home in a moral or philosophical
design of professedly universal application. Duessa, the
hateful witch of Falsehood, who endeavours to mislead the
Red Cross Knight of Holiness (bk. i.), and seeks another
victim in another knight, Sir Scudamore (bk. iv.), is no
universal pattern of vice; she is Spenser's interpretation

of the character of Mary, Queen of Scots.   Sir Artegal, the
Knight of Justice, is obviously a portrait of Arthur, Lord
Grey of Wilton, Lord Deputy of Ireland, whom Spenser
served as secretary.   Elsewhere there are undiguised refer-
ences to the poet's painful personal relation with Lord
Treasurer Burghley :—

> 'The rugged forehead, that with grave foresight,
>   Welds kingdom's causes and affairs of state.' [1]

Spenser laments that he had incurred this 'mighty peer's displeasure' by applying himself too exclusively to tales of
love (Bk. vi., canto xii., stanza xli.).   Queen Elizabeth herself constantly appears on the scene, and no halo of allegory
is suffered to encircle her.   Spenser addresses her in the key
of adulation which is a conventional note of the panegyric
of princes, but is altogether out of harmony with a broad
philosophic tone.   The Queen is apostrophised as the main
source of the poet's inspiration :—

> 'And thou, O fairest Princess under sky !
> In this fair mirror mayest behold thy face,
> And thine own realms in land of Fairy,
> And in this antique image thy great ancestry.' [2]

In another passage of the second book Prince Arthur and
the Knight of Temperance, Sir Guyon, peruse together two
old books called respectively *The Briton Moniments* and *The
Antiquity of Fairy* from which the poet pretends to draw a
chronicle of the old British kings.   He justifies the digres-
sion by a rapturous panegyric of 'my own sovereign queen,
thy realm and race,' who is descended

> 'From mighty kings and conquerors in war,
>   Thy fathers and great grandfathers of old,
>   Whose noble deeds above the Northern Star
>   Immortal fame for ever hath enrolled.' [3]

[1] Bk. iv., introd., stanza i.   [2] Bk. ii., introd., stanza iv.
[3] Bk. ii., canto x., stanza iv.

Nowhere does the fervid loyalty of the Elizabethan find more literal utterance than in Spenser's poem.

However zealous a worshipper at the shrine of 'divine philosophy,' Spenser was deeply moved by the peculiar aspirations which fired the age, and the prejudices which distorted its judgment. His resolve to preach morality that should be of universal application was not proof against such influences. The old blind woman in the first book, counting her beads and mumbling her nine hundred 'pater nosters' and nine hundred 'ave marias,' is a caricature of papistry. It is the fruit of the contemporary Protestant zeal which infected Spenser and his circle of friends. The current passion for exploring the New World moves the poet to note how every day—

> ' Through hardy enterprise
> Many great Regions are discovered,
> Which to late age were never mentioned.
> Who ever heard of th' Indian Peru ?
> Or who in venturous vessel measured
> The Amazon huge river, now found true ?
> Or fruitfullest Virginia who did ever view ? ' [1]

Identifying himself with a popular sentiment of the day, the poet lays stress on the enlightened argument that no limits can be set to the area over which man's energy and enterprise may yet gain sway :—

> ' Yet all these were, when no man did them know,
> Yet have from wisest ages hidden been ;
> And later times things more unknown shall show.
> Why then should witless man so much misween,
> That nothing is but that which he hath seen ? ' [2]

Such digressions and interpolations add greatly to the poem's charm and variety, but they interrupt the flow of the allegorical narrative and frankly ignore the allegorical design.

[1] Bk. ii., introd., stanza ii.   [2] Bk. ii., introd., stanza iii.

But it is not as a chivalric story nor as an allegory, it is not as an epic narrative nor as an ethical tractate, nor indeed is it as an exposition of Elizabethan ideals *The poetic* and sentiments, that Spenser's poem is to be *style.* finally judged. It is by its poetic style and spirit that it must be appraised. It is the fertility of the poet's imagination, the luxuriance of his pictorial imagery, his exceptional command of the music of words, which give the *Faerie Queene* its highest title to honour. Despite all his ethical professions and his patriotic zeal, it was to the muse of poetry alone that Spenser swore unswerving fealty. The spirit of his work may best be gauged by the opening stanza of his sixth and last completed book :—

'The ways through which my weary steps I guide
In this delightful land of Fairy,
Are so exceeding spacious and wide,
And sprinkled with such sweet variety
Of all that pleasant is to ear or eye,
That I, nigh ravished with rare thought's delight,
My tedious travel do forget thereby ;
And, when I gin to feel decay of might,
It strength to me supplies and cheers my dulled sprite.

Such secret comfort and such heavenly pleasures,
Ye sacred imps, that on Parnassus dwell,
And there the keeping have of learning's treasures
Which do all earthly riches far excel,
Into the minds of mortal men do well,
And goodly fury into them infuse ;
Guide ye my footing, and conduct me well,
In these strange ways, where never foot did use,
Ne none can find but who was taught them by the Muse.'

His quarry is 'all that pleasant is to ear or eye.' He dwells in ' that delightful land' where the 'sacred imps' of Parnassus infuse 'goodly fury' into the minds of mortal men. His conception of happiness is to be ' nigh ravished with rare thought's delight.' It is not study of religion or philosophy or politics that can cheer and strengthen his 'dulled sprite.' It is in the 'exceeding spacious and wide' realms of beauty, which are only accessible to the poet's imagination, that he finds 'heavenly pleasures.' Spenser abandoned himself recklessly to the pure spirit of poetry. Despite the diffuseness of utterance and lack of artistic restraint which were inevitable in so fervid a votary of the Muses, Spenser, in his *Faerie Queene*, gave being to as noble a gallery of sublime conceptions, as imposing a procession of poetic images, as ever came from the brain of man.

The form of Spenser's verse was admirably adapted to its purpose. It was his own invention, and is in itself striking testimony to the originality of his genius. The Spenserian stanza was ingeniously formed by adding an Alexandrine, a line in twelve syllables, to the eight ten-syllabled lines of the stanza which was popular in France under the name of 'Chant royal,' and in Italy under the name of 'ottava rima.' Undoubtedly there is in Spenser's metrical device a tendency to monotony and tediousness. Languor would seem to be an inevitable characteristic. Dr. Johnson complained that the stanza was 'tiresome to the ear by its uniformity, and to the attention by its length.' But Spenser's rare poetic instinct enabled him to hold such defect in check by variety in the pauses. In his hands the stanza is for the most part an instrument of sustained spirit, even though the closing Alexandrine imposes a gentle and leisurely pace on the progress of the verse. One stanza glides into the next with graceful, natural flow, and at times with rapidity. The movement has been compared, not perhaps quite appositely, to that of the magic gondola which Spenser describes in his account of the Lady of the Idle Lake; the vessel slides

The
Spenserian
stanza.

The flow of
the verse.

' More swift than swallow shears the liquid sky ;
    It cut away upon the yielding wave,
    Ne cared she her course for to apply ;
    For it was taught the way which she would have,
    And both from rocks and flats itself could wisely save.' [1]

Spenser does not altogether avoid 'rocks and flats.' Horace
Walpole called attention to a certain want of judgment in
devising a nine-line stanza in a language so barren of rhymes
as the English tongue, with only three different rhymes; of
these one is twice repeated, the second three times, and the
third four times. This rhyming difficulty was not capable
of complete mastery, and Spenser's rhyming failures are not
inconspicuous. There are in every canto some stanzas in
which an awkward strain is put, by the exigencies of rhyme,
on the laws of syntax, prosody, and even good sense. But
the great passages of the poem are singularly free from
irregularities of metre, and fascinate us by the dexterity of
the rhymes. In view of the massive proportions of the work,
Spenser's metrical success moves almost boundless admiration. In the Spenserian stanza, as Spenser handled it, are,
if anywhere, 'the elegancy, facility, and golden cadence of
poetry.' [2]

[1] Bk. ii., canto vi., stanza v.

[2] Every canto offers examples of carelessness. Turning to bk. iv.,
canto ii., we find Spenser in a single stanza (xxxiii.) rhyming 'waste' with
'defaced' (which is spelt 'defaste' in order to cover up the irregularity);
'writs' for purposes of rhyme are used for 'writings,' and the closing
Alexandrine sinks to such awkward tautology as this :—

> 'Sith works of heavenly wits
> Are quite devoured, *and brought to naught by little bits.*'
>
>> (Stanza xxxiii.)

In stanza lii. the Alexandrine again offends :—

> 'That both their lives may likewise be annext
> Unto the third, that his may so be trebly wext.'

The last stanza of the canto ends lamely and with burlesque effect, thus :—

> 'The which, for length, I will not here pursew,
> But rather will reserve it for a Canto new.'
>
>> (Stanza liv).

Spenser in the *Faerie Queene,* as in his earliest poetic effort, *The Shepheards Calender,* deliberately used a vocabu-
The
vocabulary. lary that was archaic for its own day. Many contemporary critics were doubtful of his wisdom. The poet Daniel, who fully recognised Spenser's genius, deemed his meaning needlessly obscured by 'aged accents and untimely (*i.e.* obsolete) words.' But a tendency to preciosity, a predilection for the unfamiliar, a passion for what was out of date, were characteristic of Spenser's faculty. Archaic language lent, in his view, the beauty of mellowness to his work and removed it from the rawness or 'wearisome turmoil' of current speech.

It was his filial devotion to Chaucer which mainly kept alive Spenser's love for archaisms of speech. Chaucer's
The debt
to Chaucer. verse had from earliest days lingered in his memory, and he occasionally quotes lines of his predecessor word for word.[1] In book iv. canto ii., he completes the Squire's Tale, which in Chaucer's text was left unfinished. Spenser fulfils Chaucer's promise to tell of the chivalric contests in which suitors for the hand of the fair Canace engaged. This episode was preluded in the *Faerie Queene* by a splendid invocation to his master, to revive whose 'English undefiled' was one of his primary ambitions.

---

[1] With Spenser's

> 'Ne may Love be compelled by mastery :
> For soon as mastery comes, sweet Love anon
> Taketh his nimble wings, and soon away is gone.'
> > (Bk. iii., canto i., stanza xxv.)

compare Chaucer's

> 'Love wolle not be constreyn'd by maistery ;
> When maistery cometh, the God of Love anone
> Betith his winges, and farewell he is gone.
> > (*Franklin's Tale,* lines 2310-2.)

' Dan Chaucer, well of English undefiled,
On fame's eternal beadroll worthy to be filed.

.   .   .   .   .

Then pardon, O most sacred happy spirit !
That I thy labours lost may thus revive,
And steal from thee the meed of thy due merit,
That none durst ever whilst thou wast alive,
And being dead in vain yet many strive :
Ne dare I like ; but, through infusion sweet
Of thine own spirit which doth in me survive,
I follow here the footing of thy feet,
That with thy meaning so I may the rather meet.' [1]

Spenser's artistic nature was many-sided. Plato's idealism,
equally with Chaucer's homely gaiety and insight,
moulded his mind. But his varied knowledge
of literature and philosophy went hand in hand
with a different type of endowment—a sensuous sensitiveness
to external aspects of nature.

His sensi-
tiveness to
beauty.

' Every sight
And sound from the vast earth and ambient air
Sent to his heart its choicest impulses.'

Especially perfect is the art with which he depicts fountains
and rivers and oceans.   The magical canto in which he
describes the marriage of the river Thames with the river
Medway is rich alike in classical allusion and intimate knowledge of British topography.   But the varied learning is
fused together by an exuberance of pictorial fancy and
sympathy with natural scenery, which give individuality to
almost every stream that may have come within the poet's
cognisance either in literature or in life.   Spenser's power
as the poet of nature owes its finest quality to his rare
genius for echoing in verse the varied sounds which natural
phenomena produce in the observer's ear.   When he represents a gentle flowing river, the metre glides with a corresponding placidity.   When he describes a tempestuous wind,

_____
[1] Bk. iv., canto ii., stanzas xxxii. and xxxiv.

the words rush onwards with an unmistakable roar. In the familiar stanzas which follow we hear in living harmonies the voices of the birds :—

> ' Eftsoones they heard a most melodious sound,
> Of all that mote delight a dainty ear,
> Such as at once might not on living ground,
> Save in the Paradise, be heard elsewhere :
> Right hard it was for wight which did it hear,
> To read what manner music that mote be,
> For all that pleasing is to living ear
> Was there consorted in one harmony ;
> Birds, voices, instruments, winds, waters, all agree.
>
> The joyous birds, shrouded in cheerful shade
> Their notes unto the voice attempred sweet ;
> Th' Angelical soft trembling voices made
> To th' instruments divine respondence meet ;
> The silver sounding instruments did meet
> With the base murmurs of the waters fall ;
> The waters fall with difference discreet,
> Now soft, now loud, unto the wind did call ;
> The gentle warbling wind low answered to all.' [1]

Spenser did not depict physical beauty in men or women with quite the same abandonment that he brought to the sights and sounds of earth or air. But although Spenser studied as thoroughly as any poet the aspects of physical beauty—' the goodly hue of white and red with which the cheeks are sprinkled '—his philosophic idealism would seldom allow him to content himself with the outward appearance. To him as to Plato the fair body was merely the external expression of an inner spiritual or ideal beauty, which it was the duty of reasoning man to worship :—

> ' So every spirit, as it is most pure
> And hath in it the more of heavenly light,
> So it the fairer body doth procure
> To habit in, and is more fairly dight
> With cheerful grace and amiable sight,

---

[1] Bk. II., canto xii., stanzas lxx.-lxxi.

For of the soul the body form doth take,
For soul is form, and doth the body make.' [1]

Spenser's influence on the poetic endeavours of his own age
was very great. Imitations of his allegorical method abounded,
and one at least of his disciples, Phineas Fletcher, Spenser's
produced in his *Purple Island* an elaborate alle- influence.
gorical description of the human body, a poem which,
despite its defects and dependence on the *Faerie Queene,*
does no dishonour to its source. Charles Lamb justly
called Spenser 'the poet's poet.' Probably no poem is qualified equally with the *Faerie Queene* to endow the seeds of poetic
genius in youthful minds with active life. Cowley's confession is capable of much pertinent illustration in the biography
of other poets. 'I believe,' wrote Cowley, 'I can tell the
particular little chance that filled my head first with such
chimes of verse as have never since left ringing there; for I
remember, when I began to read and take some pleasure in
it, there was wont to lie in my mother's parlour (I know not
by what accident, for she herself never in her life read any
book but of devotion); but there was wont to lie Spenser's
Works; this I happened to fall upon, and was infinitely
delighted with the stories of the knights and giants, and
monsters, and brave horses which I found everywhere there
(though my understanding had little to do with all this);
and by degrees with the tinkling of the rhyme and dance of
the numbers, so that I had read him all before I was twelve
years old, and was thus made a poet.'

The variety of Spenser's excellences caused his work to
appeal in different ways to different men. The
boy Cowley was fascinated by his chivalric tales of his excel-
of wonder and the ringing harmony of his verse. lences.
Milton was chiefly impressed by the profundity of his ideal

---

[1] *An Hymne in Honour of Beautie,* ll. 127-133.

philosophy; Bunyan by his moral earnestness. Dryden did homage to him as his master in poetic speech, although he deemed his learning his crowning merit. In the eighteenth century the impulse to poetic effort which was inherent in his writings showed no sign of decay. James Thomson and Robert Burns, Shelley and Keats, Byron and Campbell, worked with varying skill in the Spenserian stanza, and, by the uses to which they put their master's metrical instrument, added to the masterpieces of English poetry. The poems penned in the stanza of the *Faerie Queene* include the *Cotter's Saturday Night* by Burns, the *Eve of St. Agnes* by Keats, and *Childe Harold* by Byron, and all reflect glory on the stanza's inventor. But Spenser's work is an inexhaustible fountain of poetic inspiration, and none can define the limits of its influence.

FRANCIS BACON, VISCOUNT ST. ALBAN.

From the portrait by Paul Van Somer in the National Portrait Gallery.

VI

FRANCIS BACON

'The mind is the man. . . . A man is but what he knoweth.'
BACON, *Praise of Knowledge*, 1592.

[BIBLIOGRAPHY.—Bacon's life and work may be studied in full in the *Life and Letters*, by James Spedding, 7 vols., 1861-74, and in the *Works*, edited by J. Spedding, R. L. Ellis, and D. D. Heath, 7 vols., 1857-9. The best summary of his life and work is *Francis Bacon, an Account of his Life and Works*, by the Rev. E. A. Abbott, D.D., 1885. The text of his chief English writings was published in a convenient volume, at a small price, by George Newnes, Limited, in 1902. Of modern annotated reprints of the *Essays*, those edited respectively by Dr. Abbott (1879), and by Samuel Harvey Reynolds (Clarendon Press, 1890), are most worthy of study. A valuable *Harmony of the Essays*—the text of the four chief editions in parallel columns — was prepared by Professor Edward Arber in 1869. The *Advancement of Learning* was edited by Dr. Aldis Wright for the Clarendon Press in the same year.]

I

WE now approach the highest but one of the peaks of intellectual greatness which were scaled in England by sons of the Renaissance. Spenser was a great poet and moralist, one who sought to teach men morality by means of poetry, one who could weave words into harmonious sequence, one who could draw music from ordinary speech, with a sureness of touch that only two or three men in the world's history—Virgil, perhaps, alone among the classical poets, and Milton most conspicuously among the modern poets—have excelled.

An ascending scale of greatness.

But if we deduct Spenser's æsthetic power and moral enthusiasm from the sum of his achievement, if we turn to measure the calibre of Spenser's intellect or the width of his mental horizon, if we estimate the extent by which he advanced human thought beyond the limits that human thought had already commanded, we cannot fail to admit (difficult as any precise comparison may be) that Bacon, with whom I now deal, is Spenser's intellectual superior.

Not that Bacon himself is the highest peak in the range of sixteenth-century English enlightenment. Giant as Bacon was in the realm of mind, in the empire of human intellect, Shakespeare, his contemporary, manifested an intellectual capacity that places Bacon himself in the second place.

From every point of view the interval that separates Bacon from Shakespeare is a wide one. An illogical tendency has of late years developed in undisciplined minds to detect in Bacon and Shakespeare a single personality. One has heard of brains which, when subjected to certain excitements, cause their possessors to see double, to see two objects when only one is in view; but it is equal proof of unstable, unsteady intellectual balance which leads a man or woman to see single, to see one individuality when they are in the presence of two individualities, each definite and distinct. The intellect of both Shakespeare and Bacon may well be termed miraculous. The facts of biography may be unable to account for the emergence of the one or the other, but they can prove convincingly that no two great minds of a single era pursued literary paths more widely dissevered. To assume, without an iota of sound evidence, that both Shakespeare's and Bacon's intellect were housed in a single brain is unreal mockery. It is an irresponsibly fantastic dream which lies outside the limits of reason.

Bacon's and Shakespeare's distinct individualities.

II

The accessible details of Bacon's biography are more numerous and more complicated than in the case of Shakespeare, or any other writer of the age.   His life, intellectually and materially, is fuller of known incident ; his writings are more voluminous ; his

The study of Bacon's life and work.

extant letters and private memoranda are more accessible. His work is noble ; his life is ignoble.   But in order to understand his intricate character, in order fully to appreciate his psychological interest, in order fully to appreciate his place in the history of literature and science, both his biography and his work demand almost equally close study.

Bacon came of no mean stock.   His father, Sir Nicholas Bacon, was Lord Keeper of the Great Seal, the chief Law Officer of England, who exercised the authority of Lord High Chancellor.   Sir Nicholas was thus

Bacon's parents.

a successor of Sir Thomas More.   He was of a merry, easygoing disposition, with a pronounced love of literature and a gift of eloquent speech.   He freely and without compunction engaged in the political intrigue which infected the queen's court, and made no greater pretence than his contemporaries to superfine political virtue.   Bacon's mother, his father's second wife, was a woman of paradoxical character.   Her great learning and scholarship were of the true Renaissance type ; she was at home in most of the classical and post-classical authors of Greece and Rome.   But her main characteristic was a fiery religious zeal.   She belonged to the narrowest and least amiable sect of the Calvinists, and her self-righteous temper led her to rule her household and her children with a crabbed rigour that did not diminish with age.   In feature Bacon closely resembled his stern-complexioned mother, and although her sour pietism did not descend to him, her love of literature, as well as the resolute self-esteem which her creed harboured in her, was woven into the web of his character. Lady Bacon was highly connected : her sister married Lord Burghley, Queen Elizabeth's powerful Treasurer and Prime Minister. The Prime Minister of the day therefore stood to Bacon in the relation of uncle.

Bacon thus began life with great advantages. He was son of the Lord Chancellor and nephew of the Prime Minister. It is difficult in England to be more influentially related. His family was not rich, but it was reasonably provided for. As far as social position went, he could not have been better placed.

His advantage of birth.

Francis Bacon was born in 1561 at his father's official residence in London, York House in the Strand, of which the water-gate alone survives. Queen Elizabeth had come to the throne three years before. Shakespeare was born three years after. When he was a child, before he was thirteen, Bacon was sent, as the custom then was, to a university—to Trinity College, Cambridge, a recently founded institution which was even then acquiring great educational traditions. He was there for two years, and at the age of fifteen returned to London to study law.

Birth and education.

Bacon was an extraordinarily thoughtful boy, full of great ambitions, all lying within a well-defined compass. He wished to be a great man, to do work by which he might be remembered, to do work that should be beneficial to the human race. With that self-confidence which he owed to his mother, he judged himself to be, almost from childhood, capable of improving man's reasoning faculties; of extending the range of man's knowledge, especially his knowledge of natural science and the causes of natural phenomena. When his father first brought him to court as a boy, the queen was impressed by his thoughtful demeanour, and laughingly dubbed him, in allusion to his

His precocity.

father's office, her 'young Lord Keeper.' It is difficult to
match in history—even in the fertile epoch of the Renaissance—either Bacon's youthful precocity, or the closeness
and fidelity with which he kept before his mind through life
the ambitions which he formed in youth.

III

Three impressionable years of Bacon's youth—from his
fifteenth to his eighteenth year—were spent at the English
Embassy in Paris in the capacity of a very junior secretary.
The experience widened his outlook on life and gave him a
first taste of diplomacy. But his father had destined Francis
for his own profession of law, and the lad returned to England
to follow his father's wishes. He worked at his   The profes-
profession with industry. But it excited in him no   sion of law.
enthusiasm. He regarded it as a means to an end. His father
died when Francis was eighteen. His example endowed the
lad with the belief that intrigue was the key to worldly
prosperity. A very narrow income was his only tangible
bequest. But a competence, an ample supply of money, was
needful if Bacon were to achieve those advances in science, if
he were to carry to a successful issue those high resolves to
extend the limit of human knowledge which he held to be his
mission in life. ' He knew himself,' he repeatedly   His
declared, ' to be fitter to hold a book than to play   idealism.
a part on the active stage of affairs.' For affairs he said he
was not ' fit by Nature and more unfit by the preoccupation
of his mind.' Yet he did not hesitate to seek early admission to ' the active stage of affairs.' His nature was so framed
that he felt it his duty to devote himself to work in the world
in which he felt no genuine interest, in order to   His
acquire that worldly fortune, that worldly position   materialism.
and worldly influence without which he regarded it to be

impossible to carry into effect his intellectual ambition, his intellectual mission. Never were materialism and idealism woven so firmly together into the texture of a man's being. ' I cannot realise the great ideal,' he said in effect, ' which I came into the world and am qualified to reach, unless I am well off and influential in the merely material way.' The inevitable sequel was the confession that much of his life was misspent ' in things for which he was least fit, so, as I may truly say, my soul hath been a stranger in the course of my pilgrimage.'

The profession of the law had prizes which he hoped that the influence of his uncle, the Prime Minister, might open to him. But Lord Burghley, unlike English officers of state of later periods, was not always eager to aid his relatives, and Bacon's early hopes of legal preferment were not fulfilled. However, when Bacon was twenty-three, his uncle did so much service for him as to secure for him a seat in Parliament. He entered the House of Commons in 1584, and he remained a member of the House for more than thirty years. A lawyer in England often finds it extremely advantageous to himself in the material sense to identify himself with politics at the same time as he practises at the bar. This plan Bacon readily adopted. He at once flung himself into the discussion of the great political questions of the day in the same spirit as that in which he approached the profession of the law. At all hazards he must advance himself, he must build up a material fortune. If the intellectual work to which he was called were to be done at all, no opportunity of securing the material wherewithal was he justified in rejecting. That is the principle which inspired Bacon's attitude to politics as well as to law ; that is the principle which inspired every action of his life outside the walls of his study.

His entrance into politics.

Naturally as a politician he became an opportunist. His intellectual abilities enabled him to form enlightened views of political questions, views in advance of his age. His attitude But his ideal was not in politics. His scheme of to politics. life compelled him to adapt his private views in politics to suit the views of those in authority, so as to gain advancement from them. In his early days in the House of Commons he sought to steer a middle course—his aim being so to express his genuine political opinions or convictions, which were wise in themselves, as to give them a chance of acceptance from those in authority. He urged on the Government the wisdom of toleration in matters of religion. Aggressive persecution of minorities appeared to him in his heart to be unstatesmanlike as well as inhuman. But he carefully watched the impression his views created. He was not prepared to sacrifice any chance of material advancement to his principles. If his own political views proved unacceptable to those who could help him on, he must substitute others with which the men of influence were in fuller sympathy.

Very methodical by nature, Bacon systematised as a young man practical rules of conduct on which he relied for the advancement of his material interests, and for the consequent acquisition of the opportunity His working scheme of working out his philosophical aims in the of life. interests of mankind. He drew up a series of maxims, a series of precepts for getting on, for bettering one's position—for the architecture, as he called it, of one's fortune. Of these precepts, which form a cynical comment on Bacon's character and on his conception of social intercourse, this much may be said in their favour,—that they get behind the screen of conventional hypocrisies. They are not wholly original. In spirit, at any rate, they resemble the unblushing counsel which Machiavelli, the Florentine statesman and historian

of the sixteenth century, offered to politicians.   The utility of
Machiavellian doctrines Bacon's father had acknowledged.
Machiavelli and his kind were among Bacon's heroes : ' We
are much beholden to Machiavelli and others,' he remarked
in the *Advancement of Learning*, 'that wrote what men do, not
what they ought to do.'   But Bacon's compendium of proverbial philosophy, whatever its debt to others, reveals his
individuality as clearly as anything to which he set his pen.

Bacon laid it down that the best way to enforce one's views
upon those in authority was by appearing to agree with
His   them, and by avoiding any declared disagree-
precepts.   ment with them.   'Avoid repulse,' he said ;
' never row against the stream.'   Practise deceit, dissimulation, whenever it can be made to pay, but at the same time
secure the reputation of being honest and outspoken.   'Have
openness in fame and repute, secrecy in habit; dissimulation in seasonable use, and a power to feign if there be no
remedy ; mixture of falsehood is like alloy in coin of gold
and silver which may make the metal work better.'   Always
show off your abilities to the best advantage ; always try to
do better than your neighbours.   But on none of his rules
of conduct does Bacon lay greater stress, than on the suggestion that the best and most rapid way of getting on is
The uses of   to accommodate oneself to the ways of great
great men.   men, to bind oneself hand and foot to great men.
This rule Bacon sought with varying success to put into
practice many times during his life.

IV

In 1591, when Bacon was thirty, a first opportunity of
coming advancement through intimate association with a
man of position seemed to present itself.   He obtained an
introduction to a young nobleman of great ambition and

no little influence, the Earl of Essex. He was Bacon's
junior by six years. He was as passionate and
impulsive a young gentleman as could be found
among Elizabethans, but he was not altogether
without consciousness of his own defects. He was not
blind to the worth of sobriety and foresight in others.
The cool and wary good sense of Bacon attracted him;
Bacon's abilities impressed him. Bacon deliberately planned
his relationship with Essex to secure his own preferment.
He attached himself to Essex, he said, 'in a manner which
happeneth rarely among men.' He would do the best he
could with him in all ways. Essex might prove a fit instrument to do good to the State as well as to himself. He
would persuade Essex to carry through certain political
reforms which required great personal influence to bring
them to the serious notice of the authorities. At the same
time Essex was either to secure for his mentor dignified and
remunerative office, or to be swept out of his path.

The first episode of the partnership was not promising.
The high legal office of Attorney-General fell vacant.
Bacon's enthusiastic patron, Essex, was readily
induced to apply for the post in Bacon's behalf.
But Essex met with a serious rebuff. A deaf ear was
turned by the queen and the Prime Minister to the proposal.
Essex was as disappointed as Bacon himself. He quixotically
judged himself in honour bound to compensate Bacon for the
loss. He gave him a piece of land at Twickenham, which
Bacon afterwards sold for £1800. For a moment this failure
daunted Bacon. After so discouraging an experience he
seriously considered with himself whether it were not wiser
for him altogether to forsake the law, the prizes in which
seemed beyond his reach, and devote himself entirely to the
scientific study which was his true end in life. It would

*Bacon's
relations
with Essex.*

*An un-
promising
opening.*

have been better for his fame had he yielded to the prompt-
ings of the inner voice. But he was in need of money.
With conscious misgivings he resolved to keep to the difficult
path on which he had embarked.

The outlook did not immediately grow brighter. Closer
acquaintance with Essex convinced Bacon that he was not
the man either to carry through any far-reaching
political reforms or to aid his own advancement.
He was proving himself captious and jealous-
tempered. He was not maintaining his hold upon the
queen's favour. Bacon energetically urged on him petty
tricks of conduct whereby he might win and retain the
queen's favour. He drew up a series of obsequious speeches
which would fit a courtier's lips and might convince a
sovereign that the man who spoke them to her deserved
her confidence.

*Essex dis-
appoints
Bacon.*

Finally Bacon sought a bold means of release from a
doubtful situation. He thoroughly appreciated the difficult
problem which the government of Ireland offered
Elizabethan statesmen, and he plainly told Essex
that Ireland was his destiny ; Ireland was 'one of
the aptest particulars for your Lordship to purchase
honour on.' Bacon steadily pressed his patron to seek the
embarrassing post of Governor or Lord-Deputy of the distracted country. The counsel took effect. The arduous
office was conferred on Essex. His patron's case, as it presented itself to Bacon's tortuous mind, was one of kill or
cure. Glory was to be gained by pacifying Ireland, by
bringing her under peaceful rule. Infamy, enforced withdrawal from public life, was the reward of failure. The
task was admittedly hard, and called for greater prudence
than any of which Essex had yet given signs. But Bacon,
from his point of view, thought it desirable that Essex should

*The govern-
ment of
Ireland.*

have the opportunity of achieving some definite triumph in life which would render his future influence supreme. Or if he were incapable of conspicuous success in life, then the more patent his inefficiency became, and the quicker he was set on one side, the better for his protégé's future.

Essex completely failed in Ireland, and he was ordered to answer for his conduct in the arbitrary Court of the Star Chamber. Thereupon Bacon set to work with Machiavellian skill to turn an apparently unpromising situation to his own advantage. He sought and obtained permission to appear at the inquiry into Essex's conduct as one of the Counsel for the Crown. He protested to the end that he was really working diplomatically in Essex's behalf, but he revealed the secret of his conduct when he also plainly told Essex that the queen's favour was after all more valuable to him than the earl's. His further guarded comment that he loved few persons better than his patron struck a hardly less cynical note.

Downfall of Essex.

Essex was ultimately released from imprisonment on parole; but he then embarked on very violent courses. He sought to stir up a rebellion against the queen and her advisers in London. He placed himself in a position which exposed him to the penalties of high treason. Bacon again sought advantage from his patron's errors. He again appeared for the Crown at Essex's formal trial on the capital charge of treason. His advocacy did much to bring Essex's guilt home to the judges. With inhuman coolness Bacon addressed himself to the prisoner, and explained to him the heaviness of his offence. Finally Essex was condemned to death and was executed on 25th February 1601.

Essex's death.

Bacon sacrificed all ordinary considerations of honour in his treatment of Essex. But his principles of active life deprived friendship of meaning for him. The material

benefit to be derived by one man from association with
Bacon's
perfidy. another alone entered into his scheme of self-
advancement, and self-advancement was the only
principle which he understood to govern 'the active stage of
affairs.'

v

The death of Elizabeth opened new prospects to Bacon,
but the story of his life followed its old drift. He naturally
Bacon and
James I. sought the favour of the new king, James I.
Naturally he would accommodate his own political
opinions to those of a new king. The royal influence must,
if it were possible, be drawn his way, be drawn towards him,
be pressed into his individual service. Bacon probably at the
outset had hopes of inducing the king to accept and act
upon the good counsel that he should offer him, just as at
the opening of their relations he thought it possible that he
might lead Essex to take his enlightened advice. It was
reported that the king was not devoid of large ideas. Bacon,
who was never a good judge of men, may have credited
the report. He may not have seen at first that James was
without earnest purpose in life; that the king's intellect was
cast in a narrow mould; that an extravagant sense of his own
importance mainly dominated its working. Yet there was
this excuse for Bacon's misapprehension: James was inquisi-
tively minded. He was at times willing to listen to the
exposition of good principles, however great his disinclina-
tion to put them into practice.

By way of experiment, Bacon at the outset proffered King
James I. some wise counsel. He repeated his old arguments
Advice to
the king. for toleration in matters of religion. Bacon
set forth these views as mere *ballons d'essai*, as
straws to show him which way the wind blew. As soon
as Bacon saw that the wind in the royal quarter was

not blowing in the direction of toleration, he tacked about to win the breeze of royal approval some other way. He supported persecution. Happily another proposal of his was grateful to the new king. Bacon recommended a political union, a political amalgamation of the two kingdoms of England and Scotland, of both of which James was now king. It was a wise plan in the circumstances, and one entirely congenial to the new Scottish monarch of England. James was not slow to mark his approval of Bacon's advice on the point, and Bacon's material prospects brightened.

James's reign was a critical period in English history. Bacon's depth of intellectual vision enabled him to foresee, perhaps more clearly than any other man of his age, the growing danger of a breach between the king and the people's representatives in the House of Commons. The English people was learning its political strength; the English people was learning the value of personal liberty, although the mass of them only hazily recognised the importance of self-government. Sir Walter Ralegh had enunciated the principle that 'in every just state some part of the government is or ought to be imparted to the people.' There was a growing conviction that government for the good of the many, rather than for the good of any one man, was essential to the full enjoyment of life. Government for the good of a sovereign who failed to move in the people any personal enthusiasm was certain to prove sooner or later an intolerable burden. Bacon acknowledged it to be the duty of a true statesman to seek to reconcile the two conflicting forces, the power of the king and the reasonable claims of the people. He had no faith in democracy; he believed in the one-man rule probably as sincerely as he believed in any political principle. The future peace of the country depended, in Bacon's view, on the king

The political situation.

—on his power and will to dispense equal justice among his subjects, and to conform to his subjects' just wishes on matters affecting their personal liberties. The king should be persuaded to exert his power and will to this end. But the problem of how best to reconcile king and people was not one that could be solved by mere assumption of the king's benevolent intentions. Unless a man championed great principles, and applied them to the problem without fear of forfeiting royal favour, he wasted breath and ink. Bacon had no intention of imperilling his relations with the king, of sacrificing his personal chances of preferment. However clearly he may have diagnosed the situation, he had not moral fibre enough materially to shape its course of development.

VI

Bacon was eager to derive personal profit from any turn of the political wheel. Yet with the singular versatility that characterised him, he, amid all the bustle of the political world in which he had immersed himself, found time to pursue his true vocation. Before Queen Elizabeth died he had produced the first edition of his *Essays,* those terse observations on life which placed him in the first rank of Elizabethan men of letters.[1] They were penetrating reflections on human nature and conduct

Literary occupations.

---

[1] The first edition of the *Essays* appeared in 1597, and consisted only of ten essays together with two pieces called respectively 'Sacred Meditations,' and 'Colours of Good and Evil.' This volume was reprinted without alteration in 1598 and 1606. A revised version which came out in 1612 brought the number of essays up to thirty-eight. Other editions followed, including a Latin translation by the author and translations by English friends into both Italian and French. The final edition, the publication of which Bacon superintended, is dated 1625 (the year before his death), and supplied as many as fifty-eight essays. An addition to the collection, a fragment of an essay of 'Fame,' appeared posthumously. This was included by Dr. William Rawley, Bacon's chaplain, into whose hands his master's manuscripts passed at his death, in the miscellaneous volume which Rawley edited in 1657 under the title of *Resuscitatio.*

which seemed to come from a sober observer of affairs,
from one of infinitely varied experience, from a thinker
not unduly biassed by his material interests. Revision and
enlargement of his *Essays* constantly occupied Bacon's
scanty leisure till his death.

In 1605, two years after James's accession, there appeared
a far more convincing proof of disinterested devotion to
things of the mind. Bacon then published his greatest contribution in English to philosophical literature, his *Advancement of Learning*. It was a popular work, treating eloquently
of the excellence of knowledge and noting in detail the
sufficiency and insufficiency of its present state. Bacon
surveyed fairly and sagaciously all existing departments of
knowledge, and indicated where progress was most essential.
The noble volume was intended to prepare the minds of
readers for the greater venture which absorbed Bacon's
thoughts, the exposition of a new philosophy, a new instrument of thought, the *Novum Organum*. This new instrument
was designed first to enable man to interpret nature and
thereby realise of what the forces of nature were capable,
and then to give him the power of adapting those forces to
his own purposes. In the completion of that great design lay
Bacon's genuine ambition; from birth to death, political
office, the rewards of the legal profession, money profits,
anxious as he was to win them, were means to serve his
attainment of that great end. All material successes in life
were, in his view, crude earthworks which protected from
assault and preserved intact the citadel of his being.

Slowly but surely the material recognition, the emoluments
for which he hungered, came Bacon's way. In 1606, at the
age of forty-five, he married. His wife was the
daughter of an alderman in the city of London, **Marriage.**
and brought him a good dowry. Little is known of Bacon's

domestic life, and some mystery overhangs its close. He had no children, but according to his earliest biographer he was a considerate and generous husband.[1] In the last year of his life, however, he believed he had serious ground of complaint against his wife, and the munificent provision which he made for her in the text of his will he in a concluding paragraph, 'for just and grave causes, utterly revoked and made void, leaving her to her right only.' He acquired a love of magnificence in his domestic life, which he indulged to an extent that caused him pecuniary embarrassments. It was soon after he entered the estate of matrimony that he put in order, at vast expense, the property at Gorhambury, near St. Albans, which his father had acquired, and he built upon the land there a new country residence of great dimensions, Verulam House. In the decoration and furnishing of the mansion he spent far more than he could afford. There he maintained a retinue of servants the number of whom, it was said, was hardly exceeded in the palace of the king.

Bacon's material resources rapidly grew after his marriage. A year later he received his first official promotion. In 1607 he was made Solicitor-General, a high legal office, and one well remunerated. He had waited long for such conspicuous advancement. He was now forty-six years old, and the triumph did not cause him undue elation. He suffered, he writes, much depression during

His first promotion.

---

[1] Dr. William Rawley, Bacon's chaplain, in his *Life*, ed. 1670, p. 6, writes with some obvious economy of truth :—'Neither did the want of children detract from his good usage of his consort during the intermarriage ; whom he prosecuted, with much conjugal love and respect : with many rich gifts, and endowments ; besides a robe of honour, which he invested her withal : which she wore until her dying day, being twenty years and more, after his death.' According to Aubrey, after Bacon's death she married her gentleman-usher, Sir Thomas Underhill, and survived the execution of Charles I. in 1649.

the months that followed. But his ambition was far from
satiated. A repetition of the experience happily brought him greater content. Six years later, at fifty-two, he was promoted to the more responsible and more highly remunerated office of Attorney-General.

Attorney-General.

VII

The breach between the king and his people was meanwhile widening. The Commons were reluctant to grant the king's demand for money without exacting guarantees of honest government—guarantees for the expenditure of the people's money in a way that should benefit them. Such demands and criticism the king warmly resented. He was bent on ruling autocratically. He would draw taxes from his people at his unfettered will. The hopelessness of expecting genuine benefit to the nation from James's exercise of authority was now apparent. Had Bacon been a high-minded, disinterested politician, withdrawal from the king's service would have been the only course open to him ; but he had an instinctive respect for authority, his private expenses were mounting high, and he was at length reaping pecuniary rewards in the legal and political spheres. Bacon deliberately chose the worser way. He abandoned in practice the last shreds of his political principles ; he gave up all hope of bringing about an accommodation on lines of right and justice between the king and the people. He made up his mind to remain a servant of the crown, with the single and unpraiseworthy end of benefiting his own pocket.

The political peril.

Tricks and subterfuges, dissimulation, evasion, were thenceforth Bacon's political resources. He soon sought assiduously the favour of the king's new and worthless favourite, the Duke of Buckingham. For a fleeting moment he seems to have tried to deceive himself, as he had

Bacon and Bucking- ham.

tried to deceive himself in the case of Essex and of the king, into the notion that this selfish, un- principled courtier might impress a statesmanlike ideal on the king's government. Bacon offered Buckingham some advice under this misconception. But Bacon quickly recognised his error. The good counsel was not repeated. He finally abandoned himself exclusively to the language of unblushing adulation in his intercourse with the favourite in order to benefit by the favourite's influence.

Bacon's policy gained him all the success that he could have looked for. A greater promotion than any he had en-

Lord Keeper.

joyed soon befell him. The Lord Keepership of the Great Seal, the highest legal office, to which belonged the functions of the Lord Chancellor, became vacant. It was the post which Bacon's father had filled, and the son proposed himself to Buckingham as a candidate. Bacon secured the lofty dignity on the ground that the favourite thought he might prove a useful, subservient tool. But a rough justice governed the political world even in James I.'s reign. Bacon's elevation to the high office proved his ruin.

Bacon was now not only the foremost judge in the land, but was also chief member of the King's Council. He had

Lord Veru- lam and Viscount St. Alban.

become, however, the mere creature of the crown, and all his political intelligence he suffered to run to waste. The favourite, Buckingham, was supreme with the king, and Bacon played a very subordinate part in discussions of high policy. He obsequiously as- sented to measures which he knew to be disastrous, and even submitted meekly to the personal humiliations which sub- servience to Buckingham—an exacting master—required. For a time his pusillanimity continued to bring rewards. In 1618 he was raised to the peerage, as Baron Verulam ; in

1619 he exchanged without alteration of functions the title
of Lord Keeper of the Great Seal for the more dignified
style of Lord High Chancellor of England. Two years
later he was advanced to a higher rank of nobility as
Viscount St. Alban. His paternal estate, on which he had
built his sumptuous pleasure-house, lay near the city of St.
Albans, and that city occupied the site of the Roman city
of Verulamium. He felt a scholar's pride in associating his
name with a relic of ancient Rome.

It may be admitted that Bacon's quick intelligence
rendered him a very efficient and rapid judge in his court,
the Court of Chancery. He rapidly cleared off *His judi-*
arrears of business, and seems to have done as a *cial work.*
rule substantial justice to suitors. But he was not, even
in his own court, his own master. The favourite, Buckingham, inundated him with letters requesting him to show
favour to friends of his who were interested in causes
in Bacon's court. Bacon's moral sense was too weak to
permit resistance to the favourite's insolent demands.

Bacon's moral perception was indeed blurred past recovery.
Servility to the king and his favourite had obvious dangers,
of which he failed to take note. Resentment
was rising in the country against the royal power, *The ap-*
proaching
and that rebellious sentiment was certain sooner *danger.*
or later to threaten with disaster those who for worldly gain
bartered their souls to the king and his minion. The wheel
was coming full circle.

VIII

Yet so full of contradiction is Bacon's career, that it was
when he stood beneath the shadow of the ruin
The Novum
which was to destroy his worldly fortune and repute *Organum,*
that he crowned the edifice of his philosophical *1620.*
ambition, which was to bring him imperishable glory. In

1620 he published his elaborate Latin treatise, *Novum Organum.* It is only a fragment—an unfinished second instalment—of that projected encyclopædia in which he designed to unfold the innermost secrets of nature. But such as it is, the *Novum Organum* is the final statement of his philosophic and scientific position. It expounds 'the new instrument,' the logical method of induction whereby nature was thenceforth to be rightly questioned, and her replies to be rightly interpreted. The book is the citadel of Bacon's philosophic system. To this exposition of his ultimate aim in life Bacon justly attached the highest importance. Twelve times amid the bustle of public business had he rewritten the ample treatise before he ventured on its publication. For twelve years, amid all the preoccupation of his public career, a draft of the volume had never been far from his hand.

The *Novum Organum* was obsequiously dedicated to the king. A very few months later, the irony of fate was finally **The wrath of Parliament.** to bring home to Bacon the error of dividing his allegiance between intellectual ideals and worldly honours and riches. For eight years James had suspended the sittings of Parliament. But money difficulties were growing desperate. At length the king resolved on the perilous device of making a fresh appeal to Parliament to extricate him from his embarrassments. Bacon was well aware of the exasperated state of public feeling, but with a curiously mistaken faith in himself and in his reputation, he deemed his own position perfectly secure. When Parliament met he discovered his error. At first he sought to close his eyes to the true character of the crisis, but they were soon rudely opened. His enemies were numerous in the House of Commons, and were in no gentle mood.

Heated censure was passed on Bacon and on others of the

king's associates as soon as the session opened.   Quickly a
specific charge was brought against him.   Two
petitions were presented to the House of Com- *The charge of corruption.*
mons by suitors in Bacon's court charging him with
taking bribes in his court, of corrupting justice.   The charge
was undisguised.   There was no chance of misapprehending
its gravity, but with characteristic insensibility, Bacon
affected to regard the attack as some puerile outcome of
spite.   He asserted that it was unworthy of consideration.
The House of Commons, however, referred the complaints to
the House of Lords, and the Lords took the matter too
seriously to leave Bacon longer in doubt of his danger.

As soon as the scales dropped from his eyes, the shock
unmanned him.   He fell ill, and was unable to leave his
house.   Fresh charges of corrupting justice were *Bacon's collapse.*
brought against him, and he was called upon for
an answer.   Seeking and obtaining an interview with the
king, he confessed to his sovereign that he had taken
presents from suitors, but he solemnly asseverated that he
had received none before the cause was practically decided.
He denied that gifts had ever led him to pervert justice.
Unluckily, evidence was forthcoming that at any rate he took
a bribe while one cause was pending.

As soon as he studied the details of the indictment, Bacon
perceived that defence was impossible, and his failing nerve
allowed him to do no more than throw himself on the mercy
of his peers.   His accusers pressed for a definite *His confession of guilt.*
answer to the accusation, but he gave none.   He
declined to enter into details.   He declared in
writing that he was heartily sorry and truly penitent for the
corruption and neglect of which he confessed himself guilty.

The story is a pitiful one.   Bacon, reduced to the last
stage of nervous prostration, figures in a most ignoble light

throughout the proceedings.   He turned his back to the

His punish-   smiter in a paroxysm of fear.   On the 1st of
ment.   May 1621 he was dismissed from his office of Lord
Chancellor, and two days later, in his absence through illness, sentence was pronounced upon him by the House of
Lords.   He was ordered to pay a fine of £40,000 and to be
imprisoned for life, and was declared incapable of holding any
office in the State.

Thus ended in deep disgrace Bacon's active career.   The
king humanely relieved him of his punishment, and he was

His retire-   set free with the heavy fine unpaid.   He retired
ment.   from London to his house at St. Albans.   Driven
from public life, he naturally devoted himself to literature and
science—to those spheres of labour which he believed himself brought into the world to pursue.   Although his health

His literary   was broken, his intellect was unimpaired by his
and scienti-
fic occupa-   ruin, and he engaged with renewed energy in
tion.   literary composition, in philosophical speculation,
and in scientific experiment.   The first fruit of his enforced
withdrawal from official business was a rapidly written mono-
graph on Henry vii.   He essayed history, he boldly said,
because, being deprived of the opportunity of doing his
country 'service,' 'it remained to him to do it honour.'
His *Reign of King Henry VII.* is a vivid historical picture,
independent in tone and of substantial accuracy.   More
germane to his previous labours was a first instalment of a
large collection of scientific facts and observations, which he
published in Latin in the same year as his account of
Henry vii. (1622), under the title *Historia Naturalis et
Experimentalis ad Condendam Philosophiam* (Natural and
Experimental History for the Foundation of Philosophy).
Next year there followed *De Augmentis Scientiarum,* an
enlarged version in Latin of his *Advancement of Learning.*

To the last Bacon, with characteristic perversity, declined to realise the significance of his humiliation. Of the sentence passed upon him, he remarked before he died, 'It was the justest censure in Parliament that was these two hundred years.' But he prefaced this opinion with the qualification, 'I was the justest judge that was in England these fifty years.' As his life was closing, he cherished wild hopes of regaining the king's favour, even of returning to the domain of politics out of which he had passed so ignominiously. He offered to draw up a Digest of the Law, to codify the Law. He still addressed his patron of the past, King James, with the same adulation as of old. But fortunately for himself these ill-conceived efforts failed. When Charles I. came to the throne on the death of his father James I., Bacon imagined that a new opportunity was opened to him, and he petitioned for that full pardon which would have enabled him to take his seat in Parliament. But his advances were then for a last time brusquely repulsed.

His vain hope of rehabilitation.

IX

Although Bacon's health was shattered and he could not yield himself in patience to exclusion from the public stage of affairs, his scientific enthusiasm still ran high. The immediate cause of his death was an adventure inspired by scientific curiosity. At the end of March 1626, being near Highgate, on a snowy day, he left his coach to collect snow with which he meant to stuff a hen in order to observe the effect of cold on the preservation of its flesh.[1] He was thus a pioneer of the art of refrigeration,

His death.

[1] This circumstance rests on the testimony of the philosopher Hobbes, who was thirty-eight years old at the time of Bacon's death, and was in constant personal intercourse with him during the previous ten years. Hobbes's story, which Aubrey took down from his lips and incorporated in his life of

of preserving food by means of cold storage. In performing
the experiment he caught a chill and took refuge in the
house of a neighbouring friend, the art-connoisseur, Lord
Arundel, who happened to be from home. Bacon was sixty-
five years old, and his constitution could bear no new strain.
At Lord Arundel's house he died on the 9th of April of
the disease now known as bronchitis. He was buried at
St. Michael's Church, St. Albans, where his tomb may still be
visited. The monument represents him elaborately attired
and seated in a contemplative attitude. It was set up by a
loving disciple, Sir Thomas Meautys. A Latin inscription,
which was penned by another admirer, Sir Henry Wotton,
may be rendered in English thus :—

> 'Thus was wont to sit FRANCIS BACON, LORD VERULAM,
> VISCOUNT ST. ALBANS, (or to call him by his more illus-

Bacon (*cf.* Aubrey's *Lives*, vol. ii. part ii. p. 602), runs as follows :—'The
cause of his Lordship's death was trying an experiment. As he was taking an
aire in a coach with Dr. Witherborne (a Scotchman, Physician to the King)
towards Highgate, snow lay on the ground, and it came into my Lord's
thoughts, why flesh might not be preserved in snow as in salt. They were
resolved they would try the experiment presently. They alighted out of
the coach, and went into a poore woman's house at the bottome of Highgate
Hill, and bought a hen, and made the woman exenterate it, and then stuffed
the bodie with snow, and my Lord did help to doe it himselfe. The snow
so chilled him, that he immediately fell so extremely ill, that he could not
returne to his lodgings (at Graye's Inne) but went to the Earl of Arundell's
house at Highgate, where they putt him into a good bed warmed with a
panne, but it was a damp bed that had not been layn in about a yeare
before, which gave him such a cold that in 2 or 3 dayes he dyed of
suffocation.' Bacon carried the frozen hen with him to Lord Arundel's
house and lived long enough to assure himself that his experiment was
successful. Lord Arundel happened to be absent from home on Bacon's
arrival, and Bacon managed, before he understood the fatal character of his
illness, to dictate a letter—the last words which he is known to have uttered
—to his host explaining the situation. 'I was likely to have had the
fortune,' the letter began, 'of Caius Plinius the elder, who lost his life by
trying an experiment about the burning of the mountain Vesuvius. For
I was also desirous to try an experiment or two, touching the conservation
and induration of bodies. As for the experiment itself, it succeeded excel-
lently well.' ('A Collection of Letters made by Sr. Tobie Mathews, Kt.,
1660,' p. 57.)

trious titles) the light of the sciences, the standard of
eloquence, who, after he had discovered all the secrets of
natural and moral philosophy, fulfilled nature's law of
dissolution, A.D. 1626, aged 66.—To the memory of so
eminent a man THOMAS MEAUTYS, a disciple in life, an
admirer in death, set up this monument.'

'For my name and memory,' Bacon wrote in his will,
'I leave it to men's charitable speeches, and to foreign
nations and the next ages.' These legatees have His
not proved themselves negligent of the trust that character.
Bacon reposed in them; yet, when his personal career is
surveyed, it is impossible for man's charitable speeches or
foreign nations or the next ages to apply to it the language
of eulogy. An unparalleled faith in himself, a blind self-
confidence, is the most striking feature of his personal character. It justified in his mind acts on his part which defied
every law of morality. That characteristic may have been
partly due to his early training. The self-righteous creed
which his narrowly Puritan mother implanted in him was
responsible for much. The Calvinistic doctrine of predes-
tination and election gave him, unconsciously, at the outset,
confidence in his eternal salvation, whatever his personal
conduct in life. But, if this were the result of his mother's
teaching, his father, who was immersed in the politics of the
day, made him familiar as a boy with all the Machiavellian
devices, the crooked tricks of policy and intrigue which
infected the political society of Queen Elizabeth's court.
While these two influences—his mother's superstition and
his father's crafty worldliness—were playing on his receptive
mind, a third came from his own individuality. He grew
convinced of the possession of exceptional intellectual power
which, if properly applied, would revolutionise man's relations with nature and reveal to him her hidden secrets.
As years advanced, he realised that material wealth and

position were needful to him if he were to attain the goal
of his intellectual ambition. With a moral sense

His neglect
of moral
sanctions.

weakened by his early associations with Calvinism
on the one hand and with utilitarianism on the
other, he was unable to recognise any justice in moral
obstacles intervening between him and that material prosperity which was essential, in his belief, to the fulfilment
of his intellectual designs. The higher he advanced in the
material world, the more independent he became of the
conventional distinctions between right and wrong. His
mighty fall teaches the useful lesson that intellectual genius,
however commanding, never justifies breaches of those eternal
moral laws which are binding on men of great mental endowments equally with men of moderate or small intellectual
capacities.

Nor in the practical affairs of life did Bacon have at command that ordinary faculty, that *savoir faire*, which is often
to be met with in men of smaller capacity, and

His want
of *savoir
faire*.

can alone ensure success or prosperity. In money
matters his carelessness was abnormal, even among
men of genius. Whether his resources were small or great,
his expenditure was always in excess of them. He was
through life in bondage to money-lenders, yet he never
hesitated to increase his outlay and his indebtedness. He
saw his servants robbing him, but never raised a word in
protest. By a will which he drew up in the year before
he died, he was munificent in gifts, not merely to friends,
retainers, and the poor, but to public institutions, which he
hoped to render more efficient in public service. Yet when
all his assets were realised, the amount was only sufficient
to defray two-thirds of his debts, and none of his magnanimous bequests took effect. With his thoughts concentrated on his intellectual ambitions, he neglected, too, the

study of the men with whom he worked.   Although human nature had revealed to him many of its secrets, and he could disclose them in literature with rare incisiveness, he failed to read character in the individual men with whom chance brought him into everyday association.   He misunderstood Essex ; he misunderstood James I.; he misunderstood Buckingham ; his wife and his servants deceived him.

X

In the conduct of his affairs, as in the management of men, Bacon stands forth as a pitiable failure.   It is only in his scientific and his literary achievements that he is great, but there few have been greater.   *His true greatness.*

Bacon's mind was a typical product of the European Renaissance.   His intellectual interests embraced every topic ; his writings touched almost every subject of intellectual study.   To each he brought the *His literary versatility.* same eager curiosity and efficient insight.   He is the despair of the modern specialist.   He is historian, essayist, logician, legal writer, philosophical speculator, writer on science in every branch.

At heart Bacon was a scholar scorning the applause which the popular writer covets.   It is curious to note that he set a higher value on his skill as a writer of Latin than on his skill as a writer of English.   Latin *His reverence for the Latin tongue.* he regarded as the language of the learned of every nationality, and consequently books written in Latin were addressed to his only fit audience, the learned society of the whole civilised globe.   English writings, on the other hand, could alone appeal to the (in his day) comparatively few persons of intelligence who understood that tongue. Latin was for him the universal language.   English books could never, he said, be citizens of the world.

So convinced was he of the insularity of his own tongue, that at the end of his life he deplored that he had wasted time in writing books in English. He hoped all his works might be translated into Latin, so that they might live for posterity. Miscalculation of his powers governed a large part of Bacon's life, and find signal illustration in this regret that he should have written in English rather than in Latin. For it is not to his Latin works, nor to the Latin translations of his English works, that he owes the main part of his immortality. He lives as a speculator in philosophy, as one who sought a great intellectual goal; but he lives equally as a great master of the English tongue which he despised.

His contempt for English.

For terseness and pithiness of expression there is nothing in English to match Bacon's style in the *Essays*. His reflections on human life which he embodied there, his comments on human nature, especially on human infirmities, owe most of their force to the stimulating vigour which he breathed into English words. No man has proved himself a greater master of the pregnant apophthegm in any language, not even in the French language, which far more readily lends itself to aphorism.

The style of his Essays.

Weighty wisdom, phrased with that point and brevity which only a master of style could command, is scattered through all the essays, and many sentences have become proverbial. It is the essay 'Of Marriage and Single Life' that begins: 'He that hath wife and children hath given hostages to fortune; for they are impediments to great enterprises either of virtue or mischief.' That 'Of Parents and Children' has 'Children sweeten labours, but they make misfortunes more bitter; they increase the cares of life, but they mitigate the remembrance of death.' Of 'Building' he made the prudent

Phrases from the Essays.

and witty remark : ' Houses are built to live in and not to look on; therefore let use be preferred before uniformity, except where both may be had. Leave goodly fabrics of houses for beauty only to the enchanted palaces of the poets who build them with small cost.' Equally notable are such sentences as these :—' A crowd is not company, and faces are but a gallery of pictures, and talk but a tinkling cymbal where there is no love.' On the scriptural proverb about riches making themselves wings, Bacon grafted the practical wisdom : ' Riches have wings and sometimes they fly away of themselves, sometimes they must be set flying to bring in more.' Equally penetrating are these aphoristic deliverances :—' Some books are to be tasted, others to be swallowed, and some few to be chewed and digested ' (Essay I., of ' Studies '). ' A little philosophy inclineth a man's mind to atheism, but depth in philosophy bringeth man's mind about to religion ' (Essay XVI., of ' Atheism '). Sometimes he uses very homely language with singular effect. ' Money is like muck—not good except it be spread '(Essay XV., of ' Seditions and Troubles '). Thus he summarised a warning which he elsewhere elaborately phrased, that it is an evil hour for a State when its treasure and money are gathered into a few hands.

But Bacon's style is varied. The pithy terseness of his essays is not present in all his works. In addition to his terse mode of English expression, he had at command a *His majes-* rich exuberance and floridity abounding in rhetori- *tic style.* cal ornament and illustration. He professed indifference to mere questions of form in composition. But whatever his theoretical view of style, he was a singularly careful writer, and his philosophical English writings—his *Advancement of Learning* especially—are as notable for the largeness of their vocabulary, the richness of their illustration, and the rhythmical flow of their sentences as for their philosophic suggestiveness.

All that Bacon wrote bore witness to his weighty and robust intellect, but his style was coloured not merely by intellectual strength, but by imaginative insight. So much imaginative power, indeed, underlay his majestic phraseology and his illuminating metaphors, that Shelley in his eloquent *Defence of Poetry* figuratively called him a poet.[1] It is only figuratively that Bacon could be called a poet. He is only a poet in the sense that every great thinker and observer of nature has a certain faculty of imagination. But his faculty of imagination is the thinker's faculty, which is mainly the fruit of intellect. The great poet's faculty of imagination, which is mainly the fruit of emotion, was denied Bacon. Poetry in its strict sense, the modulated harmony of verse, the emotional sympathy which seeks expression in lyric or drama, was out of his range.

The writing of verse was probably the only branch of intellectual endeavour which was beyond Bacon's grasp. He was ambitious to try his hand at every literary exercise. At times he tried to turn a stanza. The results are unworthy of notice. Bacon's acknowledged attempts at formal poetry are uncouth and lumbering; they attest congenital unfitness for that mode of expression. Strange arguments have indeed been adduced to credit Bacon with those supreme embodiments of all poetic excellence—Shakespeare's plays. The number of works that Bacon claimed to have penned, when combined

His verse.

---

[1] Shelley fancifully endeavours to identify poets and philosophers. 'The distinctions,' he writes, 'between philoscphers and poets have been anticipated. Plato was essentially a poet. . . . Lord Bacon was a poet. His language has a sweet and majestic rhythm, which satisfies the sense no less than the almost superhuman wisdom of his philosophy satisfies the intellect. . . . Shakespeare, Dante, and Milton . . . are philosophers of the very loftiest power.'—*Defence of Poetry*, ed. A. S. Cook, pp. 9-10.

with the occupations of his professional career, so filled every
nook and cranny of his adult time, that on no showing was
leisure available for the conquest of vast fields of poetry
and drama.   But whoever harbours the delusion that Bacon
was responsible for anything that came from Shakespeare's
pen, should examine Bacon's versified paraphrase of *Certaine
Psalmes* which he published in a volume the year before he
died.   He dedicated the book to the poet George Herbert,
in terms which attest, despite some conventional self-
depreciation, the store he set by this poor experiment.   The
work represents the whole of the extant metrical efforts
which came, without possibility of dispute, from Bacon's pen.
If the reader of that volume be not promptly disabused of
the heresy that any Shakespearean touch is discernible in the
clumsy and crude doggerel, he deserves to be condemned
to pass the rest of his days with no other literary company
to minister to his literary cravings than this '*Translation
of Certaine Psalmes into English Verse,* by the Right Honourable Francis, Lo. Verulam, Viscount St. Alban.' [1]

[1] Despite his incapacity for verse Bacon, like many smaller men, seems
to have assiduously courted the muse in private.   Writing to a poetic friend,
Sir John Davies, in 1603, he numbers himself among 'concealed poets,'
and the gossiping biographer, Aubrey, applies to him the same designation.
Apart from his verse-rendering of the psalms, he has only been credited
on any sane grounds with two pieces of verse, and to one of these he has
certainly no title. The moralising jingle, beginning 'The man of life upright,'
figures in many seventeenth-century manuscript miscellanies of verse as
'Verses made by Mr. Francis Bacon,' but its true author was Thomas
Campion (cf. *Poems,* ed. A. H. Bullen, p. 20). The other poetic performance
assigned to Bacon is variously called 'The World,' 'The Bubble,' and 'On
Man's Mortality.' It opens with the lines,

'The world's a bubble, and the life of man
Less than a span,'

and was first printed after Bacon's death in 1629 in Thomas Farnaby's
Florilegium Epigrammaticum Græcorum, a Latin translation of selections
from the *Greek Anthology.* The poem in question is the only English verse
in Farnaby's book, and is ascribed by him on hazy grounds to 'Lord
Verulam.' It is a rendering of the epigram in the *Palatine Anthology,*

It is Bacon's scientific or philosophic labour which forms
the apex of his history. Although he wrote many scattered
treatises which dealt in detail with scientific phenomena, Bacon's scientific and philosophic aims can
best be deduced from his two great works, the
Advancement of Learning, which was written in English, and
the *Novum Organum,* which was written in Latin. The first,
which was greatly amplified in a Latin paraphrase (at least
one-third being new matter) called *De Augmentis Scientiarum,*
is a summary survey in English of all knowledge. The
second work, the Latin *Novum Organum,* is a fragment of
Bacon's full exposition of his scientific system ; it is the only
part of it that he completed, and mainly describes his
inductive method of scientific investigation.

His
philosophic
works.

Bacon's attitude to science rests on the convictions that
man's true function in life is to act as the interpreter of
nature; that truth cannot be derived from authority,
but from man's experience and experiments ; that
knowledge is the fruit of experience and experiment. Bacon's philosophic writings have for their main
object the establishment of a trustworthy system whereby
nature may be interpreted by man, and brought into his

His atti-
tude to
science.

x. 359, which is sometimes assigned to Posidippus and sometimes to Crates
(*cf.* Mackail's *Greek Anthology,* sect. xii. No. xxxix. p. 278). The English
lines, the authorship of which remains uncertain, paraphrase the Greek
freely and effectively, but whoever may be their author, they cannot be
ranked among original compositions. A copy was found among Sir Henry
Wotton's papers, and printed in the *Reliquiæ Wottonianæ* (1651) above the
signature 'Ignoto.' They were also put to the credit, in early manuscript
copies, of Donne, of 'Henry Harrington,' and of 'R. W.' The Greek
epigram, it is interesting to note, was a favourite with Elizabethan versifiers.
English renderings are extant by Nicolas Grimald (in Tottel's *Songes and
Sonnettes,* ed. Arber, p. 109), by Puttenham (in *Arte of English Poesie,* ed.
Arber, p. 214), by Sir John Beaumont, and others.

service, whereby the study of natural science may be set on a firm and fruitful foundation.

The first aim was to overthrow the deductive methods of Aristotle and mediæval schoolmen, by virtue of which it had been customary before Bacon's time to seek to prove preconceived theories without reference to actual fact or experience. The formal logic of the syllogism was in Bacon's eyes barren verbiage. By such means elaborate conclusions were reached, which were never tested by observation and experiment, although if they were so tested, they would be summarily confuted. The deductive conclusion that bodies fall to the ground at a velocity proportioned to their weight is one of the simple fallacies which were universally accepted before observation and experiment were summoned to test its truth and brought the law of gravitation into being.

His opposition to Aristotle.

Bacon ranks as the English champion of the method of inductive reasoning. It was well known to earlier logicians that an enumeration of phenomena offered material for generalisation, but Bacon's predecessors were content with a simple and uncritical enumeration of such facts as happened to come under their notice, and their mode of generalising was valueless and futile, because the foundations were unsound as often as they were sound. Bacon argued that reports of isolated facts were to be accumulated, and were then to be systematically tested by means of observation and experiment. Phenomena were to be carefully selected and arranged. There were to be eliminations and rejections of evidence. From the assemblage and codification of tested facts alone were conclusions to be drawn.

Bacon on induction.

On man's inability, without careful training, to distinguish between fact and fiction, Bacon laid especial stress. Man's

powers were rarely in a condition to report on phenomena
profitably or faithfully. Congenital prejudice was
first to be allowed for and counteracted. Man
was liable to misapprehensions of what came
within the range of his observation, owing to inadequate
control of the senses and emotions.

Man's mental prejudices.

To an analysis of the main defects in the operation of
the human intellect in its search after truth Bacon devoted
much attention. The mind of man, Bacon pointed out, was
haunted by phantoms, and exorcism of these phantoms was
needful before reason was secure in her dominion of the
mind. Bacon called the phantoms of the mind idols—idola,
from the Greek word εἴδωλα, phantoms or images. Idols
or idola were, in Bacon's terminology, the antitheses of
ideas, the sound fruit of thought. Bacon finally reduced
the idols or phantoms which infested man's mind to four
classes—idols of the tribe, the cave, the market-place, and
the theatre.[1]

Idols of the tribe are inherent habits of mind common
to all the human tribe, such as the tendency to put more
faith in one affirmative instance of success than in
any number of negative instances of failure. An
extraordinary cure is effected by means of some drug, and
few people stop to inquire how often the drug has failed, or
whether the cure was due to some cause other than the
administration of this particular drug. Idols of the cave (a
conception which is borrowed from Plato's *Republic*) are the
prejudices of the individual person when he is imprisoned in

The doctrine of idols.

---

[1] Sections xxxviii.-lxviii. of the *Novum Organum* expound Bacon's 'doctrine of the idols' in its final shape. A first imperfect draft of the doctrine appears in the *Advancement of Learning* (Bk. ii.), and is expanded in the *De Augmentis* and in the Latin tracts *Valerius Terminus* and *Partis Secundæ Delineatio*, but the *Novum Organum* is the *locus classicus* for the exposition of the doctrine.

the cave of his own idiosyncrasy. One man's natural habit
inclines to exaggeration of statement, while another man's
habit inclines to underestimation of the importance of what
he sees or hears. The third idol—of the market-place—
is the disposition to become the slave of phrases and words
which are constantly heard in ordinary traffic, the market-
place of life. Mere words or phrases, when echoed in the
market-place of life, apart from the circumstances that give
them their full significance, breed irrational misconception.
Words like Free-trade or Protection, to take a modern
example, fall within the scope of Bacon's doctrine; they
easily become verbal fetishes, and the things of which
they are mere market-place tokens are left out of account.
Idols of the theatre mean those tendencies on the part
of masses of men and women to put faith in everything that
is said very dogmatically, as actors are wont to speak from
the stage of the theatre. Philosophies or religions, which
rest on specious dogmas, have the character, in Bacon's
judgment, of stage-plays which delude an ignorant audience
into accepting the artificial, unreal scene for nature, by
virtue of over-emphasised speech and action.

Man's vision must be purged from prejudices, whether
they are inherited or spring from environment, before he
can fully grasp the truth. The dry light of
reason is the only illuminant which permits man *The dry
light of
reason.*
to see clearly phenomena as they are; only when
idols are dispersed does the dry light burn with effectual
fire.

XII

Bacon claimed that all knowledge lay within the scope of
man's enfranchised mind. The inductive system was to
arrive ultimately at the cause, not only of scientific facts and

conditions, but of moral, political, and spiritual facts and
conditions. He refused to believe that any limits were

set beyond which human intellect when clarified

The limit-
less possi-
bilities of
man's
knowledge.

and purified could not penetrate. He argued
that, however far we may think we have advanced
in knowledge or science, there is always more

beyond, and that the tracts lying beyond our present gaze
will in due course of time come within the range of a
purified intellectual vision. There were no bounds to what
human thought might accomplish. To other children of the
Renaissance the same sanguine faith had come, but none
gave such emphatic voice to it as Bacon.

But Bacon did not go far along the road that he had
marked out for himself. His great system of knowledge

The frag-
mentary
character
of his work.

was never completed. He was always looking
forward to the time when, having exhausted his
study of physics, he should proceed to the study

of metaphysics—the things above physics, spiritual things—
but metaphysics never came within his view, nor did he, to
speak truth, do much more than touch the fringe of physical
investigation. He failed to keep himself abreast of the

His ignor-
ance of
contem-
porary
advances
in science.

physical knowledge of his day, and some of his
guesses at scientific truth strike the modern reader as
childish. He knew nothing of Harvey's discovery
of the circulation of the blood, which that great

physician enunciated in his lectures to his students fully ten
years before Bacon died. He knew nothing of Napier's
invention of logarithms, nor of Kepler's mathematical calcu-
lations, which set the science of astronomy on a just footing.
He ignored the researches of his own fellow-countryman,
William Gilbert, in the new science of the magnet. Nor,
apparently, was he acquainted with the vast ˙ series of
scientific discoveries, including the thermometer and the

telescope, which were due to the genius of the greatest of his scientific contemporaries, Galileo.

It is doubtful whether Bacon, despite his intuitive grasp of scientific principle, had any genuine aptitude for the practical work of scientific research. News of Galileo's discovery of Jupiter's satellites reached him, but he did not apprehend its significance. Galileo's final confirmation of the Copernican system of astronomy, which proved that the earth went round the sun, never obtained Bacon's recognition. He adhered to the geocentric theory of Ptolemy, which was long accepted universally, that the earth was the fixed centre of the universe, round which sun and planets revolved. He even disrespectfully referred to those who insisted on the earth's movement round the sun as 'these mad carmen which drive the earth about.'

Yet Bacon's spacious intuition enabled him to strike out a few shrewd scientific observations that anticipated researches of the future. He described heat as a His own mode of motion, and light as requiring time for discoveries. its transmission. Of the atomic theory of matter he had, too, a shadowy glimpse. He even vaguely suggested some valuable mechanical devices which are now in vogue. In a description of instruments for the transference of sound, he foreshadowed the invention of speaking-tubes and telephones; and he died, as we have seen, in an endeavour to test a perfectly accurate theory of refrigeration.

His greatness in the history of science does not, however, consist in the details of his scientific study, nor in his applications of science to practical life, nor in his personal His place aptitude for scientific research, but rather in the history of impetus which his advocacy of inductive and science. experimental methods gave to future scientific investigation. As he himself said, he rang the bell which called the other wits together. He first indicated the practical efficiency of scientific induction, and although succeeding experimenters in science may have been barely conscious of their indebtedness to him, yet their work owes its value to the logical method which he brought into vogue.

XIII

Although he failed to appreciate the value of the scientific investigations of his contemporaries, Bacon preached with enthusiasm the crying need of practical research if his prophecy of the future of science were to be realised. His mind frequently contemplated the organisation, the endowment and equipment of research in every branch of science, theoretical or practical. A great palace of invention, a great temple of science, was one of his dreams. In later life he amused himself by describing, in fanciful language, what form such a palace might take in imaginary conditions. The sketch is one of the most charming of his writings. He called it *The New Atlantis*. It was never finished, and the fragment was not published in his lifetime.

The endowment of research.

Bacon intended the work to fulfil two objects. First he sought to describe an imaginary college, which should be instituted for the purpose of interpreting nature, and of producing great and marvellous works for the benefit of men. In the second place, he proposed to frame an ideal body of laws for a commonwealth. The second part was not begun. The only portion of the treatise that exists deals, after the manner of a work of fiction, with an ideal endowment of scientific research. It shows Bacon to advantage as a writer of orderly and dignified English, and embodies, in a short compass, as many of Bacon's personal convictions and ideals as any of his compositions.

The New Atlantis.

In the history of the English Renaissance, the *New Atlantis*

fills at the same time an important place. It is in a sense
the epilogue of the drama. It is the latest pro-
nouncement in the endeavour of the Renaissance   The
epilogue
to realise perfection in human affairs. The cry for   to the
the regeneration of the race found voice—for the   Renaissance
in England.
first time in England under the spell of the Renaissance—in
More's *Utopia*. More pleaded for the recognition of equal
social rights for all reasoning men. Bacon's *New Atlantis*
was a sequel to More's *Utopia*, but it sharply contrasted with
it in conception. Since More wrote the *Utopia*, time had
taught thinkers of the Renaissance to believe that man's
ultimate regeneration and perfectibility depended primarily
not on reform of laws of property or on social revolution,
but on the progress of science and the regulation of human
life by the scientific spirit. Bacon's *New Atlantis* proclaimed
with almost romantic enthusiasm that scientific method
alone was the ladder by which man was to ascend to perfect
living.

The opening page of Bacon's scientific romance introduces
us abruptly to a boatload of mariners on their voyage from
Peru by the South Pacific Sea to China and Japan.   The story
Storms delay them, and their food-supplies fail,   of the *New
Atlantis*
but happily they reach land, the existence of which   Utopia.
they had not suspected. The inhabitants, after careful
inquiry, permit the castaways to disembark. The land
proves to be the island of Ben Salem, to which the Christian
religion had been divinely revealed at a very early period.
The islanders practise all civic virtues, especially the virtue
of hospitality. The visitors are royally entertained. It is
curious to note that Bacon, zealous for efficiency of organisation in small things as in great, points out how the servants
refused with amused contempt the offer of gifts of money
from the strange travellers on whom they were directed to

wait ; the servants deemed it (such was their disinterested
and virtuous faith in logic) dishonour to be twice paid for
their labours—by their employers and by their employers'
guests.

The customs of the people of this unknown island are
charmingly described, and ultimately the travellers are introduced to the chief and predominating feature of
the island, a great college of science, founded by
an ancient ruler, and called Salomon's house—
' the noblest foundation that ever was upon the earth, and
the lantern of this kingdom.'

The rest of the work describes the constitution of this great
foundation for ' the finding out the true nature of all things.'
The end of this college of science is to reach ' the
knowledge of causes, and secret motions of things,
and the enlarging of the bounds of human empire to
the effecting of all things possible.'   That is the motto of the
great temple.   There is much that is fantastic in the sequel,
but it illustrates Bacon's dearest aspirations, and his anticipa-
tions of what science might, if effort were fittingly organised,
ultimately accomplish.   There are caves sunk six hundred
fathoms deep, in which 'refrigerations and conservations
of bodies' are effected, and new metals artificially contrived.
There are turrets half a mile high—in one case erected on a
mountain three miles high—for purposes of meteorological
observation.   There is a chamber of health, where the atmosphere is modulated artificially with a view to adapting it
to cure various diseases.   In the gardens, new flowers and
fruits are brought into being by dint of grafting and in-
oculation.   Vivisection is practised on beasts and birds, so
that opportunities may be at hand to test the effects of
poison and new operations in surgery, and to widen the
knowledge of physiology ; while breeding experiments pro-

*The im-
aginary
college of
science.*

*The work
of the
college.*

duce new and useful species of animals. Optics in all its branches is studied practically in the laboratories, called perspective-houses. Finally, there is an establishment where tricks that deceive the senses, like feats of juggling, or spiritualistic manifestations, or ghostly apparitions, are practised to the highest perfection, and then explained to serious students who go out into the world, and by their instruction prevent the simple-minded from being deceived by quacks and impostors.

The leading men of the island, the aristocracy, consist of a great hierarchy of fellows, or endowed students, of the House of Science. Each rank exercises different functions. Some, called 'the merchants of light,' travel to collect information. Others at home compile knowledge from books. Others codify the experiments of their colleagues. Some of the students devote themselves to applying the discoveries of theoretical science to mechanical inventions. Others extract, through the general work of the college, philosophic generalisations. Religion sheds its light on the foundation ; and the father, or chief ruler, of the house is represented as abounding in pious fervour. All the students are, indeed, described as philanthropists seeking inspiration from God. Respect for great discoverers of new truths or of new applications of science was one of the principles of Bacon's great scheme of a Temple of Science. For every invention of value a statue to the inventor was at once erected in the House, and a liberal and honourable reward was given him.

The Fellows of the college.

The scheme of this great imaginary institution is Bacon's final message to mankind. His college of science was a design, he said, fit for a mighty prince to execute. He felt that if such a design had been executed in his day, he himself would have had the opportunity

Bacon's aspiration.

which he lacked of separating himself from sordid and sophisticated society, from evil temptations which he had not the moral courage to resist, of realising his youthful ambition. History would then have known him exclusively as a benefactor of the human race, a priest of science, who consecrated every moment of his life to searching into the secrets of nature for the benefit of his fellow-men.

Bacon's idea has not yet been realised. Whether a temple of science, on the scale that Bacon imagined it, will ever come into existence remains to be seen.[1] At

Prospects of realising Bacon's ideal.

present the portents, I fear, are not favourable for its emergence in this country. It seems more likely to come to birth in Germany or in America first. For both in Germany and in America things of the mind such as Bacon worshipped receive a public consideration which is denied them here. Nothing here is comparable with the widespread eagerness in the United States among young men and women to enjoy the benefit of academic scientific training. Rich and poor alike share the passion for enlightenment. The sacrifices, the penurious living which poor students cheerfully face in order to complete their University course, form heroic chapters in the nation's life. And most important in the present connection is it to note the munificent readiness with which the legislatures of many States of America, and more especially rich individual citizens of America, respond, like the founder of Bacon's *New Atlantis*, to demands made on their resources to supply the people with fit endowment and equipment of research. Nothing in the current experience of our country enables us to realise, even dimly, the scale on

1 The passage which follows was interpolated in a repetition of this lecture at the Working Men's College in London at the opening of the Session on 3rd October 1903.

which wealth in America is appropriated to Bacon's great cause—the advancement of learning.

This is a melancholy reflection. It suggests a descent from the high level of aspiration and endeavour which England maintained in the era of the Renaissance and after. England nurtured not merely Bacon, who stimulated scientific research through all the world; she has produced a long succession of scientific investigators—'merchants of light' one might call them in Bacon's fine phrase—who, working in Bacon's spirit, enjoy the honours of universal recognition. She has moreover produced in the past a long line of benefactors who paid willing tribute to learning, who, in the cause of research, fostered educational institutions, libraries, and laboratories. England's prestige owes very much to the scientific triumphs won by men who were Bacon's disciples in methods of research, and who were indebted to ancient educational benefactions.

Bacon was well alive to the means whereby a nation's intellectual prestige could best be sustained. In this illuminating tractate of his, *The New Atlantis,* he argued in effect that it was incumbent on a nation to apply a substantial part of its material resources to the equipment of scientific work and exploration—a substantial part of its resources which should grow greater and greater with the progress of time and of population, with the increasing complexity of knowledge. Such application of material resources, in Bacon's view, was the surest guarantee of national glory and prosperity. This is perhaps at the moment the most serious lesson that Bacon's writings teach us, and patriotic pride in his achievement ought to forbid our neglect of his counsel, ought to forbid our watching supinely the superior, the better sustained efforts of foreign nations to reach his ideal.

VII

SHAKESPEARE'S CAREER

> . . . Princes sit like stars about his throne,
> And he the sun for them to reverence.
> None that beheld him, but like lesser lights
> Did vail their crowns to his supremacy.
> *Pericles,* II. iii. 39-42.

[BIBLIOGRAPHY.—The main facts are recorded in the present writer's *Life of Shakespeare,* which was published in 1898. The documentary information respecting Shakespeare's career is collected in Halliwell Phillipps's *Outlines of the Life of Shakespeare,* 2 vols., tenth Edition, 1898. The two volumes published by The New Shakspere Society: *Shakspere's Centurie of Prayse; being materials for a history of opinion on Shakspere and his works, A.D.* 1591-1693 (edited by C. M. Ingleby, and Lucy Toulmin Smith, 1879), and *Some* 300 *Fresh Allusions to Shakespeare from* 1594 *to* 1694 *A.D.* (edited by F. J. Furnivall, 1886), bear useful testimony to the persistence of the accepted tradition.]

I

THE obscurity with which Shakespeare's biography has been long credited is greatly exaggerated. The mere biographical information accessible is far more definite
The documentary material. and more abundant than that concerning any other dramatist of the day. In the case of no contemporary dramatist are the precise biographical dates and details—dates of baptism and burial, circumstances of marriage, circumstances of children, the private pecuniary transactions of his career, the means of determining the years in which his various literary works were planned and produced—equally numerous or based on equally firm documentary foundation.

WILLIAM SHAKESPEARE.

From the monument in the chancel of the parish church of Stratford-upon-Avon.

Shakespeare's father, John Shakespeare, was a dealer in agricultural produce at Stratford-on-Avon, a prosperous country town in the heart of England. John Shakespeare was himself son of a small farmer residing in the neighbouring Warwickshire village of Snitterfield. The family was of yeoman stock. Shakespeare's mother, Mary Arden, was also daughter of a local farmer, who enjoyed somewhat greater wealth and social standing than the poet's father and his kindred. William Shakespeare, the eldest child that survived infancy, was baptized in the parish church of Stratford-on-Avon on 26th April 1564, and the entry may still be read there in the parish registers.

Parentage and birth.

The more closely one studies Shakespeare's career, the plainer it becomes that his experiences and fortunes were very similar to those of many who came in adult years to follow in his day his own profession. Sprung from yeoman stock, of a family moderately supplied with the world's needs, he had the normal opportunities of education which the Grammar School of the town of his birth could supply. Elizabethan Grammar Schools gave boys of humble birth a sound literary education. Latin was the chief subject of their study. The boys talked Latin with their master in simple dialogue ; they translated it into English ; they wrote compositions in it. A boy with a native bent for literature was certain to have his interest stimulated if he went to an Elizabethan Grammar School, and mastered the Latin curriculum. Few of Shakespeare's schoolfellows at Stratford, whatever their adult fortunes, lost in later life familiarity with the Latin which they had acquired at school. Friends and neighbours of Shakespeare at Stratford, who were educated with him at the Grammar School and passed their days as grocers or butchers in the town, were in the habit of corresponding with one another in copious and fluent Latin.

Education.

Of Shakespeare's great literary contemporaries few began life in a higher social position or with better opportunities of education than he. Marlowe, who was the first writer of literary blank verse in England, and was Shakespeare's tutor in artistic tragedy, was son of a shoemaker, and was educated at the King's Grammar School of Canterbury. Spenser, the poet of the *Faerie Queene*, was son of an impecunious London tailor, and began writing poetry after passing through the Merchant Taylors' School. These schools were of the same type as the school of Stratford-on-Avon; they provided an identical course of study.

The training of literary contemporaries.

While Shakespeare was a schoolboy, his father was a prosperous tradesman, holding the highest civic office in the little town of Stratford. Unfortunately, when the eldest son William was little more than fourteen, the father fell into pecuniary embarrassment, and the boy was withdrawn from school before his course of study was complete. He was deprived of the opportunity of continuing his education at a university; his further studies he had to pursue unaided. Nothing peculiar to his experience is to be detected in the fact that his pursuit of knowledge went steadily forward after he left school. Many men of the day, whose education suffered similar abbreviation, became not merely men of wide reading, but men of immense learning. Ben Jonson, whose erudition in the Latin and Greek classics has for range and insight very rarely been equalled in England, was, according to his own account, taken from school and put as a lad to the trade of bricklaying—the least literary of all trades. Sir Walter Ralegh had a very irregular training in youth; he left Oxford soon after joining the university, without submitting to regular discipline there; yet, after a career of

His self-training.

great activity in all departments of human effort, he wrote his *History of the World,* a formidable compendium of learned and recondite research. Other great writers of the day owed little or nothing to academic teaching; their wide reading was the fruit of a natural taste; it was under no teacher's control; it was carried forward at the same time as they engaged in other employment. Shakespeare, owing to his interrupted education, was never a trained scholar; he had defects of knowledge which were impossible in a trained scholar, but he was clearly an omnivorous reader from youth till the end of his days; he was a wider reader than most of those who owed deeper debts to schools or colleges.

II

Shakespeare's father intended that he should assist him in his own multifarious business of glover, butcher, and the rest. But this occupation was uncongenial to the young man, and he successfully escaped from it. He developed early. At eighteen he married hastily, to the not unnatural annoyance of his parents. Very soon afterwards his genius taught him that he required a larger scope for its development than the narrow associations of a domestic hearth in a little country town could afford him. At twenty-two, like hundreds of other young Englishmen of ability, of ambition, and of high spirits, he set his face towards the capital city of the country, towards London, where he found his goal.

Experiences of youth.

The drama was in its infancy. The first theatre built in England was not a dozen years old when Shakespeare arrived in the metropolis. The theatre was a new institution in the social life of Shakespeare's youth. English drama was an innovation; it was one of the latest

The infant drama.

fruits of the Renaissance in England, of the commingling
of the new study of classical drama with the new expansion
of intellectual power and outlook.   A love of mimicry is
inherent in men, and the Middle Ages gratified it by their
Miracle Plays, which developed into Moralities, and Interludes.   In the middle of the sixteenth century Latin and
Greek plays were crudely imitated in English.   But of
poetic, literary, romantic, intellectual drama, England knew
practically nothing until Shakespeare was of age.   The land
was just discovered, and its exploration was awaiting a
leader of men, a master mind.

There is nothing difficult or inexplicable in Shakespeare's
association with the theatre.   It should always be borne in
mind that his conscious aims and ambitions were
those of other men of literary aspirations in this
stirring epoch.   The difference between the
results of his endeavours and those of his fellows was due
to the magic and involuntary working of genius, which,
since the birth of time, has exercised as large a charter as
the wind, to blow on whom it pleases.   Speculation or
debate as to why genius bestowed its fullest inspiration on
Shakespeare, this youth of Stratford-on-Avon, is as futile a
speculation as debate about why he was born into the world
with a head on his shoulders at all instead of, say, a block
of stone.   It is enough for prudent men and women to
acknowledge the obvious fact that genius in an era of infinite
intellectual energy endowed Shakespeare, the Stratford-on-
Avon boy, with its richest gifts.   A very small acquaintance
with the literary history of the world, and the manner in
which genius habitually plays its part there, will show
the folly of cherishing astonishment that Shakespeare, of
Stratford-on-Avon, rather than one more nobly born, or
more academically trained, should, in an age so rich in

His associa-
tion with
the theatre.

intellectual and poetic impulse, have been chosen for the glorious dignity.

In London Shakespeare's work was mainly done. There his reputation and fortune were achieved. But his London career opened under many disadvantages. A young man of twenty-two, burdened with a wife and three children, he had left his home in his little native town about 1586 to seek his fortune in the great city. Without friends, and without money, he had, like many another stage-struck youth, set his heart on a two-fold quest. He would become an actor in the metropolis, and would write the plays in which he should act. Fortune did not at first conspicuously favour him ; he sought and won the menial office of call-boy in a London playhouse, and was only after some delay promoted to humble duties on the stage itself. But no sooner had his foot touched the lowest rung of the theatrical ladder, than he felt intuitively that the topmost rung was within his reach. He tried his hand on the revision of an old play in the theatrical repertory, a play which was about to be revived. The manager was not slow to recognise the gift for dramatic writing.

His association with London.

III

Shakespeare's period of probation was not short. He did not leap at a bound to fame and fortune. Neither came in sight until he had worked for seven or eight years in obscurity and hardship. During these years he accumulated knowledge in very varied fields of study and experience. Rapid power of intuition characterised many another great writer of the day, but none possessed it in the same degree as himself. Shakespeare's biographers have sometimes failed to make adequate allowance for his power of acquiring information with almost the

The period of probation.

rapidity of a lightning flash, and they have ignored altogether the circumstance that to some extent his literary contemporaries shared this power with him.   The habit of viewing Shakespeare in isolation has given birth to many misconceptions.

The assumption of Shakespeare's personal association in early days with the profession of the law is a good illus-

Use of law tration of the sort of misunderstanding which has
terms.   corrupted accounts of Shakespeare's career.   None can question the fact of Shakespeare's frequent use of law terms.   But the theory that during his early life in London he practised law in one or other professional capacity becomes perfectly superfluous as soon as his knowledge of law is compared with that of other Elizabethan poets, and its intuitive, rather than professional, character appreciated.

It is true that Shakespeare employs a long series of law terms with accuracy and is in the habit of using legal metaphors.   But the careful inquirer will also perceive that instances of 'bad law' or unsound interpretation of legal principles are almost as numerous in Shakespeare's work as instances of 'good law' or right interpretation of legal principles.   On that aspect of the problem writers are as a rule tantalisingly silent.

If we are content to keep Shakespeare apart from his contemporaries, or to judge him exclusively by the practice of imaginative writers of recent times, the circumstance that he often borrows metaphors or terminology from the law may well appear to justify the notion that personal experience of the profession is the best explanation of his practice.

The habit   But the problem assumes a very different aspect
of contem-   when it is perceived that Shakespeare's fellow-
poraries.   writers, Ben Jonson and Spenser, Massinger and Webster, employed law terms with no less frequency and

facility than he. It can be stated with the utmost confidence that none of these men engaged in the legal profession. Spenser's *Faerie Queene* seems the least likely place wherein to study Elizabethan law. But Spenser in his romantic epic is even more generous than Shakespeare in his plays in technical references to legal procedure. Take such passages as the following. The first forms a technical commentary on the somewhat obscure law of 'alluvion,' with which Shakespeare shows no sign of acquaintance :—

Spenser's use of law terms.

> ' For that a waif, the which by fortune came
> Upon your seas, he claim'd as property :
> And yet nor his, nor his in equity,
> But yours the waif by high prerogative.
> Therefore I humbly crave your Majesty
> It to replevie, and my son reprieve,
> So shall you by one gift save all us three alive.' [1]

In the second passage a definite form of legal practice is fully and accurately described :—

> ' Fair Mirabella was her name, whereby
> Of all those crimes she there indicted was :
> All which when Cupid heard, he by and by,
> In great displeasure willed a Capias
> Should issue forth t'attach that scornful lass.
> The warrant straight was made, and there withal
> A Bailiff-errant forth in post did pass,
> Whom they by name there Portamore did call ;
> He which doth summon lovers to love's judgment hall.
> The damsel was attached, and shortly brought
> Unto the bar whereas she was arraigned ;
> But she thereto nould plead, nor answer aught
> Even for stubborn pride which her restrained.
> So judgment passed, as is by law ordained
> In cases like.' [2]

It will be noticed by readers of these quotations that

---

[1] *Faerie Queene*, Bk. iv., canto xii., stanza xxxi.
[2] *Faerie Queene*, Bk. vi., canto vii., stanzas xxxv. and xxxvi.

Spenser makes free with strangely recondite technical terms. The verb 'replevie,' in the first quotation, means 'to enter on disputed property, after giving security to test at law the question of rightful ownership'; the technicality is to modern ears altogether out of harmony with the language of the Muses, and is rarely to be matched in Shakespeare.

Spenser's recondite law phrases.

Such examples could be multiplied almost indefinitely from Spenser, Ben Jonson, and scores of their contemporaries. The questions 'Was Spenser a lawyer?' or 'Was Ben Jonson a lawyer?' have as far as my biographical studies go, not yet been raised. Were they raised, they could be summarily answered in the negative.

Shake-speare's conformity with pre-vailing habit.

No peculiar biographical significance can attach therefore, apart from positive evidence no tittle of which exists, to Shakespeare's legal phraseology. Social intercourse between men of letters and lawyers was exceptionally active in the sixteenth and seventeenth centuries. In view of the sensitiveness to environment, in view of the mental receptivity of all great writers of the day, it becomes unnecessary to assign to any more special causes the prevailing predilection for legal language in contemporary literature. The frequency with which law terms are employed by Shakespeare's contemporaries, who may justly be denied all practical experience of the profession of law, confutes the conclusion that Shakespeare, because he uses law terms, was at the outset of his career in London a practising lawyer or lawyer's clerk. The only just conclusion to be drawn by Shakespeare's biographer from his employment of law terms is that the great dramatist in this feature, as in numerous other features, of his work was merely proving the readiness with which he identified himself with the popular literary habits of his day. All Shakespeare's mental energy, it may safely be premised, was absorbed throughout his London career by his dramatic ambition. He had no time to make acquaintance at first hand with the technical procedure of another profession.

IV

It was not probably till 1591, when he was twenty-seven, that Shakespeare's earliest original play, *Love's Labour's Lost*, was performed. It showed the hand of a beginner; Shake-speare's early plays. it abounded in trivial witticisms. But above all there shone out clearly and unmistakably the dramatic and poetic fire, the humorous outlook on life, the insight into human feeling, which were to inspire Titanic achievements in the future. Soon after, he scaled the tragic heights of *Romeo and Juliet,* and he was rightly hailed as the prophet of a new world of art. Thenceforth he marched onward in triumph.

Fashionable London society befriended the new birth of the theatre. Cultivated noblemen offered their patronage to promising actors or writers for the stage, and The Earl of Southampton soon gained the ear of the young Earl of Southampton, one of the most accomplished and handsome of the Queen's noble courtiers. The earl was said to spend nearly all his leisure at the playhouse every day.

It is not always borne in mind that Shakespeare gained soon after the earliest of his theatrical successes notable recognition from the highest in the land, from Queen Elizabeth, and her Court. It was probably at the suggestion of his enthusiastic patron, Lord Southampton, that, in the week preceding the Christmas of 1594, when Shakespeare was thirty, and he had just turned the corner of his career, the Lord Chamberlain, who controlled the entertainment of the Court, sent a stirring message to the theatre in Shoreditch, where Shakespeare was at work as playwright and actor. The young dramatist was ordered to present himself at Court for two days following Christmas, and to give his sovereign on each of the two evenings a taste of his quality.

The invitation was of singular interest. It cannot have been Shakespeare's promise as an actor that led to the royal summons. His histrionic fame did not progress at the same rate as his literary repute. He was never to win the laurels of a great actor. His most conspicuous triumph on the stage was achieved in middle life as the Ghost in his own *Hamlet*, and he ordinarily confined his efforts to old men of secondary rank. Ample compensation for his personal deficiencies as an actor was provided by the merits of his companions on his first visit to Court; he was to come supported by actors of the highest eminence in their generation. Directions were given that the greatest of the tragic actors of the day, Richard Burbage, and the greatest of the comic actors, William Kemp, were to bear the young actor-dramatist company. With neither of these was Shakespeare's histrionic position then, or at any time, comparable. For years they were the leaders of the acting profession. Shakespeare's relations with Burbage and Kemp were close, both privately and professionally. Almost all Shakespeare's great tragic characters were created on the stage by Burbage, who had lately roused London to enthusiasm by his stirring representation of Shakespeare's *Richard III.* for the first time. As long as Kemp lived he conferred a like service on many of Shakespeare's comic characters, and he had recently proved his worth as a Shakespearean comedian by his original rendering of the part of Peter, the Nurse's

Shakespeare at Court.

graceless serving-man, in *Romeo and Juliet*. Thus powerfully
supported, Shakespeare appeared for the first time in the
royal presence-chamber in Greenwich Palace on the evening
of St. Stephen's Day (the Boxing-day of subsequent genera-
tions) in 1594.

Extant documentary evidence of this visit of Shakespeare
to Court may be seen in the manuscript account of the
'Treasurer of the [royal] chamber' now in the A perform-
Public Record Office in London. The document ance at
Court in
attests that Shakespeare and his two associates 1594.
performed one 'Comedy or Interlude' on that night of
Boxing-day in 1594, and gave another 'Comedy or Interlude' on the next night but one (on Innocents'-day); that
the Lord Chamberlain paid the three men for their services
the sum of £13, 6s. 8d., and that the Queen added to the
honorarium, as a personal proof of her satisfaction, the
further sum of £6, 13s. 4d. The remuneration was thus
£20 in all. These were substantial sums in those days,
when the purchasing power of money was eight times as
much as it is to-day, and the three actors' reward would
now be equivalent to £160. Unhappily the record does not
go beyond the payment of the money. What words of commendation or encouragement Shakespeare received from his
royal auditor are not handed down to us, nor do we know
for certain what plays were performed on the great occasion.
It is reasonable to infer that all the scenes came from
Shakespeare's repertory. Probably they were drawn from
Love's Labour's Lost, which was always popular in later years
at Elizabeth's Court, and from the *The Comedy of Errors*, in
which the farcical confusions and horse-play were calculated
to gratify the Queen's robust taste. But nothing can be stated
with absolute certainty except that on December 29, 1594,
Shakespeare travelled up the River Thames from Greenwich

to London with a heavier purse and a lighter heart than on his setting out. That the visit had in all ways been crowned with success there is ample indirect evidence. He and his work had fascinated his sovereign, and many a time was she to seek delight again in the renderings of his plays, by himself and his fellow actors, at her palaces on the banks of the Thames during her remaining nine years of life.

When, a few months later, Shakespeare was penning his new play of *A Midsummer Night's Dream*, he could not forbear

Shake-
speare's
gallantry.

to make a passing obeisance of gallantry (in that vein for which the old spinster queen was always thirsting) to 'a fair vestal throned by the West,' who passed her life 'in maiden meditation, fancy free.'

The interest that Shakespeare's work excited at the Court was continuous throughout his life, and helped to render his

Continu-
ance of
Court
favour.

position unassailable. When James I. ascended the throne, no author was more frequently honoured by 'command' performances of his plays in the presence of the sovereign. Then, as now, the playgoer's appreciation was quickened by his knowledge that the play he was witnessing had been produced before the Court at Greenwich or Whitehall a few days earlier. Shakespeare's publishers were not above advertising facts like these, as

Publishers'
advertise-
ments of
the fact.

the title-pages of quarto editions published in his lifetime sufficiently prove. 'The pleasant conceited comedy called *Love's Labour's Lost*' was advertised with the appended words, 'as it was presented before her highness this last Christmas.' 'A most pleasant and excellent conceited comedy of *Sir John Falstaff and the Merry Wives of Windsor*' was stated to have been 'divers times acted both before her Majesty and elsewhere.' The ineffably great play of *King Lear* was advertised with something like tradesmanlike effrontery 'as it was played before the King's

Majesty at Whitehall on St. Stephen's Night in the Christmas Holidays.'

V

But the Court never stood alone in its admiration of Shakespeare's work.   Court and crowd never differed in their estimation of his dramatic power.   There is no doubt that Shakespeare conspicuously caught the ear of the Elizabethan playgoers of all classes at a very early date in his career, and held it firmly for life. 'These plays,' wrote two of his professional associates of the reception of the whole series in the playhouse during his lifetime, 'these plays have had their trial already, and stood out all appeals.'   Equally significant is Ben Jonson's apostrophe of Shakespeare as

The favour of the crowd.

'The applause, delight, and wonder of our stage.'

A charge has sometimes been brought against the Elizabethan playgoer of failing to recognise Shakespeare's sovereign genius.   That accusation should be reckoned among popular fallacies.   It was not merely the recognition of the fashionable, the critical, the highly-educated, that Shakespeare personally received.   It was by the voice of the half-educated populace, whose heart and intellect were for once in the right, that he was acclaimed the greatest interpreter of human nature that literature had known, and, as subsequent experience has proved, was likely to know.   There is evidence that throughout his lifetime and for a generation afterwards his plays drew crowds to pit, boxes, and gallery alike.   It is true that he was one of a number of popular dramatists, many of whom had rare gifts, and all of whom glowed with a spark of the genuine literary fire.   But Shakespeare was

Popular fallacy of Shakespeare's neglect.

the sun in the firmament; when his light shone the fires of all contemporaries paled in the contemporary playgoer's eye. Very forcible and very humorous was the portrayal of human frailty and eccentricity in the plays of Shakespeare's contemporary, Ben Jonson. Ben Jonson, too, was a fine classical scholar, which Shakespeare, despite his general knowledge of Latin, was not. But when Shakespeare and Ben Jonson both tried their hands at dramatising episodes in Roman history, the Elizabethan public of all degrees of intelligence welcomed Shakespeare's efforts with an enthusiasm which they rigidly withheld from Ben Jonson's. This is how an ordinary playgoer contrasted in crude verse the reception of Jonson's Roman play of *Catiline's Conspiracy* with that of Shakespeare's Roman play of *Julius Cæsar*:—

> ' So have I seen when Caesar would appear,
> And on the stage at half-sword parley were
> Brutus and Cassius—oh ! how the audience
> Were ravished, with what wonder they went thence ;
> When some new day they would not brook a line
> Of tedious though well-laboured Catiline.'

Jonson's 'tedious though well-laboured *Catiline*' was unendurable when compared with the ravishing interest of *Julius Cæsar*.

Shakespeare was the popular favourite. It is rare that the artist who is a hero with the multitude is also a hero with the cultivated few. But Shakespeare's universality of appeal was such as to include among his worshippers from first to last the trained and the untrained playgoer of his time.

Shakespeare's universality of appeal.

VI

Shakespeare's work was exceptionally progressive in quality; few authors advanced in their art more steadily.

His hand grew firmer, his thought grew richer, as his years
increased, and apart from external evidence as to the date of
production or publication of his plays, the discern- Progres-
ing critic can determine from the versification, and sive quality
of his
from the general handling of his theme, to what work.
period in his life each composition belongs. All the differences discernible in Shakespeare's plays clearly prove the
gradual but steady development of dramatic power and
temper; they separate with definiteness early from late
work. The comedies of Shakespeare's younger days often
trench upon the domains of farce; those of his middle and
later life approach the domain of tragedy. Tragedy in his
hands markedly grew, as his years advanced, in subtlety
and intensity. His tragic themes became more and more
complex, and betrayed deeper and deeper knowledge of the
workings of human passion. Finally the storm and stress
of tragedy yielded to the placid pathos of romance. All the
evidence shows that, when his years of probation ended, he
mastered in steady though rapid succession every degree
and phase of excellence in the sphere of drama, from the
phantasy of *A Midsummer Night's Dream* to the unmatchable
humour of Falstaff, from the passionate tragedies of *King
Lear* and *Othello* to the romantic pathos of *Cymbeline* and
The Tempest.

VII

Another side of Shakespeare's character and biography
deserves attention. He was not merely a great poet and
dramatist, endowed with imagination without rival His prac-
or parallel in human history; he was a practical tical handling of
man of the world. His work proves that his unique affairs.
intuition was not merely that of a man of imaginative
genius, but that of a man who was deeply interested and

well versed in the affairs of everyday life.   With that
practical sense, which commonly characterises the man of
the world, Shakespeare economised his powers and spared
his inventive energy, despite its abundance, wherever his
purpose could be served by levying loans on the writings of
others.   He rarely put himself to the pains of inventing a
plot for his dramas ; he borrowed his fables from popular
current literature, such as Holinshed's *Chronicles,* North's
translation of Plutarch's *Lives,* widely read romances, or even
plays that had already met with more or less success on the
stage.   It was not merely ' airy nothings ' and ' forms of
things unknown '—the creatures of his imagination—that
found in his dramas ' a local habitation and a name ' ; he
depended very often on the solid fruit of serious reading.
By such a method he harboured his strength, at the same time
as he deliberately increased his hold on popular taste.   He
diminished the risk of failure to satisfy the standard of
public culture.   Naturally he altered his borrowed plots as
his sense of artistic fitness dictated, or refashioned them
altogether.   From rough ore he usually extracted pure gold,
but there was business aptitude in his mode of gathering
the ore.   In like manner the amount of work he accomplished in the twenty years of his active professional career
amply proves his steady power of application, and the
regularity with which he pursued his literary vocation.

Appreciation of his practical mode of literary work should
leave no room for surprise at the discovery that he engaged
with success in the practical affairs of life which lay outside the
sphere of his art.   As soon as the popularity of his
work for the theatre was assured, and he had acquired by way of reward a valuable and profitable
share in the profits of the company to which he was attached,
Shakespeare returned to his native place, filled with the

The return
to Strat-
ford.

ambition of establishing his family there on a sure footing. His father's debts had grown in his absence, and his wife had had to borrow money for her support. But his return in prosperous circumstances finally relieved his kindred of pecuniary anxiety. He purchased the largest house in the town, New Place, and, like other actors of the day, faced a long series of obstacles in an effort to obtain for his family a coat of arms. He invested money in real estate at Stratford; he acquired arable land as well as pasture. His Stratford neighbours, who had known him as a poor lad, now appealed to him for loans or gifts of money in their need, and for the exercise of his influence in their behalf in London. He proved himself a rigorous man in all business matters with his neighbours, asserting his legal rights in all financial relations in the local courts, where he often appeared as plaintiff, and usually came off victorious. His average income in later life was reputed by his neighbours to exceed a thousand pounds a year.

His financial competence.

No mystery attaches to Shakespeare's financial competency. It is easily traceable to his professional earnings—as author, actor, and theatrical shareholder—and to his shrewd handling of his revenues. Shakespeare's ultimate financial position differs little from that which his fellow theatrical managers and actors made for themselves. The profession of the theatre flourished conspicuously in his day, and brought fortunes to most of those who shared in theatrical management. Shakespeare's professional friends and colleagues—leading actors and managers of the playhouses—were in late life men of substance. Like him, they had residences in both town and country; they owned houses and lands; and laid questionable claim to coat armour.[1] Edward Alleyn, an actor and playhouse manager,

[1] A manuscript tract, entitled 'A brief discourse of the causes of the

began life in much the same way as Shakespeare, and was only two years his junior; at the munificent expense of ten thousand pounds he endowed out of his theatrical earnings, after making due provision for his family, the great College of God's Gift, with almshouses attached, at Dulwich, within four miles of the theatrical quarter of Southwark. The explanation of such wealth is not far to seek. The fascination of novelty still hung about the theatre even when Shakespeare retired from work. The Elizabethans, and the men and women in Jacobean England, were—excepting those of an ultra-pious disposition—enthusiastic playgoers and seekers after amusement, and the stirring recreation which the playhouse provided was generously and even extravagantly

discord amongst the officers of Arms and of the great abuses and absurdities committed to the prejudice and hindrance of the office,' was recently lent me by its owner. It is in the handwriting of one of the smaller officials of the College of Arms, William Smith, rouge dragon pursuivant, and throws curious light on the passion for heraldry which infested Shakespeare's actor-colleagues. Rouge-dragon specially mentions in illustration of his theme two of Shakespeare's professional colleagues, namely Augustine Phillipps and Thomas Pope, both of whose names are enshrined in that leaf of the great First Folio which enumerates the principal actors of Shakespeare's plays during his lifetime. Augustine Phillipps was an especially close friend, and left Shakespeare by his will a thirty shilling piece in gold. Both these men, Pope and Phillipps, according to the manuscript, spared no effort to obtain and display that hall-mark of gentility—a coat of arms. Both made unjustifiable claim to be connected with persons of high rank. When applying for coat-armour to the College of Arms, 'Pope the player,' we are told, would have no other arms than those of Sir Thomas Pope, a courtier and privy councillor, who died early in Elizabeth's reign, and perpetuated his name by founding a college at Oxford, Trinity College. The only genuine tie between him and the player was identity of a not uncommon surname. Phillipps the player claimed similar relations with a remoter hero, one Sir William Phillipps, a warrior who won renown at Agincourt, and who was allowed to bear his father-in-law's title of Lord Bardolph—a title very familiar to readers of Shakespeare in a different connection. The actor Phillipps, to the disgust of the heraldic critic, caused the arms of this spurious ancestor, Sir William Phillipps, Lord Bardolph, to be engraved with due quarterings on a gold ring. The critic tells how he went with a colleague to a small graver's shop in Foster Lane, in the City, and saw the ring that had been engraved for the player.

remunerated. There is nothing exceptional either in the amount of the profits which Shakespeare derived from connection with theatrical enterprise or in the manner in which he spent them.

VIII

Finally, about 1611, Shakespeare made Stratford his permanent home. He retired from the active exercise of his profession, in order to enjoy those honours and His last privileges which, according to the prevailing days. social code, wealth only brought in full measure to a playwright after he ceased actively to follow his career. Shakespeare practically admitted that his final aim was what at the outset of his days he had defined as 'the aim of all' :

> 'The aim of all is but to nurse this life
> Unto honour, wealth, and ease in waning age.'

Shakespeare probably paid occasional visits to London in the five years that intervened between his retirement from active life and his death. In 1613 he purchased a house in Blackfriars, apparently merely by way of investment. He then seems, too, to have disposed of his theatrical shares. For the work of his life was over, and he devoted the evening of his days to rest in his native place, and to the undisturbed tenure of the respect of his neighbours. He was on good terms with the leading citizens of Stratford, and occasionally invited literary friends from London to be his guests. In local politics he took a very modest part. There he figured on the side of the wealthy, and showed little regard for popular rights, especially when they menaced property. At length, early in 1616, when his fifty-second year was closing, his health began to fail, and he died in his great house at Stratford on Tuesday, April 23, 1616, probably on his fifty-second birthday.

Shakespeare carefully attended in the last months of his life to the disposition of his property, which consisted, apart from houses and lands, of £350 in money (nearly £3000 in modern currency), and much valuable plate and other personalty. His wife and two daughters survived him. He left the bulk of his possessions to his elder daughter, Susanna, who was married to a medical practitioner at Stratford, John Hall. He bequeathed nothing to his wife except his second best bedstead, probably because she had smaller business capacity to deal with property than her daughter Susanna, to whose affectionate care she was entrusted. Shakespeare's younger daughter, Judith, was adequately provided for; and to his granddaughter, his elder daughter's daughter, Elizabeth, who was ultimately his last direct survivor, he left most of his plate. The legatees included three of the dramatist's fellow-actors, to each of whom he left a sum of 26s. 8d., wherewith to buy memorial rings. Such a bequest well confirms the reputation that he enjoyed among his professional colleagues for geniality and gentle sympathy. Other bequests show that he reckoned to the last his chief neighbours at Stratford among his intimate friends.

His will.

Shakespeare was buried in the chancel of the church of his native town, Stratford-on-Avon. On the slab of stone covering the grave on the chancel floor were inscribed the lines:

His burial.

> 'Good frend for Jesus sake forbeare,
> To digg the dust encloased heare :
> Bleste be ye man yt spares thes stones,
> And curst be he yt moves my bones.'

A justification of this doggerel inscription is (if needed) not far to seek. According to one William Hall, who described a visit to Stratford in 1694, these crude verses were penned by Shakespeare to suit the capacity of 'clerks and sextons, for the most part a very ignorant set of people.' Had this curse not threatened them, Hall proceeds, the sexton would not have hesitated in course of time to remove Shakespeare's dust to 'the bone-house,' to which desecration Shakespeare had a rooted antipathy. As it was, the grave was made seventeen feet deep, and was never opened, even to receive his wife, although she expressed a desire to be buried in the same grave with her husband.

But more important is it to remember that a monument was soon placed on the chancel wall near his grave. The inscription upon Shakespeare's tomb in Stratford-on-Avon Church attests that Shakespeare, the native of *His monu-* Stratford-on-Avon, who went to London a poor *ment.* youth and returned in middle life a man of substance, was known in his native place as the greatest man of letters of his epoch. In these days, when we hear doubts expressed of the fact that the writer of the great plays identified with Shakespeare's name was actually associated with Stratford-on-Avon at all, this epitaph should, in the interests of truth and good sense, be learned by heart in youth by every English-speaking person. The epitaph opens with a Latin distich, in which Shakespeare is likened, not perhaps very appositely, to three great heroes of classical antiquity—in judgment to Nestor, in genius to Socrates (certainly an inapt comparison), and in art or literary power to Virgil, the greatest of Latin poets. Earth is said to cover him, the people to mourn him, and Olympus to hold him. Then follows this English verse, not brilliant verse, but verse that leaves no reader in doubt as to its significance :

'Stay, passenger, why goest thou by so fast?
Read, if thou canst, whom envious death hath plast

> Within this monument ;—Shakespeare, with whom
> Quicke nature died : [1] whose name doth deck this tombe
> Far more than cost : sith all that he hath writ
> Leaves living art but page to serve his wit.'

There follows the statement in Latin that he died on 23rd
April 1616.

> 'All that he hath writ
> Leaves living art but page to serve his wit.'

These words mean only one thing : at Stratford-on-Avon,
his native place, Shakespeare was held to enjoy a universal
reputation. Literature by all other living pens was at the
date of his death only fit, in the eyes of his fellow-townsmen,
to serve 'all that he had writ' as pageboy or menial. There
he was the acknowledged master, and all other writers were
his servants. The epitaph can be explained in no other
sense. Until the tongue that Shakespeare spoke is dead,
so long as the English language exists and is understood,
it is futile to express doubt of the traditionally accepted facts
of Shakespeare's career.

IX

The church at Stratford-on-Avon, which holds Shakespeare's bones, must always excite the liveliest sense of
His elegists. veneration among the English-speaking peoples.
It is there that is enshrined the final testimony
to his ascent by force of genius from obscurity to glory.

---

[1] It is curious to note that Cardinal Pietro Bembo, one of the most cultivated writers of the Italian Renaissance, was author of the epitaph on the
painter Raphael, which seems to adumbrate (doubtless accidentally) the
words in Shakespeare's epitaph, 'with whom Quicke Nature died.' Bembo's
lines run :

> 'Hic ille est Raphael, metuit quo sospite vinci
> Rerum magna parens, et moriente, mori.'

> ('Here lies the famous Raphael, in whose lifetime
> great mother Nature feared to be outdone, and
> at whose death feared to die.')

But great as is the importance of the inscription on his tomb to those who would understand the drift of Shakespeare's personal history, it was not the only testimony to the plain current of his life that found imperishable record in the epoch of his death.   Biographers did not lie in wait for men of eminence on their deathbeds in Shakespeare's age, but the place of the modern memoir-writer was filled in those days by friendly poets, who were usually alert to pay fit homage in elegiac verse to a dead hero's achievements.   In that regard Shakespeare's poetic friends showed at his death exceptional energy.   During his lifetime men of letters had bestowed on his 'reigning wit,' on his kingly supremacy of genius, most generous stores of eulogy.   When Shakespeare lay dead, in the spring of 1616, when, as one of his admirers technically phrased it, he had withdrawn from the stage of the world to the 'tiring-house' or dressing-room of the grave, the flood of panegyrical lamentation poured forth in a new flood.   One of the earliest of the elegies was a sonnet by William Basse, who not only gave picturesque expression to the conviction that Shakespeare would enjoy for all time a unique reverence on the part of his countrymen, but brought into strong relief the fact that national obsequies were held by his contemporaries to be his due, and that the withholding of them was contrary to a widely disseminated wish.   In the opening lines of his poem Basse apostrophised Chaucer, Spenser, and the dramatist, Francis Beaumont, the only three poets who had hitherto received the recognition of burial in Westminster Abbey.   Beaumont, the youngest of the trio, had been buried in the Abbey only five weeks before Shakespeare died.   To this honoured trio Basse made appeal to 'lie a thought more nigh' one to another so as to make room for the newly dead Shakespeare within their 'sacred sepulchre.' Then, in the second half of his sonnet, the poet justified the fact that Shakespeare was buried elsewhere by the reflection that he in right of his pre-eminence merited a tomb apart from all his fellows. With a glance at Shakespeare's distant grave in the chancel of Stratford-on-Avon church, the writer exclaimed :

> 'Under this carved marble of thine own
> Sleep, brave tragedian, Shakespeare, sleep *alone*.'

This fine sentiment found many a splendid echo.   It re-sounded in Ben Jonson's noble lines prefixed to the First Folio of 1623. 'To the memory of my beloved, the author, Mr. William Shakespeare, and what he hath left us.'

> 'My Shakespeare, rise ! I will not lodge thee by
> Chaucer, or Spenser, or bid Beaumont lie
> A little further to make thee a room.
> Thou art a monument without a tomb,
> And art alive still, while thy book doth live
> And we have wits to read and praise to give.'

Milton qualified the conceit a few years later, in 1630, when he declared that Shakespeare 'sepulchred' in 'the monument' of his writings,

> 'in such pomp doth lie,
> That kings for such a tomb would wish to die.'

Never was a glorious immortality foretold for any man with more impressive confidence than it was foretold for

Prophecy of immortality.

Shakespeare at his death by his circle of adorers. When Time, one elegist said, should dissolve his 'Stratford monument,' the laurel about Shakespeare's brow would wear its greenest hue.   Shakespeare's critical friend, Ben Jonson, was but one of a numerous band who imagined the 'sweet swan of Avon,' 'the star of poets,' shining for ever as a constellation in the firmament.

Ben Jonson did not stand alone in anticipating that his
fame would always shed a golden light on his native place
of Stratford and the river Avon which ran beside it.   Such
was the invariable temper in which literary men gave vent
to their grief on learning the death of the 'beloved author,'
'the famous scenicke poet,' 'the admirable dramaticke
poet,' 'that famous writer and actor,' 'worthy master William
Shakespeare' of Stratford-on-Avon.

x

When Shakespeare died, on the 23rd April 1616, many
men and women were alive who had come into personal
association with him, and there were many more   The oral
who had heard of him from those who had   tradition.
spoken with him.   Apart from his numerous kinsfolk, his
widow, sister, brother, daughters, nephews, and neighbours
at Stratford-on-Avon, there were in London a large society
of fellow-authors and fellow-actors with whom he lived in
close communion.   In London, where Shakespeare's work was
mainly done, and his fortune and reputation achieved, he lived
with none in more intimate social relations than with the
leading members of his own prosperous company of actors,
which, under the patronage of the king, produced his greatest
plays.   It is to be borne in mind that to the disinterested
admiration for his genius of two fellow-members of Shakespeare's company we chiefly owe the preservation and
publication of the greater part of his literary work in the
First Folio, that volume which first offered the world a full
record of his achievement, and is the greatest of England's
literary treasures.   Those actor-editors of his dramas, Heming
and Condell, acknowledged plainly and sincerely the personal
fascination that 'so worthy a friend and fellow as was our
Shakespeare' had exerted on them.   All his fellow-workers

cherished an affectionate pride in the intimacy. It was
they who were the parents of the greater part of the
surviving oral tradition concerning Shakespeare—a tradition
which combines with the extant documentary evidence to
make Shakespeare's biography as unassailable as any narrative known to history.

Some links in the chain of Shakespeare's career are still
missing, and we must wait for the future to disclose them.
The cer- But though the clues at present are in some
tainty of places faint, the trail never altogether eludes
our
knowledge. the patient investigator. The ascertained facts
are already numerous enough to define beyond risk of
intelligent doubt the direction that Shakespeare's career
followed. Its general outline is fully established by a continuous and unimpeachable chain of oral tradition, which
survives from the seventeenth century, and by documentary
evidence—far more documentary evidence—than exists in
the case of Shakespeare's great literary contemporaries. How
many distinguished Elizabethan and Jacobean authors have
shared the fate of John Webster, next to Shakespeare the
most eminent tragic dramatist of the era, of whom no
positive biographic fact survives ?

It may be justifiable to cherish regret for the loss of
Shakespeare's autograph papers, and of his familiar corre-
The absence spondence. Only five signatures of Shakespeare
of his
manu- survive, and no other fragments of his handwriting
scripts. have been discovered. Other reputed autographs
of Shakespeare have been found in books of his time,
but none has quite established its authenticity. Yet the
absence of autograph material can excite scepticism of the
received tradition only in those who are ignorant of Elizabethan literary history—who are ignorant of the fate that
invariably befell the original manuscripts and correspondence

of Elizabethan and Jacobean poets and dramatists. Save for a few fragments of small literary moment, no play of the era in its writer's autograph escaped early destruction by fire or dustbin. No machinery then ensured, no custom then encouraged, the due preservation of the autographs of men distinguished for poetic genius. The amateur's passion for autograph collecting is of far later date. Provision was made in the public record offices, or in private muniment-rooms of great country mansions, for the protection of the official papers and correspondence of men in public life, and of manuscript memorials affecting the property and domestic history of great county families. But even in the case of men, in the sixteenth or seventeenth centuries, in official life who, as often happened, devoted their leisure to literature, autographs of their literary compositions have for the most part perished, and there usually only remain in the official depositories remnants of their writing about matters of official routine. Some documents signed by Edmund Spenser, while he was Secretary to the Lord Deputy of Ireland, or holding official positions in the Government of Ireland, survive, but where is the manu-script of Spenser's poems—of his *Shepheards Calender*, or his great epic of the *Faerie Queene*? Official papers signed by Sir Walter Ralegh, who filled a large place in English public life of the period, survive, but where is any fragment of the manuscript of his voluminous *History of the World*?

Not all the depositories of official and family papers in England, it is to be admitted, have yet been fully explored, and in some of them a more thorough search than has yet been undertaken may possibly throw new light on Shake-speare's biography or work. Meanwhile, instead of mourn-ing helplessly over the lack of material for a knowledge of Shakespeare's life, it becomes us to estimate aright what we have at our command, to study it closely in the light of the literary history of the epoch, and, while neglecting no opportunity of bettering our information, to recognise frankly the activity of the destroying agencies that have been at work from the outset. Then we shall wonder, not why we know so little, but why we know so much.

VIII

FOREIGN INFLUENCES ON SHAKESPEARE

'. . . All the learnings that his time
Could make him the receiver of, . . . he took,
As we do air, fast as 'twas minister'd,
And in 's spring became a harvest.'

Cymbeline, i. i. 43-46.

'His learning savours not the school-like gloss
That most consists in echoing words and terms . . .
Nor any long or far-fetched circumstance—
Wrapt in the curious generalties of arts—
But a direct and analytic sum
Of all the worth and first effects of art.
And for his poesy, 'tis so rammed with life
That it shall gather strength of life with being,
And live hereafter more admired than now.'

BEN JONSON, *Poetaster*, Act v. Sc. i.

[BIBLIOGRAPHY.—Study of foreign influences on Shakespeare's work has not been treated exhaustively. M. Paul Stapfer's *Shakespeare and Classical Antiquity*, 1880, covers satisfactorily a portion of the ground, and much that is useful may be found in *Shakespeare's Library*, edited by J. P. Collier and W. C. Hazlitt, 1875, and *Shakespeare's Plutarch*, edited by Prof. Skeat, 1875. Mr. Churton Collins's *Shakespearean Studies*, 1904, and Mr. J. M. Robertson's *Montaigne and Shakespeare*, 1897, throw light on portions of the topic, although all the conclusions reached cannot be fully accepted. Of the indebtedness of Elizabethan writers to Italian and French poets, much has been collected by the present writer in his introduction to *Elizabethan Sonnets* (Messrs. Constable's 'An English Garner,' 2 vols., 1904).]

I

ART and letters of the supreme kind, we are warned by Goethe, know nothing of the petty restrictions of nationality. Shakespeare, the greatest poet of the world, is

claimed to be .the property of the world.　Some German
writers have carried this argument further.　They
have treated Shakespeare as one of themselves,
and the only complaint that Germans have been
known of late years to make of Shakespeare is that he had
the inferior taste to be born an Englishman.

Shakespeare's universal repute.

The interval between English and French literary sentiment is far wider than that between English and German
literary sentiment.　It is therefore significant to
note that France, too, regards Shakespeare as an
embodiment of that highest kind of power of the human
intellect which gives a claim of kinship with him to every
thinking man, no matter what his race or country.　Victor
Hugo recognised only three men as really memorable in the
world's history ; Moses and Homer were two of them,
Shakespeare was the third.　The elder Dumas, the prince
of romancers, gave even more pointed expression to his
faith in Shakespeare's pre-eminence in the Pantheon, not
of any single nation or era, but of the everlasting universe.
Dumas set the English dramatist next to God in the cosmic
system : 'After God Shakespeare has created most.'

In France.

In presence of so exalted an estimate there is something
bathetic, something hardly magnanimous, in insisting on the
comparatively minor matter of fact that Shakespeare was an Englishman, a kinsman of the
English-speaking peoples, born in the sixteenth
century in the heart of England, and enjoying experiences
which were common to all contemporary Englishmen of the
same station in life.　Yet Shakespeare's identity with England—with the English-speaking race—is a circumstance
that accurate scholarship compels us to keep well before our
minds.　It is a circumstance which Shakespeare himself
presses on our notice in his works.　Shakespeare was not

Shakespeare's patriotism.

superior to the ordinary, natural, healthy, instinct of patriotism.   English history he studied in a patriotic light, even if it be admitted that his patriotism was a well-regulated sentiment which sought the truth.   In his English History plays he made contributions to a national epic.   His Histories are detached books of an English Iliad.   They are no blind heroic glorifications of the nation ; Shakespeare's kings are more remarkable for their failings than their virtues.   But Shakespeare pays repeated homage to his own country, to the proud independence which its geographical position emphasised, to the duty laid by nature on its inhabitants of mastering the seas that encompass it :

> ' England bound in with the triumphant sea,
>   Whose rocky shore beats back the envious siege
>   Of wat'ry Neptune.'

The significance of the sea for Englishmen was recognised by Shakespeare as fully as by any English writer.   His lines glow with exceptional thrill when he writes of

> ' The natural bravery of the isle, which stands
>   As Neptune's park, ribbed and belted in
>   With rocks unscaleable, and roaring waters.'

None but an Englishman could have apostrophised England as—

> ' This precious stone, set in a silver sea,
>   This blessed plot, this earth, this realm, this England.'

Shakespeare's great contemporary, Bacon, bequeathed by will his name and memory to men's charitable speeches, and to foreign nations, and the next ages.   His next-of-kin. Shakespeare made no testamentary dispositions of his name and memory, and by default his name and memory become the heritage of the English-speaking peoples, his next-of-kin.

II

But the depth of Shakespeare's interest in his country
and her fortunes, his instinctive identification of himself with

Foreign
influence
on Eliza-
bethan
literature.

England and Englishmen, is a fact of secondary
importance in any fruitful diagnosis of his genius
or work.   Neither Elizabethan literature nor his
spacious contribution to it came to birth in insular
isolation ; they form part of the European literature of the
Renaissance.

Full of suggestiveness are the facts that Shakespeare was
born in the year of Michael Angelo's death and of Galileo's
birth, and that he died in the same year as Cervantes.   He
was sharer of the enlightenment of the great era which saw
the new birth of the human intellect in all countries of
Western Europe.

No student will dispute the proposition that Elizabethan
England was steeped in foreign influences.   Elizabethan
literature abounded in translations from Greek, Latin,
Italian, French, and Spanish, in adaptations of every manner
of foreign literary effort.   The spirit and substance of foreign
literature were among the elements of which Elizabethan
literature was compounded.   Literary forms which were im-
ported from abroad, like the sonnet and blank verse, became
indigenous to Elizabethan England.   The Elizabethan
drama, the greatest literary product of the Elizabethan epoch,
was built largely upon classical foundations, and its plots were
framed on stories invented by the novelists of the Italian
Renaissance.   Shakespeare described an Elizabethan gallant
or man of fashion as buying ' his doublet in Italy, his round
hose in France, his bonnet in Germany, and his behaviour
everywhere.'   The remark might easily be applied figuratively
to the habiliments—to the characteristics—of Elizabethan
literature.   The dress and fashion of Elizabethan literature
were more often than not Continental importations.

The freedom with which the Elizabethans adapted contemporary poetry of France and Italy at times seems inconsistent with the dictates of literary honesty. Elizabethan
Many a poem, which was issued in Elizabethan plagiarism.
England as an original composition, proves on investigation
to be an ingenious translation from another tongue. The
practice of unacknowledged borrowing went far beyond the
limits which a high standard of literary morality justifies.
Such action was tolerated to an extent to which no other
great literary epoch seems to offer a parallel. The greatest
of the Elizabethans did not disdain on occasion to transfer
secretly to their pages phrases and ideas drawn directly from
foreign books. But it is unhistorical to exaggerate the
significance of these foreign loans, whether secret or acknowledged. The national spirit was strong enough in Elizabethan
England to maintain the individuality of its literature in the
broad current. Despite the eager welcome which was
extended to foreign literary forms and topics, despite the
easy tolerance of plagiarism, the foreign influences, so far from
suppressing native characteristics, ultimately invigorated,
fertilised, and chastened them.

III

Shakespeare's power of imagination was as fertile as that
of any man known to history, but he had another power
which is rarely absent from great poets, the power Shake-
of absorbing or assimilating the fruits of reading. speare's
Spenser, Milton, Burns, Keats, and Tennyson had tive power.
the like power, but probably none had it in quite the same
degree as Shakespeare. In his case, as in the case of
the other poets, this power of assimilation strengthened,
rendered more robust, the productive power of his imagination. This assimilating power is as well worth minute

study and careful definition as any other of Shakespeare's characteristics.

The investigation requires in the investigator a wide literary knowledge and a finely balanced judgment. Short-sighted critics, misapprehending the significance of his career, have sometimes credited Shakespeare with exceptional ignorance, even illiteracy. They have oracularly declared him to be a natural genius, owing nothing to the learning and literature that came before him, or were contemporary with him. That view is contradicted point-blank by the external facts of his education, and the internal facts of his work. A more modern type of critic has gone to the opposite extreme, and has credited Shakespeare with all the learning of an ideal professor of literature. This notion is as illusory as the other, and probably it has worked more mischief. This notion has led to the foolish belief that the facts of Shakespeare's career are inconsistent with the facts of his achievement. It is a point of view that has been accepted without serious testing by those half-informed persons who argue that the plays of Shakespeare must have come from the pen of one far more highly educated than we know Shakespeare to have been.

The two views of Shakespeare's equipment of learning were put very epigrammatically by critics writing a century and a half ago. One then said ' the man who doubts the learning of Shakespeare has none of his own ' ; the other critic asserted that ' he who allows Shakespeare had learning ought to be looked upon as a detractor from the glory of Great Britain.'

Each of these apophthegms contains a sparse grain of truth. The whole truth lies between the two. Shakespeare was obviously no scholar, but he was widely read in the literature that was at the disposal of cultivated men of his day.   All that he read passed quickly into his mind, but did not long retain there the precise original form.   It was at once assimilated, digested, transmuted by his always dominant imagination, and, when it came forth again in a recognisable shape, it bore, except in the rarest instances, the stamp of his great individuality, rather than the stamp of its source.

Shakespeare's mind may best be likened to a highly sensitised photographic plate, which need only be exposed for the hundredth part of a second to anything *The instantaneous* in life or literature, in order to receive upon its *power of* surface the firm outline of a picture which could *perception.* be developed and reproduced at will.   If Shakespeare's mind for the hundredth part of a second came in contact in an alehouse with a burly good-humoured toper, the conception of a Falstaff found instantaneous admission to his brain.   The character had revealed itself to him in most of its involutions, as quickly as his eye caught sight of its external form, and his ear caught the sound of the voice. Books offered Shakespeare the same opportunity of realising human life and experience.   A hurried perusal of an Italian story of a Jew in Venice conveyed to him the mental picture of Shylock, with all his racial temperament in energetic action, and all the background of Venetian scenery and society accurately defined.   A few hours spent over Plutarch's *Lives* brought into being in Shakespeare's brain the true aspects of Roman character and Roman aspiration.   Whencesoever the external impressions came, whether from the world of books or the world of living men, the same mental process was at work, the same visualising instinct which made the thing, which he saw or read of, a living and a lasting reality.

IV

In any estimate of the extent of foreign influence on Shakespeare's work, it is well at the outset to realise the opportunities of acquaintance with foreign literatures that were opened to him in early life. A great man's education or mental training is not a process that stops with his school or his college days; it is in progress throughout his life. But youthful education usually suggests the lines along which future intellectual development may proceed.

At the grammar school at Stratford-on-Avon, where Shakespeare may be reasonably presumed to have spent seven years of boyhood, a sound training in the elements of classical learning was at the disposal of all comers. The general instruction was mainly confined to the Latin language and literature. From the Latin accidence, boys of the period, at schools of the type of that at Stratford, were led, through Latin conversation books,—books of Latin phrases to be used in conversation, like the *Sententiae Pueriles* and Lily's *Grammar,*—to the perusal of such authors as Seneca, Terence, Cicero, Virgil, Plautus, Ovid, and Horace. Nor was modern Latin literature altogether overlooked. The Latin eclogues of a popular Renaissance poet of Italy, Baptista Mantuanus—'the good old Mantuan' Shakespeare familiarly calls him—were often preferred to Virgil's for youthful students. Latin was the warp and woof of every Elizabethan grammar school curriculum.

Early instruction in Latin.

The rudiments of Greek were occasionally taught in Elizabethan grammar schools to very promising pupils; but it is doubtful if Greek were accessible to Stratford schoolboys. It is unlikely that Shakespeare knew anything of Greek at first hand. Curious verbal coincidences have been

detected between sentences in the great Greek plays and
in Shakespearean drama. Striking these often are. In
the *Electra* of Sophocles, which is akin in its lead- Apparent
ing motive to *Hamlet*, the chorus consoles Electra ignorance of Greek
for the supposed death of Orestes with the same language.
expressions of sympathy as those with which Hamlet's
mother and uncle seek to console him on the loss of his
father :—

'Remember Electra, your father whence you sprang is mortal,
wherefore grieve not much, for by all of us has this debt of suffering
to be paid.'

In *Hamlet* are the familiar sentences—

'Thou know'st 'tis common ; all that live must die ;
But, you must know, your father lost a father ;
That father lost, lost his . . . but to persever
In obstinate condolement is a course
Of impious stubbornness.'

Shakespeare's 'prophetic soul,' which is found both in
Hamlet and in the *Sonnets*, is matched by the πρόμαντις
θυμὸς of Euripides's *Andromache* (1075). Hamlet's 'sea of
troubles' exactly translates the κακῶν πέλαγος of Æschylus's
Persae (442). Such parallels could be easily Accidental
extended. But none compels us to admit textual coincid-
knowledge of Æschylus or Sophocles or Euripides ences.
on Shakespeare's part. They barely do more than suggest
the community of sentiment that binds all great thinkers
together.

Something of the Greek spirit lived in Latin, French,
Italian, and English translations and adaptations of the
masterpieces of Greek literature. Shakespeare gained
some conception of the main features of Greek literature
through those conduits. At least one epigram of the Greek
anthology he turned through a Latin version into a sonnet.

But there was no likelihood that he sought at first hand in
Greek poetry for gnomic reflections on the commonest vicissitudes of human life.   Poets, who write quite independently
of one another, often clothe such reflections in almost identical phrase.   When we find a universal sentiment common
to Shakespeare and a foreign author, it is illogical to infer
that the sentiment has come to Shakespeare from that
foreign author, unless we can establish two most important
propositions.   First, external fact must render such a transference probable or possible.   There must be reasonable
ground for the belief that the alleged borrower had direct
access to the work from which he is supposed to borrow.
Secondly, either the verbal similarity or the peculiar dis-
tinctiveness of the sentiment must be such as to render it
easier to believe that the utterance has been directly borrowed
than that it has arisen independently in two separate minds.

In the case of the Greek parallels of phrase it is easier to
believe that the expressions reached Shakespeare independently—by virtue of the independent working of the
intuitive faculty—than that he directly borrowed them of
their Greek prototypes.   Most of the parallelisms of thought
and phrase between Shakespearean and the Attic drama are
probably fortuitous, are accidental proofs of consanguinity of
spirit rather than evidences of Shakespeare's study of
Greek.

But although the Greek language is to be placed outside
Shakespeare's scope at school and in later life, we may safely
Knowledge defy the opinion of Dr. Farmer, the Cambridge
of French scholar of the eighteenth century, who enunciated
and
Italian. in his famous *Essay on Shakespeare's Learning* the
theory that Shakespeare knew no tongue but his own, and
owed whatever knowledge he displayed of the classics and of
Italian and French literature to English translations.   English

translations of foreign literature undoubtedly abounded in Elizabethan literature. But Shakespeare was not wholly dependent on them. Several of the books in French or Italian, whence Shakespeare derived the plots of his dramas, were not in Elizabethan days rendered into English. Belleforest's *Histoires Tragiques* is the source of Hamlet's history. In Ser Giovanni's Italian collection of stories, called *Il Pecorone*, alone may be found the full story of the Merchant of Venice. Cinthio's *Hecatommithi* alone supplies the tale of Othello. None of these foreign books were accessible in English translations when Shakespeare wrote. On more general grounds the theory of his ignorance is adequately confuted. A boy with Shakespeare's exceptional alertness of intellect, during whose school days a training in Latin classics lay within reach, would scarcely lack in future years the means of access to the literatures of France and Italy which were written in cognate languages.

With Latin and French and with the Latin poets of the school curriculum, Shakespeare in his early writings openly and unmistakably acknowledged his acquaintance. In *Henry V.* the dialogue in many scenes is carried on in French which is grammatically accurate if not idiomatic. In the mouth of his schoolmasters, Holofernes in *Love's Labour's Lost* and Sir Hugh Evans in *The Merry Wives of Windsor*, Shakespeare placed Latin phrases drawn directly from Lily's popular school grammar, and from the *Sententiae Pueriles*, the conversation book used by boys at school. The influence of a popular school author, the voluminous Latin poet Ovid, was especially apparent throughout his earliest literary work, both poetic and dramatic. Ovid's *Metamorphoses* was peculiarly familiar to him. Hints drawn directly from it are discernible in all his early poems and plays as well as in *The Tempest*, his latest play (v. i. *33 seq.*).

Latin and French quotations.

Ovid's Latin, which was accessible to Shakespeare since his school days, never faded altogether from his memory.

We have, however, to emphasise at every turn the obvious fact that Shakespeare was no finished scholar and that he was no scholarly expert in any language but his own. He makes, in classical subjects, precisely those mistakes which are impossible in a finished scholar. Homer's Ὑπερίων, a name of the sun, which Ovid exactly reproduces as Hўpĕriōn, figures in Shakespeare's pages as Hȳpērĭŏn—'Hyperion to a satyr'—with every one of the four syllables wrongly measured. The wholesale error in quantity would be impossible in a classical scholar, and Keats's submissive repetition of it is clear evidence that, despite his intuitive grasp of the classical spirit, he had no linguistic knowledge of Greek. Again, Shakespeare's closest adaptations of Ovid's *Metamorphoses*, despite his personal knowledge of Latin, reflect the tautological phraseology of the popular English version by Arthur Golding, of which some seven editions were issued in Shakespeare's lifetime. From Plautus Shakespeare drew the plot of *The Comedy of Errors*, but there is reason to believe that Shakespeare consulted an English version as well as the original text. Like many later students of Latin, he did not disdain the use of translations when they were ready to his hand. Shakespeare's lack of exact scholarship explains the 'small Latin and less Greek' with which he was credited by his scholarly friend Ben Jonson. But the report of his early biographer, Aubrey, 'that Shakespeare understood Latin pretty well,' need not be contested. His knowledge of French in early life may be estimated to have equalled his knowledge of Latin, while he probably had quite sufficient acquaintance with Italian to enable him to discern the drift of any Italian poem or novel that reached his hand.

Lack of scholarship.

V

There is no evidence that Shakespeare was a widely travelled man.   It is improbable that he completed his early education in a foreign tour, and that he came under foreign literary influences at their fountain-heads, in the places of their origin.   Young Elizabethans of rank commonly made a foreign tour before completing their education, but Shakespeare was not a young man of rank.   It was indeed no uncommon experience for men of the humbler classes to work off some of the exuberance of youth by 'trailing a pike' in foreign lands, serving as volunteers with foreign armies.   From the neighbourhood of Stratford itself when Shakespeare was just of age many youths of his own years crossed to the Low Countries. They went to Holland to fight the Spaniards under the command of the great Lord of Warwickshire, the owner of Kenilworth, the Queen's favourite, the Earl of Leicester. A book was once written to show that one of these adventurous volunteers, who bore the name of Will Shakespeare, was Shakespeare himself, but the identification is a mistake. William Shakespeare, the Earl of Leicester's soldier, came from a village in the neighbourhood of Stratford where the name was common.   He was not the dramatist.

Some have argued that in his professional capacity of actor Shakespeare went abroad.   English actors in Shakespeare's day occasionally combined to make professional tours through foreign lands where court society invariably gave them a hospitable reception.   In Denmark, Germany, Austria, Holland, and France, many dramatic performances were given before royal audiences by English actors throughout Shakespeare's active career.   But it is improbable that Shakespeare joined any of these expeditions.

Shakespeare no traveller abroad.

Actors of small account at home mainly took part in them, and Shakespeare quickly filled a leading place in the theatrical profession. Lists of those Englishmen who paid professional visits abroad are extant, and Shakespeare's name occurs in none of them.

It seems unlikely that Shakespeare ever set foot on the Continent of Europe in either a private or professional capacity. He doubtless would have set foot there if he could have done so, but the opportunity did not offer. He knew the dangers of insular prejudice :—

Views of foreign travel.

> ' Hath Britain all the sun that shines ? Day, night,
> Are they not but in Britain ? . . . prithee, think
> There 's livers out of Britain.'

He acknowledged the educational value of foreign travel when rightly indulged in. He points out in one of his earliest plays how wise fathers

> ' Put forth their sons, to seek preferment out,
> Some to the wars to try their fortune there ;
> Some to discover islands far away ;
> Some to the studious universities [on the Continent]' ;

how the man who spent all his time at home was at a disadvantage

> ' In having known no travaile in his youth.'

' A perfect man ' was one who was ' tried and tutored in the world ' outside his native country.

> ' Home-keeping youth have ever homely wits.'

Some touch of a counsel of perfection may be latent in these passages. Elsewhere Shakespeare betrayed the stay-at-home's impatience of immoderate enthusiasm for foreign sights and customs. He denounced with severity the uncontrolled passion for travel. He scorned the travelled

Englishman's affectations, his laudation of foreign manners, his exaggerated admiration of foreign products as compared with home products :—

'Farewell, monsieur traveller,' says Rosalind to the melancholy Jaques. ' Look you lisp and wear strange suits and disable all the benefits of your own country, and be out of love with your nativity, and almost chide God for making you that countenance you are, or I will scarce think you have swam in a gondola.'

But many who reject theories of Shakespeare's visits to Florence or Germany or Flanders are unwilling to forgo the conjecture that Shakespeare had been in Italy. To Italy—especially to cities of Northern Italy, like Venice, Padua, Verona, Mantua, and Milan—Shakespeare makes frequent and familiar reference, *Imaginative affinity with Italy.* and he supplies many a realistic portrayal of Italian life and sentiment. But the fact that he represents Valentine in *The Two Gentlemen* (i. i. 71) as travelling from Verona to Milan (both inland cities) by sea, and the fact that Prospero in *The Tempest* embarks in a ship at the gates of Milan (i. ii. 129-44) renders it almost impossible that he could have gathered his knowledge of Northern Italy from personal observation. Shakespeare doubtless owed all his knowledge of Italy to the verbal reports of travelled friends and to Italian books, the contents of which he had a rare power of assimilating and vitalising. The glowing light which his quick imagination shed on Italian scenes lacked the literal precision and detailed accuracy with which first-hand exploration must have endowed it.

VI

The only safe source of information about Shakespeare's actual knowledge in his adult years either of the world of literature or of the world of men is his extant written work. It is a more satisfying source than any conjectures of his personal experiences.   What are the general tracts of foreign

knowledge, what are the spheres of foreign influence with which Shakespeare's work—his plays
and poems—prove him to have been familiar ?   It
is quite permissible to reply to such questions without further
detailed consideration of the precise avenues through which
those tracts of knowledge were in Shakespeare's day ap-
proachable.   With how many of the topics or conceptions
of great foreign literature does the internal evidence of his
work show him to have been acquainted ?

Firstly, it is obvious that the tales and personages of
classical mythology—the subject-matter of classical poetry
—were among his household words.   When the
second servant in *The Taming of the Shrew* asks
the drunken Kit Sly :—' Dost thou love pictures?'
Shakespeare conjures up stories of classical folk-lore with
such fluent ease as to imply complete familiarity with most
of the conventional themes of classical poetry.   ' Dost thou
love pictures?' says the servant.   He answers his own
question thus :—

> ' Then we will fetch thee straight
>   Adonis painted by a running brook,
>   And Cytherea all in sedges hid,

.   .   .   .   .

Lord.   We 'll show thee Io as she was a maid,

.   .   .   .   .

3rd Serv. Or Daphne roaming through a thorny wood,
>   Scratching her legs that one shall swear she bleeds,
>   And at that sight shall sad Apollo weep.'

All that it was of value for Shakespeare to know of Adonis,
Cytherea, Io, Daphne, Apollo, flowed in the current of his
thought.   Without knowledge of Greek he assimilated the
pellucid fancy and imagery that played about Greek verse.
The Greek language was unknown to him.   But he compre-

hended the artistic significance of Greek mythology, of
which Greek poetry was woven, as effectively as the learned
poets of the Italian and French Renaissance

So, too, with the general trend and leading episodes
of Greek history. Greek tradition, both in mythical and in
historic times, was as open a book to him as Greek
poetic mythology. He had not studied Greek
history in the spirit of an historical scholar. *Troilus* Mythical history of Greece.
and Cressida indicates no critical study of the authorities for
the Trojan War, but the play leaves no doubt of Shakespeare's
intuitive grasp of the leading features and details of the
whole story of Troy as it was known to his contemporaries.
In Athens—the capital city of Greece, the main home of
Greek culture—he places the scene of more than one of his
plays. The names of Greek heroes from Agamemnon,
Ulysses, Nestor, and Theseus, to Alcibiades and Pericles,
figure in his *dramatis personæ*. The names are often so
employed as to suggest little or nothing of the true historic
significance attaching to them, but their presence links
Shakespeare with the interest in Greek achievement which
was a corner-stone of the Renaissance. The use to which
he put Greek nomenclature is an involuntary act of homage
o 'the glory that was Greece.'

'The grandeur that was Rome' made, however, more
bundant appeal to Shakespeare. The history of Rome in its
reat outlines and its great episodes clearly fascinated him as
deeply as it fascinated any of the leaders of the Renaissance.
The subject in one shape or another was always inviting
his thought and pen. His chief narrative poem *Lucrece*—one
of his first efforts in literature—treats with exuberant eagerness of a legend of an early period in Roman history
—of regal Rome. When Shakespeare's dramatic History of Rome.
powers were at their maturity he sought with concen-

trated strength and insight dramatic material in the history
of Rome at her zenith, as it was revealed in the pages of
the Greek biographer Plutarch.   No lover of Shakespeare
would complain if the final judgment to be pronounced on
his work were based on his three Roman tragedies: the
austere *Coriolanus*, with its single but unflaggingly sustained
dramatic interest, the scene of which is laid in the early
days of the Roman Republic; the tragedy of *Julius Cæsar*,
a penetrating political study of the latest phase of the
Roman Republic, and the tragedy of *Antony and Cleopatra*,
a magical presentment and interpretation of an episode in
the early history of the Roman Empire.   To Shakespeare's
mind, any survey of human endeavour, from which was excluded the experience of Rome with her 'conquests, glories,
triumphs, spoils,' would have 'shrunk to little measure.'

Of Shakespeare's acquaintance with the literature of Rome
as represented by Ovid, the proofs are too numerous and
familiar to need rehearsal.   But there are more recondite
signs that he had come under the spell of the greatest
of Latin poems, the *Æneid* of that poet Virgil, to whom
he was likened in his epitaph.   'One speech in it I
chiefly loved,' said Hamlet: ''twas Æneas' tale to Dido;
and thereabout of it especially, where he speaks of Priam's
slaughter.'   Shakespeare recalls the same Virgilian story in
his beautiful and tender lines :—

> 'In such a night
> Stood Dido with a willow in her hand
> Upon the wild sea banks, and waft her love
> To come again to Carthage.'

Not Roman poetry only, but also Roman drama, fell within
the scope of Shakespeare's observation.   The humours of
Plautus are reproduced with much fidelity in *The Comedy of
Errors*.

If we leave classical history and literature for the foreign literatures that were more nearly contemporary with Shakespeare, evidence of devotion to one of the greatest and most prolonged series of foreign literary efforts crowds upon us.   With Italy—the Italy of the *Italian history and literature.* Renaissance—his writings show him to have been in full sympathy through the whole range of his career.   The name of every city of modern Italy which had contributed anything to the enlightenment of modern Europe finds repeated mention in his plays.   Florence and Padua, Milan and Mantua, Venice and Verona are the most familiar scenes of Shakespearean drama.   To many Italian cities or districts definite characteristics that are perfectly accurate are allotted. Padua, with its famous university, is called the nursery of the arts; Pisa is renowned for the gravity of its citizens; Lombardy is the pleasant garden of great Italy.   The mystery of Venetian waterways excited Shakespeare's curiosity.   The Italian word ' traghetto,' which is reserved in Venice for the anchorage of gondolas, Shakespeare transferred to his pages under the slightly disguised and unique form of ' traject.'

In the early period of his career Shakespeare's discipleship to Italian influences was perhaps most conspicuous. In his first great experiment in tragedy, his *Romeo and Juliet,* he handled a story wholly of Italian origin and identified himself with the theme with a completeness that admits no doubt of his affinity with Italian feeling.   That was the earliest of his plays in which he proved himself the possessor of a poetic and dramatic instinct of unprecedented quality. But Italian influences and signs of sympathy with the spirit of Italy mark every stage of his work.   They dominate the main plot of the maturest of his comedies, *Much Ado about Nothing*; they colour one of his latest works, his serious romantic play of *Cymbeline*.

The Italian novel is one of the most characteristic forms
of Italian literature, and the Italian novel constituted the
The Italian main field whence Shakespeare derived his plots.
novel. Apart from *Love's Labour's Lost* and *A Midsummer
Night's Dream*, the plots of which, while compounded of
many borrowed simples, are largely of Shakespeare's own
invention, apart, too, from *The Comedy of Errors*, which was
adapted from Plautus, there is no comedy by Shakespeare of
which the fable does not owe something to an Italian novel.
The story of *All's Well that Ends Well*, and the Imogen story
of *Cymbeline*, are of the invention of Boccaccio—of Boccaccio,
the master-genius of the Italian novelists. *Much Ado about
Nothing* and *Twelfth Night* come from Bandello, the chief
of Boccaccio's disciples, and *Measure for Measure* is from
Cinthio, a later disciple of Boccaccio, almost Shakespeare's
contemporary. *The Two Gentlemen of Verona*, although
based on a Spanish pastoral romance, derives hints from the
Italian of both Bandello and Cinthio.

How far Shakespeare had direct recourse to Boccaccio,
Bandello, and Cinthio is an open question. The chief Italian
Means of novels were diffused in translations and adapta-
access to tions throughout Europe. The work of Bandello,
the Italian
novel. who enjoyed, of all Italian novelists, the highest
popularity in the sixteenth century, was constantly reappear-
ing in Italian, French, and English shapes, which rendered
easy the study of his tales in the absence of access to
the original version. Shakespeare readily identified himself
with the most popular literary currents of his epoch, and
worked with zest on Bandello's most widely disseminated
stories. Before he wrote *Much Ado about Nothing*, the story
by Bandello, which it embodies, had experienced at least
four adaptations; it had been translated into French; it had
been retold in Italian by Ariosto in his epic of *Orlando*

Furioso ; it had been dramatised in English by one student of Ariosto, and had been translated into English out of the great Italian poet by another (Sir John Harington). Similarly, Bandello's tale, which gave Shakespeare his cue for *Twelfth Night*, had first been rendered into French; it was then translated from French into English; it was afterwards adapted anew in English prose from the Italian; it was dramatised in Italian by three dramatists independently, and two of these Italian dramas had been translated into French. Shakespeare's play of *Twelfth Night* was at least the ninth version which Bandello's fable had undergone.

There are two plays of Shakespeare which compel us in the present state of our knowledge to the conclusion that Shakespeare had recourse to the Italian itself. The story of Othello as far as we know was solely accessible to him in the Italian novel of Cinthio. *Othello* and *Merchant of Venice.* Many of Cinthio's stories had been translated into English; many more had been translated into French, but there is no rendering into either French or English of Othello's tragical history. Again in the *Merchant of Venice* we trace the direct influence of *Il Pecorone,* a fourteenth-century collection of Italian novels by Ser Giovanni Fiorentino; that collection remained unpublished till 1558, and was in Shakespeare's day alone to be found in the Italian original. The bare story of the Jew and the pound of flesh was very generally accessible. But it is only in Shakespeare's play and in *Il Pecorone* that the defaulting Christian debtor, whose pound of flesh is demanded by his Jewish creditor, is rescued through the advocacy of ' The Lady of Belmont,' wife of the Christian debtor's friend. The management of the plot in the Italian novel is indeed more closely followed by Shakespeare than was his ordinary habit.

The Italian fable, it is to be admitted, merely formed as

a rule the basis of his structure. Having surveyed all its

Shakespeare's radical methods of alteration. possibilities, he altered and transmuted the story with the utmost freedom as his artistic spirit moved him. His changes bear weighty testimony to the greatness of his conceptions of both life and literature. In *Measure for Measure*, by diverting the course of an Italian novel at a critical point he not merely showed his artistic ingenuity but gave dramatic dignity and unusual elevation to a degraded and repellent theme. Again, in *Othello*, the tragic purpose is planned by him anew. The scales never fall from Othello's eyes in the Italian novel. He dies in the belief that his wife is guilty. Shakespeare's catastrophe is invested with new and fearful intensity by making Iago's cruel treachery known to Othello at the last, after Iago's perfidy has compelled the noble-hearted Moor in his groundless jealousy to murder his gentle and innocent wife Desdemona. Too late Othello sees in Shakespeare's tragedy that he is the dupe of Iago and that his wife is guiltless. But, despite the magnificent freedom with which Shakespeare often handled the Italian novel, it is to the suggestion of that form of Italian literary art that his dramatic achievements owe a profound and extended debt.

Not that in the field of Italian literature, Shakespeare's debt was wholly confined to the novel. Italian lyric poetry

Petrarch. left its impress on the most inspiring of Shakespeare's lyric flights. Every sonnetteer of Western Europe acknowledged Petrarch (of the fourteenth century) to be his master, and from Petrarchan inspiration came the form and much of the spirit of Shakespeare's sonnets. Petrarch's ambition to exalt in the sonnet the ideal type of beauty, and to glorify ethereal sentiment, is the final cause of Shakespeare's contributions to sonnet-literature. At first

hand Shakespeare may have known little or even nothing
of the Italian's poetry which he once described with a touch
of scorn as 'the numbers that Petrarch flowed in.' But
English, French, and contemporary adaptations of Petrarch's
ideas and phrases were abundant enough to relieve Shakespeare of the necessity of personal recourse to the original
text while the Petrarchan influence was ensnaring him.
The cultured air of Elizabethan England was charged with
Petrarchan conceits and imagery. Critics may differ as to
the precise texture or dimensions of the bonds which unite
the two poets, but they cannot question their existence.

Nor was Shakespeare wholly ignorant of another mode in
which Italian imaginative power manifested itself. He was
not wholly ignorant of Italian art. In *The Winter's*
Tale he speaks of a contemporary Italian artist, Italian art.
Giulio Romano, with singular enthusiasm. He describes
the supposed statue of Hermione as 'performed by that rare
Italian master, Giulio Romano, who, had he himself eternity
and could put breath into his work, would beguile Nature of
her custom, so perfectly is he her ape.' No loftier praise
could be bestowed on a worker in the plastic arts. Giulio
Romano is better known as a painter than a sculptor, but
sculpture occupied him as well as painting in early life, and
although Michael Angelo's name might perhaps have been
more appropriate and obvious, Shakespeare was guilty of no
inaccuracy in associating with Romano's name the surpassing
qualities of Italian Renaissance sculpture.

VII

Of the great foreign authors who, outside Italy, were more
or less contemporary with the Elizabethans, those of France
loom large in the Shakespearean arena. No Eliza- Poetry of
bethan disdained the close study of sixteenth- France.
century literature of France. Elizabethan poetry finally

ripened in the light of the lyric effort of Ronsard and his
fellow-masters of the Pléiade School.   Ronsard and his
friends, Du Bellay and De Baïf, had shortly before Shakespeare's birth deliberately set themselves the task of refining
their country's poetry by imitating in French the classical
form and spirit.   Their design met with rare success.   They
brought into being a mass of French verse which is comparable by virtue of its delicate imagery and simple harmonies with the best specimens of the Greek anthology.
It was under the banner of the Pléiade chieftains and as
translators of poems by one or other of their retainers, that
Spenser and Daniel, Lodge and Chapman, set forth on
their literary careers.   Shakespeare could not escape
altogether from the toils of this active influence.   It
was Ronsard's example which introduced into Elizabethan
poetry the classical conceit, which Shakespeare turned to
magnificent advantage in his sonnets, that the poet's verses
are immortal and can alone give immortality to those whom
he commemorates.   Insistence on the futility of loveless
beauty which lives for itself alone, adulation of a patron in
terms of affection which are borrowed from the vocabulary
of love, expressions of fear that a patron's favour may be
alienated by rival interests, were characteristic motives of
the odes and sonnets of the Pléiade, and, though they came
to France from Italy, they seem to have first caught Shakespeare's ear in their French guise.

When Shakespeare in his *Sonnets* (No. xliv.) reflects with
vivid precision on the nimbleness of thought which

> ' can jump both sea and land
> As soon as think the place where he would be,'

he seems to repeat a note that the French sonnetteers
constantly sounded without much individual variation.   It
is difficult to believe that Shakespeare's description of

Thought's triumphs over space, and its power of leaping 'large lengths of miles,' did not directly echo Du Bellay's apostrophe to 'Penser volage,' or the address of Du Bellay's disciple Amadis Jamyn to

> 'Penser, qui peux en un moment grand erre
> Courir leger tout l'espace des cieux,
> Toute la terre, et les flots spacieux,
> Qui peux aussi penetrer sous la terre.' [1]

[1] Sonnets to Thought are especially abundant in the poetry of sixteenth-century France, though they are met with in Italy. The reader may be interested in comparing in detail Shakespeare's *Sonnet* xliv. with the two French sonnets to which reference is made in the text. The first sonnet runs :

> 'Penser volage, et leger comme vent,
>   Qui or' au ciel, or' en mer, or' en terre
>   En un moment cours et recours grand' erre,
>   Voire au seiour des ombres bien souvent.
> En quelque part que voises t'eslevant
>   Ou rabaissant, celle qui me fait guerre,
>   Celle beauté tousiours deuant toy erre,
>   Et tu la vas d'un leger pied suyvant.
> Pourquoy suis tu (ô penser trop peu sage)
>   Ce qui te nuit ? pourquoy vas-tu sans guide,
>   Par ce chemin plain d'erreur variable ?
> Si de parler au moins eusses l'usage,
>   Tu me rendrois de tant de peine vuide,
>   Toy en repos et elle pitoyable.'—(Du Bellay, *Olive* xliii.)

The second sonnet runs :

> 'Penser, qui peux en vn moment grand erre
>   Courir leger tout l'espace des cieux,
>   Toute la terre, et les flots spacieux,
>   Qui peux aussi penetrer sous la terre :
> Par toy souvent celle-là qui m'enferre
>   De mille traits cuisans et furieux,
>   Se represente au devant de mes yeux,
>   Me menaçant d'vne bien longue guerre
> Que tu es vain, puis-que ie ne sçaurois
>   T'accompagnant aller où ie voudrois,
>   Et discourir mes douleurs à ma Dame !
> Las ! que n'as tu le parler comme moy,
>   Pour lui conter le feu de mon esmoy,
>   Et lui ietter dessous le sein ma flame ? '
>   (Amadis Jamyn, Sonnet xxi.)

Tasso's sonnet (Venice 1583, i. p. 33) beginning : 'Come s'human pensier

But Shakespeare's interest in French literature was not confined to the pleasant and placid art or the light ethereal philosophy of Ronsard's school. The burly humorist Rabelais, who was older than Ronsard by a generation, and proved the strongest personality in the whole era of the French Renaissance, clearly came within the limits of Shakespeare's cognisance. The younger French writer, Montaigne, who was living during Shakespeare's first thirty-eight years of life, was no less familiar to the English dramatist as author of the least embarrassed and most suggestive reflections on human life which any autobiographical essayist has produced. From Montaigne, the typical child of the mature Renaissance in France, Shakespeare borrowed almost verbatim Gonzalo's description in *The Tempest* of an ideal socialistic commonwealth.

Rabelais and Montaigne.

VIII

This brief survey justifies the conclusion that an almost limitless tract of foreign literature lent light and heat to Shakespeare's intellect and imagination. He may not have come to close quarters with much of it. Little of it did he investigate minutely. But he perceived and absorbed its form and pressure at the lightning pace which his intuitive faculty alone could master. We may apply to him his own words in his description of the training of his hero Posthumus, in *Cymbeline*. He had at command—

Alertness in acquiring foreign knowledge.

> '. . . All the learnings that his time
> Could make him the receiver of; which he took,
> As we do air, fast as 'twas ministered,
> And in 's spring became a harvest.'

di giunger tenta Al luogo,' and Ronsard's sonnet (*Amours*, I. clxviii.) beginning: 'Ce fol penser, pour s'envoler trop haut,' should also be studied in this connection.

The world was Shakespeare's oyster which he with pen could open. The mere geographical aspect of his dramas proves his width of outlook beyond English boundaries. In no less than twenty-six plays of the whole thirty-seven are we transported for a space to foreign towns. In *A Midsummer Night's Dream*, in *Timon of Athens*, Athens is our home, and so occasionally in *Antony and Cleopatra*. Ephesus was the scene of *The Comedy of Errors* and part of the play of *Pericles*. Messina, in Sicily, is presented in *Much Ado about Nothing*, as well as in *Antony and Cleopatra*, which also takes us to Alexandria, to a plain in Syria, and to Actium. *Pericles* introduces us to Antioch, Tarsus, Pentapolis, Mytilene, together with Ephesus; *Troilus and Cressida* to Troy; and *Othello* to Cyprus. In no less than five plays the action passes in Rome. Not only is the ancient capital of the world the scene of the Roman plays *Titus Andronicus, Coriolanus, Julius Cæsar*, and *Antony and Cleopatra*, but in *Cymbeline* much that is important to the plot is developed in the same surroundings. Of all the historic towns of northern Italy can the like story be told. Hardly any European country is entirely omitted from Shakespeare's map of the world. *The Winter's Tale* takes us to Sicily and Bohemia; *Twelfth Night* to an unnamed city in Illyria; *Hamlet* to Elsinore in Denmark; *Measure for Measure* to Vienna, and *Love's Labour's Lost* to Navarre.

The geographical point of view.

Shakespeare's plays teach much of the geography of Europe. But none must place unchecked reliance on the geographical details which Shakespeare supplies. The want of exact scholarship which is characteristic of Shakespeare's attitude to literary study, is especially noticeable in his geographical assertions. He places a scene in *The Winter's Tale* in Bohemia ' in a desert country near the sea.' Unluckily Bohemia has no seaboard. Shakespeare's

Geographical blunders.

looseness of statement is common to him and at least one contemporary. In this description of his Bohemian scene, Shakespeare followed the English novelist, Robert Greene, from whom he borrowed the plot of *A Winter's Tale*. A fantastic endeavour has been made to justify the error by showing that Apulia, a province on the seacoast of Italy, was sometimes called Bohemia. The only just deduction to be drawn from Shakespeare's bestowal of a seacoast on Bohemia, is that he declined with unscholarly indifference to submit himself to bonds of mere literal fact.

Shakespeare's dramatic purpose was equally well served, whether his geographical information was correct or incorrect, and it was rarely that he attempted independent verification. In his Roman plays he literally depended on North's popular translation of Plutarch's *Lives*. He was content to take North as his final authority, and wherever North erred Shakespeare erred with him. In matters of classical geography and topography he consequently stumbled with great frequency, and quite impenitently. In *Antony and Cleopatra* Shakespeare includes Lydia among the Queen of Egypt's provinces or possessions. Lydia is a district in Asia Minor with which Cleopatra never had relation. Plutarch wrote quite correctly that the district of Libya in North Africa was for a time under the Queen of Egypt's sway. Shakespeare fell blindly into the error, caused by a misprint or misreading, of which no scholar acquainted with classical geography was likely to be guilty.

Again, in *Julius Cæsar*, there are many errors of like kind due to like causes—to casual acts of carelessness on the part of the English translator, which Shakespeare adopted without scruple. Mark Antony in Shakespeare describes the gardens which Cæsar bequeathed to the people of Rome as on *this* side of the Tiber—on the same side as the Forum— where the crowded streets and population left no room for

gardens.   Plutarch had correctly described the Tiber gardens
as lying across the Tiber, on the opposite side to that where
the Forum lay.   A very simple mistake had been committed
by North or his printers : ' on that side of the Tiber ' had
been misread ' on this side.'   But Shakespeare was oblivious
of a confusion, which would be readily perceived by one
personally acquainted with Rome, or one who had studied
Roman topography.

IX

But more interesting than the mere enumeration of
details of Shakespeare's scenes or of the literature that he
absorbed is it to consider in broad outline how   The
his knowledge of foreign literature worked on   foreign
                                                  spirit in
his imagination, how far it affected his outlook   Shakespeare.
on life.   How far did Shakespeare catch the distinctive
characteristics of the inhabitants of foreign lands and cities
who fill his stage ?   How much genuine foreign spirit did
he breathe into the foreign names ?   Various answers have
been given to this inquiry.   There are schools of critics
which deny to Shakespeare's foreign creations—to the Roman
characters of *Julius Cæsar,* or to the Italian characters of
Romeo and Juliet and *Othello*—any national or individual
traits.   All, we are told by some, are to the backbone
Elizabethan Englishmen and Englishwomen.   Others insist
that they are universal types of human nature in which
national idiosyncrasies have no definite place.

Neither verdict is satisfactory.   No one disputes that
Shakespeare handled the universal features of humanity,
the traits common to all mankind.   On the surface the
highest manifestations of the great passions—ambition,
jealousy, unrequited love—are the same throughout the

world and have no peculiarly national colour. But, to the
seeing eye, men and women, when yielding to emotions that
are universal, take something from the bent of their education, and from the tone of the climate and scenery that
environs them. The temperament of the untutored savage
differs from that of the civilised man; the predominating mood
of northern peoples differs from that of southern peoples.
Shakespeare was far too enlightened a student of human
nature, whether he met men or women in life or literature,
to ignore such facts as these. His study of foreign literature
especially brought them home to him, and gave him opportunities of realising the distinctions in human character that
are due to race or climate. Of this knowledge he took
full advantage. Love-making is universal, but Shakespeare
recognised the diversities of amorous emotion and expression which race and climate engender. What contrast can
be greater than the boisterous bluntness in which the
English king, Henry v., gives expression to his love, and
Historic   the pathetic ardour in which the young Italians
sensibility. Romeo and Ferdinand urge their suits ? Intuitively, perhaps involuntarily, Shakespeare with his unrivalled
sureness of insight impregnated his characters with such
salient features of their national idiosyncrasies as made
them true to the environment that was appointed for them
in the work of fiction or history on which he founded his
drama. As the poet read old novels and old chronicles, his
dramatic genius stirred in him a rare force of historic imagination and sensibility. Study developed in Shakespeare an
historic sense of a surer quality than that with which any
professed historian has yet been gifted. Cæsar and Brutus,
of whom Shakespeare learned all he knew in the pages of
Plutarch, are more alive in the drama of *Julius Cæsar* than
in the pages of the historian Mommsen. Cleopatra *is* the

historic queen of Egypt, and no living portrait of her is known outside Shakespeare. No minor errors in detail destroy the historic vraisemblance of any of Shakespeare's dramatic pictures.

The word 'atmosphere' is hackneyed in the critical jargon of the day. Yet the term has graphic value. Shakespeare apprehended the true environment of the heroes and heroines to whom his reading of history or romance introduced him, because no writer had a keener, quicker sense of atmosphere than he. *Fidelity to 'atmosphere.'* The comedies and tragedies, of which the scene is laid in Southern Europe, in Italy or Greece or Egypt, are all instinct with the hot passion, the gaiety, the lightness of heart, the quick jest, the crafty intrigue, which breathe the warm air, the brilliant sunshine, the deep shadows, the long days of southern skies.

The great series of the English history plays, with the bourgeois supplement of *The Merry Wives*, is, like the dramas of British legend, *Macbeth* and *King Lear* and *Cymbeline*, mainly confined to English or British scenery. Apart from them, only one Shakespearean play carries the reader to a northern clime, or touches northern history. The rest take him to the south and introduce him to southern lands. The one northern play is *Hamlet*. The introspective melancholy that infects not the hero only, but his uncle, and to a smaller extent his friend Horatio and his mother—a melancholy which is almost peculiar to them in the range of Shakespearean humanity—belongs to the type of mind which is reared in a land of mists and long nights, of leaden skies and cloud-darkened days. Such are the distinguishing features of the northern Danish climate. Shakespeare's historic sense would never have allowed him to give Hamlet a local habitation in Naples or Messina, any more than it would have suffered him to represent Juliet or Othello as natives of Copenhagen or London.

Another point is worth remarking. Shakespeare took a very wide view of human history, and few of the conditions that moulded human character escaped his notice.

Width of historic outlook.

His historic insight taught him that civilisation progressed in various parts of the world at various rates. He could interpret human feeling and aspirations at any stage of development in the scale of civilisation. Under the spur of speculation, which was offered by the discovery of America, barbarism interested him hardly less than civilisation. Caliban is one of his greatest conceptions. In Caliban he depicts an imaginary portrait conceived with the utmost vigour and vividness of the aboriginal savage of the new world, of which he had heard from travellers or read in books of travel. Caliban hovers on the lowest limits of civilisation. His portrait is an attempt to depict human nature when just on the verge of the evolution of moral sentiment and intellectual culture.

Shakespeare was no less attracted by the opposite extreme in the scale of civilisation. He loved to observe civilisation that was over-ripe, that had overleaped itself, and was descending on the other side to effeteness and ruin. This type Shakespeare slightly sketched at the outset in his portrait of the Spanish Armado in *Love's Labour's Lost*, but the painting of it only engaged his full strength, when he turned in later life to Egypt. Queen Cleopatra, the ‘serpent of old Nile,’ who by her time-honoured magic brings ‘experience, manhood, honour’ to dotage, is Shakespeare's supreme contribution to the study of civilised humanity's decline and fall.

X

But it was the thought and emotion that animated the living stage of his own epoch which mainly engaged Shakespeare's pencil.   He cared not whether his themes and scenes belonged to England or to foreign countries.   The sentiments and aspirations which filled the air of his era were part of his being, and to them he gave the crowning expression.

Shakespeare's relation to his era.

Elizabethan literature, which was the noblest manifestation in England of the Renaissance, reached its apotheosis in Shakespeare.   It had absorbed all the sustenance of the new movement—the enthusiasm for the Greek and Latin classics, the passion for extending the limits of human knowledge, the resolve to make the best and not the worst of life upon earth, the ambition to cultivate the idea of beauty, the conviction that man's reason was given him by God to use without restraint.   All these new sentiments went to the formation of Shakespeare's work, and found there perfect definition.   The watchword of the mighty movement was sounded in his familiar lines :

Elizabethan literature and the Renaissance.

> ' Sure, He that made us with such large discourse,
>   Looking before and after, gave us not
>   The capability and god-like reason,
>   To fust in us unused.'

Upon the new faith of the Renaissance in the perfectibility of man, intellectually, morally, and physically, Shakespeare pronounced the final word in his deathless phrases : ' What a piece of work is man !   How noble in reason !   how infinite in faculties !   in form and moving, how express and admirable !   in action, how like an angel !   In apprehension, how like a god !'   Renaissance authors of France, Italy, and Spain expressed themselves to like intent.   But probably in these words of Shakespeare is enshrined with best effect the true significance of the new enlightenment.

Shakespeare's lot was cast, by the silent forces of the universe, in the full current of this movement of the Re-
Shake-
speare's
foreign
contem-
poraries. naissance which was in his lifetime still active in every country of Western Europe. He was the contemporary of Tasso, Ariosto's successor on the throne of Italian Renaissance poetry and its last occupant. Ronsard and the poets of the French Renaissance flourished in his youth. Montaigne, the glory of the French Renaissance, whose thought on man's potentialities ran very parallel with Shakespeare's, was very little his senior. Cervantes, the most illustrious figure in literature of the Spanish Renaissance, was his senior by only seventeen years, and died only ten days before him. All these men and their countless coadjutors and disciples were subject to many of the same influences as Shakespeare was. The results of their efforts often bear one to another not merely a general resemblance, but a specific likeness, which amazes the investigator. How many poets and dramatists of six-teenth-century Italy, France, and Spain, applied their energies to developing the identical plots, and the identical traditions of history as Shakespeare? Almost all countries of Western Europe were producing at the same period, under the same incitement of the revival of learning, and the renewal of intellectual energy, tragedies of Julius Cæsar, of Antony and Cleopatra, of Romeo and Juliet, and of Timon of Athens. All countries of Western Europe were producing sonnets and lyrics of identical pattern with unprecedented fertility; all were producing prose histories and prose essays of the like type; all were surveying the same problems of science and philosophy, and offering much the same solutions.

The direct interchange, the direct borrowings are not

the salient features of the situation.   Less material influences than translation or plagiarism were at   The diffu-
work ; allowance must be made for the community   sion of the
of feeling among all literary artificers of the day,   Renais-
for the looking backwards to classical literature,   sance.
for the great common stock of philosophical sentiments and
ideas to which at that epoch authors of all countries under
the sway of the movement of the Renaissance had access
independently.

National and individual idiosyncrasies deeply coloured the
varied literatures in which the spirit of the Renaissance
was embodied.   But that unique spirit is visible amid all
the manifestations of national and individual genius and
temperament.

When we endeavour to define the foreign influences at
work on Shakespeare's achievement, we should beware of
assigning to the specific influence of any individual   Misappre-
foreign writers those characteristics which were   hensions to
really the property of the whole epoch, which be-   against.
longed to the stores of thought independently at the disposal
of every rational being who was capable at the period of
assimilating them.   Much has been made of the parallelisms
of sentiment between Shakespeare and his French contemporary Montaigne, the most enlightened representative of
the spirit of the Renaissance in France.   Such parallelisms
stand apart from that literal borrowing by Shakespeare of
part of a speech in *The Tempest* from Montaigne's essay on
' cannibals.'   The main resemblances in sentiment concern
the two men's attitude to far-reaching questions of philosophy.   But there is little justice in representing the one
as a borrower from the other.   Both gave voice in the same
key to that demand of the humanists of the Renaissance for
the freest possible employment of man's reasoning faculty.

Shakespeare and Montaigne were only two of many who were each, for the most part independently, interpreting in the light of his individual genius, and under the sway of the temperament of his nation, the highest principles of enlightenment and progress, of which the spirit of the time was parent.

Direct foreign influences are obvious in Shakespeare; they are abundant and varied; they compel investigation. But no study of them can throw true and trustworthy light on any corner of Shakespeare's work, unless we associate with our study a full recognition, not merely of the personal pre-eminence of Shakespeare's genius and intuition, but also of the diffusion through Western Europe of the spirit of the Renaissance. That was the broad basis on which the foundations of Shakespeare's mighty and unique achievement were laid.

INDEX